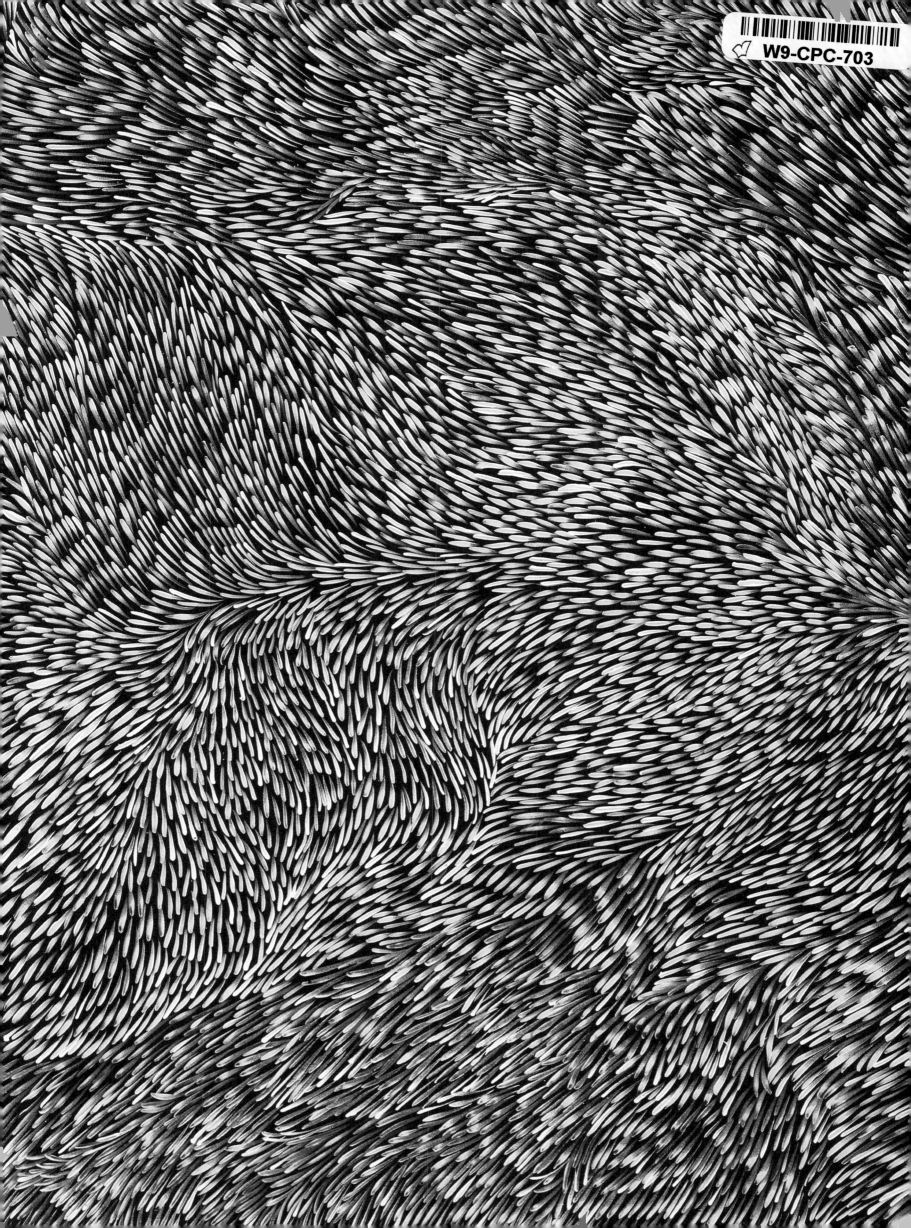

A Community of Collectors

75th Anniversary Gifts to the Seattle Art Museum

Edited by   Chiyo Ishikawa

Essays by   Barbara Brotherton
               Michael Darling
               Julie Emerson
               Chiyo Ishikawa
               Patricia Junker
               Pamela McClusky
               Marisa C. Sánchez
               Yukiko Shirahara
               Josh Yiu

Seattle Art Museum

Contents

Donors and Funders
of Works of Art Given or Promised
in Honor of the 75th Anniversary
of the Seattle Art Museum

Foreword

Why does art matter? Art has the uncanny ability to provoke new ways of thinking about and seeing the world. The beauty of art has the potential to lift our spirits and pleasurably slow our pace. The late Museum of Modern Art curator Kirk Varnedoe, speaking at Stanford University's 1992 commencement, suggested the profound transformative power of art on our individual lives: "One of art's crucial functions, personally and socially, is to propose new worlds, different from the ones you know. . . . But perhaps even more crucially, and potentially more important still for society, art can make you pay attention to things you take for granted." Art questions what we think we know, and for this reason, it is indispensable.

Seattleites appreciate the essentiality of arts and culture in building the fabric of community. In Seattle, the strong core of cultural institutions, large and small, provides the full range of performing arts, from theater and ballet to symphony and opera, and every kind of museum—art, music, science, history, and air/space. Visitors and newcomers are often surprised to find the depth and breadth of human achievement so well represented in the Northwest, a region best known for its preservation of natural beauty and its adventuresome corporations. Strong cultural institutions, as well as major universities, foster creativity, risk-taking, and imaginative thinking; they make our city vibrant and a place where companies want to locate and people want to live, work, and play. Above all, Seattle is a place where community-minded residents pull together to strengthen our young dynamic city. Seattleites at their best unite and collaborate in the interest of all.

The collectors whose names appear in this volume constitute a cohesive group with a shared aim: to ensure that Seattle and the Pacific Northwest have a celebrated art museum whose marvelously diverse collections exemplify artistic excellence and are accessible to all. These generous-spirited individuals, each and every one, deserve our deep heartfelt gratitude, and to them we dedicate this publication. The Seattle Art Museum occupies pride of place in the visual arts of the Pacific Northwest because of their philanthropy.

Indeed, our rapid growth in recent years has been fueled by the considerable number of passionate collectors in our area who possess extraordinary works of art. These impressive individuals, many of whom serve on the museum's board of trustees, understand that, in addition to how well an art museum is grounded in the broad community, its excellence depends on the depth, breadth, and quality of its collections. Great collections lie at the heart of all great art museums. Special exhibitions come and go, but the collections that belong to the museum shape its identity and provide long-term benefit for present and future generations.

The superb works of art, high in quality and broad in cultural reach, that populate this volume offer a glimpse of the Seattle Art Museum's brilliant future. While some works have already been given to the museum, many are pledged to come in the years ahead. Extraordinary also is the fact that space to display the Seattle Art Museum's expanded art collections has already been built. Eight floors of the new north building, currently leased to Washington Mutual as office space and available to the museum as early as spring 2017, will be additional gallery space when we need it. The museum's trustees, led by Chairman Jon Shirley and President Susan Brotman, were truly visionary in negotiating this innovative agreement. Their farsightedness leaves a distinguished artistic and architectural legacy.

The collectors themselves deserve our heartfelt gratitude and that of generations to come for making these extraordinary gifts, which together constitute one of the largest commitments of art in the history of U.S. philanthropy. These contributions were galvanized by the 75th Anniversary Art Acquisition Initiative Committee, under the leadership of Tom Barwick, Susan Brotman, Barney Ebsworth, Lyn Grinstein, and Virginia Wright. Besides making major pledges to the initiative, this group played the role of Pied Piper in leading fellow collectors to join in this magnificent demonstration of generosity.

Leadership and vision from the staff were also key. Maryann Jordan, senior deputy director, and Chiyo Ishikawa, Susan Brotman deputy director for art and curator of European painting and sculpture, enthusiastically led the effort. The museum's inspiring team of curators—Barbara Brotherton, Michael Darling, Julie Emerson, Patricia Junker, Pamela McClusky, Marisa Sánchez, Yukiko Shirahara, and Josh Yiu—ensured that our aspirations matched the

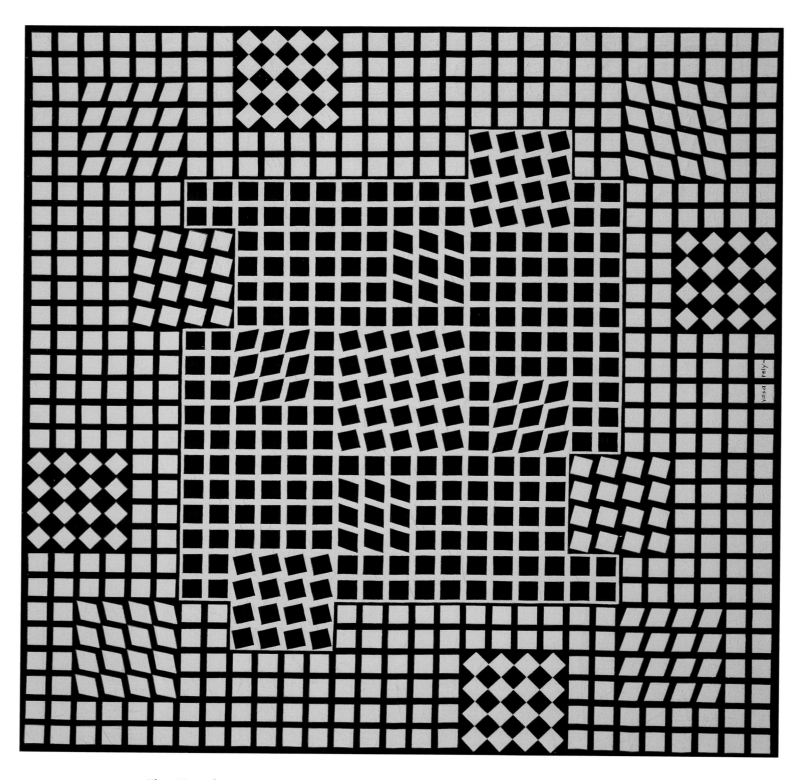

Victor Vasarely
French, 1908–1997
Tlinko-B, 1951
oil on canvas, 45¼ × 45¼ in.
Promised gift of Charles Simonyi, in honor of
the 75th Anniversary of the Seattle Art Museum,
T2008.83.1

accomplishments of our donors by making the case for exactly how each gift of art would enhance our collection. The foresight of past museum curators, especially Patterson Sims, Trevor Fairbrother, Lisa Corrin, Susan Rosenburg, Jay Xu, and William Rathbun, had set the stage for many of these decisions. Our curators were expertly supported in their efforts by Sarah Berman, Lauren Mellon, Jennifer Aydelott, and Michele Hasson. The promise of more than one thousand works and this publication are testaments to their collective dedication and success.

I also want to acknowledge the superb work of Zora Hutlova Foy in directing our publications program and specifically in bringing this book to fruition. Sarah Berman created the institutional timeline, which was thoughtfully reviewed by Pat Baillargeon. Thanks also go to Heather Pederson for her careful coordination; Susan Cole, helped by Paul Macapia and Eduardo Calderón, for the beautiful photography; Suzanne Kotz for her patience and editing skills, and John Hubbard for his sensitive design.

For the past seventy-five years, the Seattle Art Museum has reflected and in some cases catalyzed the vibrant evolution of this community. One can only imagine the landmarks ahead as the museum progresses toward its century mark, but I have no doubt that the generous benefactors involved in realizing this unprecedented initiative to build the museum's collections will have a starring role.

Mimi Gardner Gates
The Illsley Ball Nordstrom Director

A Community of Collectors

Make no little plans; they have no magic to stir men's blood.

—Daniel H. Burnham, architect of the 1893
World's Columbian Exposition

I'm living in the future. I feel wonderful.

—Talking Heads, "The Book I Read"

London's *Art Newspaper*, a must-read in the art world, posted a stunning headline in its February 2007 issue: "$1bn donations put Seattle on the map."[1] In an amazing surge of generosity and foresight, local collectors had donated or promised more than a thousand works of art valued at $1 billion to the Seattle Art Museum. The story behind the headline had unfolded over the previous eighteen months, as a determined group of museum supporters and staff developed a strategy for keeping Seattle collections in Seattle. They succeeded in securing the gift or promise of eight entire collections to the museum, and more than forty (the number has since grown to over sixty) collectors promised individual works. All of the museum's major collecting areas were represented in the gift, with the majority coming in modern and contemporary art. Highlights included Brancusi's iconic *Bird in Space,* Edward Hopper's *Chop Suey,* a pristine example of Hokusai's *Under the Wave, off Kanagawa,* and in-depth groupings of work by several artists, including Willem de Kooning, Mark Rothko, and Gerhard Richter. What better announcement as the museum prepared for its seventy-fifth anniversary celebration in 2008!

We owe our enviable position to far-sighted leaders whose ambition and vision for the museum and their city are boundless. As Seattle collector Tom Barwick put it, "You have to be thinking in terms of fifty and one hundred years from now. . . . If you can envision it, it has a lot better chance of happening than if you don't."[2] It was that forethought, and simple determination, that created Seattle's success story.

In 2005 the Seattle Art Museum was in the midst of its greatest metamorphosis since the founding of the institution in 1933. We were building a nine-acre sculpture park on the Seattle waterfront, a new venture merging art and the environment, and we were expanding our 1991 building in downtown Seattle in an innovative collaboration with Washington Mutual Bank. To fund these undertakings, and the projected renovation of our original art deco structure, home to our Asian collection, the museum had launched a $180 million capital campaign, "The Transformation of SAM." Seattle's vaunted tradition of civic philanthropy would bring major gifts from corporations, foundations, and nearly ten thousand private donors contributing anywhere between $1 and $25 million. The expansion of the downtown building and the creation of the waterfront park were widely embraced and welcomed by the city, which had recently experienced another cultural milestone with the opening of the new Seattle Public Library. That building's tradition-shattering design by Rem Koolhaas seemed to fit the city's eagerness to take risks. As the Getty Museum's director emeritus John Walsh put it, "This city relies not just on its financial success, but also on imagination."[3]

The museum board and staff directed all their efforts toward the success of the capital campaign and the realization of the simultaneous downtown and waterfront projects. As Illsley Ball Nordstrom Director Mimi Gates cheerfully observed during the course of the capital campaign, no institution would ever choose to do two capital projects at once, but these were opportunities the museum could not turn down, and the results were sure to be great for Seattle. The downtown expansion was an occasion for reinvention on several levels. Newly designed, innovative installations emphasize intersections among our global collections, and more ample galleries invite fresh ambition in the exhibition program.

The energy, optimism, and ambition of these projects parallel Seattle's amazing success in global business over the last twenty-five years. What had been a one-industry town for decades, dependent on the shifting fortunes of the Boeing Company, is now a metropolis crowded with major players. Microsoft is the biggest, but Nintendo, Costco, Starbucks, Amazon, Washington Mutual Bank, RealNetworks, Nordstrom, Safeco, and Alaska Air all base their corporate headquarters in the Seattle area, and many of them make a point of being involved with their hometown. These companies share a commitment to strengthening Seattle; some have formed foundations to distribute donations, and often their CEOs or founders have made substantial personal gifts. Seattle parks, libraries, museums, symphony, opera, and many other cultural and social institutions have benefited considerably from local philanthropy, which steps in with the kind of support that in many other American cities is largely provided by public funding. In part because of this healthy financial base, a 2005 economic impact study rated Seattle's "creative vitality index" at five times the national average.[4] As British cultural commentator James Fenton has observed, "People in Seattle and nearby Portland, in my experience, are used to being the inhabitants of somewhat remote cities, and do not need to have it explained to them that the more they support their local art institutions and events, the richer and more interesting life becomes for everyone."[5]

If Seattle's sense of personal responsibility and civic pride were not sufficiently challenged by the capital campaign, in 2005 the Seattle Art Museum embarked on another ambitious initiative: an acquisitions campaign to honor its seventy-fifth anniversary in 2008. The campaign would not emphasize monetary contributions—virtually all funds being raised were directed to the building projects—but gifts of art itself. At the time the strongest collections at the museum were historical Asian art, reflecting founder Richard E. Fuller's personal taste and early acquisitions; African art from the celebrated collection of Katherine White; and Northwest Coast Native American art from the collection of Seattle businessman John H. Hauberg. We also had an important collection of European porcelain, some fine European painting and sculpture as well as ancient Mediterranean art, a handful of American works, and a medium-sized collection of modern and contemporary art. Much of Seattle's reputation in the art world rested on collections that were still in private hands, and there would never be a better time to seek commitments of art now that the museum was on the verge of realizing its potential in so many ways. We were determined to keep Seattle's art in Seattle—and the museum expansion itself made the most compelling and timely argument for donating art now.

There were many internal discussions before we proposed this initiative to the board of trustees. Were we asking too much of our trustees and supporters? Many collectors had already made generous monetary donations and might not be so happy to see us back on their doorsteps again. Staff members were spread thin with installation planning and publication deadlines. Thinking first of what was manageable, we initially considered a fairly contained program, soliciting seventy-five stellar works for our seventy-five years. But almost immediately we realized that the symbolic gesture could in fact be very problematic as we would have to select what—and whom—to exclude.

So we took a deep breath and began a campaign that matched our building program in ambition and intensity. We assembled a committee of collectors to lead the effort. Working with staff, they identified prospective donors, strategized timing, and discussed how potential donations would complement our collections. Since most of the museum's donors are relatively young, we knew they would want to continue to live with their collections, which led us to focus on strategies for the future. We identified three principal ways in which works could be offered to the museum: outright gift, transferring title and the work to the museum; pledge, a commitment that a work would come to the museum upon the death of the owner; and fractional gift, the donation of a percentage of a work, giving the museum the right to exhibit the work for a period commensurate with its percentage of ownership. Early strategic announcements from the seventy-fifth anniversary committee established a satisfyingly high level of commitment to the initiative from the outset. At our first two meetings, in 2005, prominent collectors Virginia and Bagley Wright, Barney Ebsworth, Marshall Hatch, and Tom Barwick each announced major pledges to the museum.

The Wrights promised their collection of approximately 250 modern and contemporary works. These internationally known collectors are the acknowledged godparents of the Seattle art scene, and they have inspired two generations of collectors in their wake. They met in New York City in the mid-1950s, where Jinny, a Seattle native and recent Barnard graduate, was working at the Sidney Janis Gallery. By the time they settled in Seattle in 1955, they had already acquired works by Mark Rothko, Jackson Pollock, and Philip Guston. Their collection introduced wary Seattleites to abstraction at a time when most were exclusively interested in art from the Northwest. From their Seattle base, the Wrights continued to buy, always purchasing art of the moment. The resulting collection is a brilliant accounting of the major movements in American art since 1950, with important works by James Rosenquist, Andy Warhol, Jasper Johns, Robert Rauschenberg, Donald Judd, Cindy Sherman, Julian Schnabel, Eric Fischl, and Jeff Koons. In the 1990s their interests

expanded to include European artists such as Anselm Kiefer, Katharina Fritsch, Gerhard Richter, and Maurizio Cattelan.

Barney Ebsworth began acquiring early twentieth-century American art in the 1970s when it was so little studied that his emerging collection helped to define the field. It is studded with masterpieces by Edward Hopper, Georgia O'Keeffe, Charles Sheeler, and Marsden Hartley but also includes less well-known contributors such as Byron Browne and George Tooker. Ebsworth attributes his belief in the power of museums to change lives to the childhood visits he made to his hometown Saint Louis Art Museum. Many museums courted Ebsworth, including the National Gallery of Art, which showed his collection in 2000. In a stroke of luck for the Pacific Northwest, Ebsworth chose Seattle for his retirement and built a stunning showcase for his collection on the banks of Lake Washington. At an early seventy-fifth anniversary committee meeting, he declared that he would give eleven major works to the museum, including *Chop Suey*, the finest painting by Edward Hopper in private hands. A few months later, he followed this amazing announcement by committing sixty-five works of American modernism—the core of his collection—to the museum. Ebsworth explained why he chose the Seattle Art Museum: "I feel very blessed to have moved here because this is a community that is growing in all kinds of good ways. The other museums I've been involved in all have been around for a long time. And the collection would have been good in any of those places because it was formed to be a museum collection. But here I feel that it is not only filling a gap; it is also a bigger presence in the museum."[6]

A prime collection of Northwest modern art, featuring major figures Mark Tobey, Leo Kenney, Guy Anderson, and especially Morris Graves, was lovingly assembled over four decades by the late Marshall and Helen Hatch, who were close friends of Graves. They built a definitive collection spanning Graves's sixty-year career, from his earliest paintings on burlap bags to the delicate flower paintings of his last years. The announcement before the committee that five of the most important works in this coveted collection would come to the Seattle Art Museum was followed several months later by the revelation that Hatch would leave his entire collection of Northwest art to the museum. This pledge was particularly meaningful in light of the institutional commitment to artists of the region made by founder Richard Fuller, who had built up significant holdings of their work. The Hatch donation, made a year before his death in 2008, establishes the museum with the premier collection of Northwest modern art in the nation.

Tom and the late Ann Barwick began their collection of American art in the 1980s with the purchase of a modest drawing by Andrew Wyeth. Over time they became passionate students of the field and acquired major examples of American painting and sculpture, including works by Willard Metcalf, Frederic Remington, John LaFarge, Thomas Eakins, and William Kensett, among others. Tom Barwick's plain-spoken eloquence has converted many people to the museum and broadened local interest in American art. He even spearheaded the creation in 2004 of a curatorial department of American art, recognizing that the museum's tiny collection had significant potential for growth. In front of the anniversary committee, Barwick promised seven of the most important works from his collection.

These early commitments by four important collectors gave the museum tremendous momentum, not to mention the beginnings of a major, unbroken sweep of American art from the nineteenth century to the present day. This impressive narrative was propelled even further by the commitment of one of the most formidable collections of postwar American art anywhere. Jane Lang Davis had begun collecting with her husband, Richard Lang, in the late 1960s, and to their first acquisition, *Painting No. 11* by Franz Kline, they quickly added superb works by an array of leading American artists including Mark Rothko, Willem de Kooning, Adolph Gottlieb, Philip Guston, David Smith, and Jackson Pollock. They later added several impressive works by Francis Bacon. Jane Davis often says that they collected with the museum in mind.

The museum also received commitments for significant individual gifts. In addition, we agreed to retroactively acknowledge as seventy-fifth anniversary gifts certain major donations made since 2000. While most of the more than sixty collectors who eventually participated gave modern or contemporary art, nearly all collections at the museum benefited significantly, as will be seen in the following pages.

The range of donors and their interests are revealing about the museum and the city of Seattle. For example, Mark Groudine, deputy director of Seattle's Fred Hutchinson Cancer Research Center, collects African and Oceanic art. After he and his wife, Cynthia Putnam, donated seven works to the museum, Groudine explained, "What we like about having the pieces in the museum is that other people can enjoy them when they are displayed. And when they are not displayed, they are there for research."[7] Another donor, New Yorker Hester Diamond, gave a Mannerist painting by Flemish artist Vincent Sellaer. She knew it would make a difference to the small European collection in Seattle, whereas the painting would probably have gone unnoticed at her hometown museum, the Metropolitan Museum of Art.

Lyn and Jerry Grinstein have built a stunning collection that is particularly strong in painting. In addition to featuring the historical range of work of their favorite artist, Philip Guston, they collect some of the leading masters active today. They promised the museum an enveloping seascape by Gerhard Richter. Allan and Mary Kollar have participated for more than a decade in the museum's American Art Council. Kollar, a prominent American art dealer, first came to art as a printmaker inspired by the Japanese woodblock prints known as ukiyo-e. Over the last several decades he has amassed a stellar collection of rare early ukiyo-e examples, patiently holding out for works in excellent condition. The Kollars' gift of fifty-one prints of the highest quality, including a pristine example of the most famous Japanese woodblock of all, Hokusai's *Under the Wave, off Kanagawa,* overcomes an enormous gap in our otherwise distinguished collection of Japanese art.

Richard and Betty Hedreen's knockout collection of post–World War II painting and sculpture took a provocative turn several years ago when they purchased several examples of old master painting. The works they have promised to the museum—a major devotional painting by Bartolomé Esteban Murillo, which dramatically transforms our European collection, and a striking portrait by American painter Alex Katz—are emblematic of the range of their collection.

WE ARE ALL IN THIS TOGETHER

Contemporary collectors Rebecca and Alexander Stewart have used their knack for spotting talent early to enrich many area arts institutions. From them, the museum received several works, including a video by Los Angeles artist Sterling Ruby, a sculpture by Italian artist Enrico David, and a witty sculpture by Sonny Assu that is at home in both the contemporary and Native American collections. Margaret Levi, a political scientist at the University of Washington, and her husband, Seattle lawyer Robert Kaplan, developed a passion for Australian Aboriginal art in the 1980s. Their generous commitment of eleven paintings and eleven sculptures enabled us to inaugurate the first gallery of Australian Aboriginal art in an American museum. Businessman and philanthropist Sam Rubinstein and his wife, Gladys, were unique among area collectors in accumulating examples of early European modernism; they promised the museum works by Robert Delaunay, Roberto Matta, Max Ernst, and Alexei Jawlensky, among others. After her husband's death in February 2007, Gladys Rubinstein summed up his support of local arts organizations with the simple statement, "He always wanted to make things better for Seattle,"[8] an attitude that characterizes many of the museum's donors.

Not all gifts came through the traditional route of the art market. Simon Ottenberg, a professor emeritus of anthropology at the University of Washington, donated the fruits of more than fifty years of field research. He gave sixty-five pieces of African masquerade material, collected on-site since the 1950s from the Afikpo people

of Nigeria. The fully realized masquerade, along with footage of its performance, is a centerpiece of the new African galleries.

As these exciting donations were committed, our initiative received a potential setback in August 2006 with the announcement that Congress had signed a pension bill with a provision that imposed severe restrictions on new fractional gifts to museums. The loss of this popular option meant that we needed a way to appeal to donors who were not ready to fully commit specific individual works. We looked to the Dallas Museum of Art, which in 2005 had made the impressive announcement that three contemporary collectors, the Hoffman, Rachofsky, and Rose families, had jointly promised their collections to the museum. The donors did not specify particular works but looked to shape their collections so that they would merge seamlessly once they came to the museum. We were inspired by the foresight and collaborative nature of this approach and invited Dallas's director, Jack Lane, to address our board of trustees.

The Dallas model was enthusiastically embraced in Seattle and led to the second phase of our campaign. It harnessed some of the thinking that was already in the minds of forward-looking collectors. For example, Seattle board president (2000–2007) Susan Brotman and her husband, Jeffrey, cofounder and chairman of Costco, have built a rich contemporary collection. Thinking back to before the anniversary initiative, Susan Brotman recalled, "There began to be a lot of thought toward who was collecting what and how we were going to work together as a community of collectors."[9] The Brotmans made a point of acquiring works by significant British and German artists (for example, Antony Gormley, Damien Hirst, Anselm Kiefer, Sigmar Polke, Georg Baselitz) of the last two decades who were not widely represented in other Seattle collections. When they committed their collection to the museum in October 2006, the Brotmans also agreed to encourage other collectors to do the same.

Jon and Mary Shirley have been dedicated supporters of the museum since the early 1990s. Jon, former president of Microsoft, became chairman of our board of trustees in 2001, and the $25 million gift he and Mary made to the Olympic Sculpture Park, primarily to endow its operations, ensured its success. In 2005 they donated more than one hundred works of studio glass, many from the renowned Pilchuck Glass School founded by Dale Chihuly. The rest of their collection, displayed in a spectacular home on Lake Washington, has great depth in the work of Alexander Calder and Chuck Close, who became a close friend of the Shirleys. They have also collected works unlike anything else in Seattle, including paintings by Frida Kahlo and Yves Klein, a wondrous bronze *Bird in Space* by Constantin Brancusi, and a large sculptural installation by Magdalena Abakanowicz. In October 2006 they promised the collection to the Seattle Art Museum.

Griffith and Patricia Way promised an important collection of modern Japanese painting. A Seattle lawyer who spent much of his career in Tokyo, Griffith Way first became acquainted with Japanese culture when he was stationed in Japan at the end of World War II. He did not become a full-fledged collector until the 1980s, when he discovered early twentieth-century artists such as Tsuji Kakō who were not yet recognized by the wider art world. The Ways offered eighty paintings, which, with the ukiyo-e prints from the Kollar collection, forcefully brought our excellent historical collection of Japanese art into the modern era.

By the time we were ready to publicly announce the remarkable results of the initiative in February 2007, more than a thousand works of art had been given or promised to the museum. Richard Fuller would have been astonished to see what his Seattle Art Museum had become in the twenty-first century. The breadth and variety of art promised to the museum are impressive, but he might have been even more surprised by the collective enterprise that made it all possible. Fuller was a visionary who understood that vibrant cities need great cultural institutions, and seventy-five

years ago he founded the Seattle Art Museum with his own money and art collection. During his forty-year tenure as director, the museum broadened its original scope, but it was always identified with this single remarkable man. The late collector and former board chairman John Hauberg recalled that when local supporters had offered financial donations to the museum, Fuller turned them away: "There were people who would have been more than willing to give to the art museum, but they had never been asked."[10] How different from the community-minded Seattle Art Museum of today! Director Mimi Gates speaks about the importance of the arts in building the social fabric of the city. And Susan Brotman, board president throughout the two capital projects and chair of the capital campaign, borrowed a phrase from a work of art in our collection—"we are all in this together"—to fashion a compelling slogan that helped to rally widespread support. As the Seattle Art Museum reaches its seventy-fifth anniversary, we have learned that we are only as strong as our supporters make us. Thanks to the community of collectors who rallied to our call, the museum is stronger than ever.

Chiyo Ishikawa
Susan Brotman Deputy Director for Art
Curator of European Painting and Sculpture

NOTES
1. *The Art Newspaper*, February 2007, 1.
2. Interview, December 19, 2006.
3. John Walsh, "SAM's Buildings in Historical Perspective," unpublished lecture, Seattle Art Museum, April 27, 2007.
4. "City & County of Denver Creative Vitality Index 2007," WESTAF, 2007.
5. "You Shouldn't Have: James Fenton on the Art of Giving," *The Guardian*, May 12, 2007.
6. Interview, December 5, 2006.
7. Interview, February 17, 2007.
8. Obituary, *Seattle Times*, February 2, 2007.
9. *Art & Auction* (September 2007): 115.
10. John H. Hauberg, *Recollections of a Civic Errand Boy* (Seattle: University of Washington Press, 2003), 302.

Chiyo Ishikawa

Semblance without Being
New Still Lifes

1 **Balthasar van der Ast**
Dutch, 1593/94–1657
Still Life with Cherries, signed and dated 1617
oil on wood panel, 12¼ × 18¼ in.
Private collection, T2007.6.2

Two immaculately preserved seventeenth-century Dutch still lifes by Balthasar van der Ast and Willem Claesz. Heda will greatly enhance the Seattle Art Museum's collection of European art. These artists meticulously recorded natural and man-made objects, using the atmospheric illusionism possible with oil paint to contrast the fleetingness of life with the longevity of art. Here they also provide a context for three more recent works by Roy Lichtenstein, Cindy Sherman, and Maurizio Cattelan. These contemporary artists address some of the issues traditional still-life painters faced, but their renderings of reality add a layer of self-conscious comment on the Western art historical tradition. Verisimilitude, the goal of European artists for centuries, is the vehicle through which all five of these works make their cases.

In the painting by Balthasar van der Ast, a Chinese porcelain bowl brimming with delectable red cherries sits on a plain gray shelf (plate 1). These elements would make a perfectly pleasing picture in themselves, with the bowl neatly centered and the ripe cherries glowing invitingly. But the artist added the flamelike forms of greenish gold leaves, still attached to a fruit-bearing branch. Spanning the bowl, they impart depth and visual drama and, with their curling edges and chewed edges, the slightest hint of decay. The leaves writhe and twist against the black wall and cast dark shadows on the shelf—but not on the perfect fruit itself, which seems to burn with its own internal light source.

Like many still-life artists, Van der Ast used cunning artifice to illuminate aspects of nature. To complete the composition, he added three peaches, which offset the symmetry of the arrangement, and beautifully rendered specimens of insects and garden creatures. A butterfly seems to have just alighted on the edge of the shelf—but it will be there each time you look. The fruit will never rot, and the butterfly will never fly away. The artist has trumped nature and caught it in its perfection, forever.

Why does the painting by Willem Claesz. Heda seem so grown-up when compared to the flirtatious little bowl of cherries? The arrangement of oysters, hazelnuts, and lemons on pewter plates with a flagon and glasses is dignified, aloof, understated (plate 2). The viewpoint is lower, making the objects less accessible to us, and the whole arrangement seems farther away. Dutch still lifes often include a partially peeled lemon whose curling rind dangles over the edge of the table; Heda did not allow any such transgression of his rigorous boundaries. Everything is contained. The muted, silvery tones and the repetition of oval forms give the painting the calming, magisterial effect of a stately musical composition.

There is hushed drama available to the alert observer who notices the edges of the plates protruding beyond the lip of the table, especially the one more off than on, heavy with a lemon half and knife. Shouldn't their weight topple the plate? It doesn't. It is as if the artist is telling us that the plate stays put because he told it to—a defiance of the natural order of things.

2 **Willem Claesz. Heda**
Dutch, 1594–1680
Still Life with a Tankard, a Plate of Oysters, and Glasses on a Table, signed and dated 1636
oil on wood panel, 19¾ × 32⅞ in.
Private collection, T2007.6.1

3 **Roy Lichtenstein**
American, 1923–1997
Still Life with Silver Pitcher, 1972
oil and magna on canvas, 51 × 60 in.
Promised gift of the Virginia and Bagley Wright Collection,
in honor of the 75th Anniversary of the Seattle Art Museum,
T98.84.38

The choice and arrangement of objects in Dutch still lifes often depended on aberration, excess, or disarray to convey moralizing messages about moderation and resistance to worldly pleasures. Van der Ast's quivering butterfly is a gentle reminder of the fleetingness of life. Heda's half-full glasses and even light can be interpreted to suggest moderation, but the artist seems equally concerned with formal issues, particularly the degree of tension needed to hold a composition together and the sleight of hand required to coax believability from the physically impossible.

Three hundred years later we find a different approach to illusionism in *Still Life with Silver Pitcher* (plate 3). American pop artist Roy Lichtenstein, who maintained an ongoing dialogue with art history throughout his forty-year career, painted a series of still lifes in the early 1970s. While seventeenth-century artists mimicked the appearance of real objects, he was interested in replicating the

idea of the appearance of those objects in paintings. His schematic renderings offer a set of visual codes signaling glossy reflection, light and shadow, three-dimensionality, and textural variation. The rounded pitcher gets its bulbous shape from the placement of highlights and shadows, while the fruit at the left is merely a flat disk with an outline. Lichtenstein borrows graphic conventions from comic books—short zigzags of black against white suggest a pitcher as shiny as Dick Tracy's hair.

The entire painting is flat and looks as if it could have been plotted out with tape or decals, not oil paint, which has always been associated with seductive illusionism. Lichtenstein talked about this intentionally mechanical appearance: "I want [the painting] to look as though I never corrected anything and it just came out that way. But I go through all sorts of contortions to make it look that way. Because I want [it] to look kind of like a commercial product

4 **Cindy Sherman**
American, born 1954
Untitled No. 210, 1989
Cibachrome print, 34⅛ × 21⅛ in.
Promised gift of the Virginia and Bagley Wright Collection,
in honor of the 75th Anniversary of the Seattle Art Museum,
T98.84.63

but at the same time I want [it] to be an interesting painting."[1] A Dutch still life makes a direct appeal to multiple senses and might even make your mouth water, but Lichtenstein engages your eyes and your brain. Sensual appreciation is arrived at through intellectual processing.

Untitled No. 210 by photographer Cindy Sherman shares the burnished glow of Heda's still life, and its candle and pewter goblet are reminiscent of the domestic implements in that painting. Sherman's warmly lit portrait of a Renaissance gentleman can be viewed as a kind of still life itself, only the subject is not nature and the familiar objects of daily life but art history (plate 4). Sherman created the work as part of a series of thirty-five images based on historical portraiture. As she has done throughout her career, she composed each portrait as though staging a film, using props and costumes to create a character, situation, and setting. Here she recalls Hans Holbein the Younger's exacting portraits of humanists surrounded by exquisitely rendered letters and books, scientific instruments, and other objects of personal significance. Holbein's

5 Maurizio Cattelan
Italian, born 1960
Good Boy, 1998
taxidermized dog and chair, 16 × 11 × 5 in.
Promised gift of the Virginia and Bagley Wright Collection,
in honor of the 75th Anniversary of the Seattle Art Museum,
T98.107

marvelous images were emblematic distillations of a person and his place in the world, encompassing past worldly accomplishments and ongoing intellectual interests. Sherman's portrait recalls all of these associations, but in a generic way. She has concocted a type but has not gone so far as to create a logical narrative or individual personality for this gentleman.

Sherman's approach contains a critique of the tradition of painting and portraiture, as critic Arthur Danto noted: "Sherman has done something startling and strange, draining the old masters and their subjects at once of a certain power, by showing the artifice, the convention, the transparent fakeness of the worlds they believed were solid and unshakable and real—reducing them to conventions one can slip in and out of without believing them to be the final truth of being."[2]

Finally, Maurizio Cattelan's *Good Boy* offers an unsettling variation on the issue of illusion and artifice that has characterized the history of the still life (plate 5). Consisting of a taxidermized Jack Russell terrier curled up on a cheap modern chair, this still life is not a replica of the real; it is real. Tucked away in a corner in an installation at the Seattle Art Museum, the seemingly unstaged sculpture draws visitor responses ranging from shock and distaste to distressed empathy to knowing, amused delight.

Cattelan often uses replication in his work. After completing one project in which he exactly reproduced an entire exhibition of another artist's work, he explained, "The idea was to create confusion . . . to question identity."[3] A similar disorientation is created by this sleeping dog which isn't really sleeping, which looks lifelike because it has been artificially preserved after death. Cattelan's dog inspires the same kind of double take—"Is that real?"—as the butterfly in Van der Ast's painting. Van der Ast and his contemporaries used their remarkable skill to argue that art conferred immortality and was therefore superior to life. Beneath the one-liner jokiness of *Untitled (Cheap to Feed)* lies a concern about the same issues of life and death that transfixed seventeenth-century still-life painters.

NOTES

1. *Roy Lichtenstein: All About Art* (Humlebaek, Denmark: Louisiana Museum of Modern Art, 2003), 59.

2. Arthur Danto, *History Portraits: Cindy Sherman* (New York: Rizzoli, 1991), 13.

3. Calvin Tomkins, "The Prankster," *The New Yorker*, Oct. 4, 2004.

Michael Darling

A Story in Paint

For many years now, the Seattle Art Museum's holdings of post–World War II American paintings have been a strength of its modern and contemporary collections. Built from an early acquisition of an important Jackson Pollock painting, broad holdings of Mark Tobey and Morris Graves, seminal works by Arshile Gorky and Mark Rothko, as well as other paintings, the collection demonstrated the major happenings of the period in a very credible way. As a result of the recent gifts made as part of our seventy-fifth anniversary acquisitions initiative, however, Seattle now boasts one of the most compelling collections of material from this time of any museum in the country. The anniversary gifts have both deepened the holdings of artists already represented in the collection and, equally important, broadened the collection with the addition of works by artists such as Lee Krasner, Barnett Newman, Adolph Gottlieb, Clyfford Still, and Franz Kline. And in every category, the gifts presented are more than works on paper or prints that superficially burnish a roster of big names; they are major, representative paintings that record high-water marks in the artists' careers.

Just as important is the museum's new ability to communicate to audiences about the historical repercussions of this significant era of painting. We can now document how subsequent generations of painters have attempted to push their field forward and address the concerns of their day. The works that have come to the museum on the occasion of its anniversary provide a fascinating portrait of the last sixty years of painting, revealing both recognizable

patterns and surprising new perspectives. When the anniversary gifts are considered alongside paintings already in the collection, they bring the period to life with amazing clarity and insight. One is struck with the sense that painters increasingly felt limited by the conventional rectangle filled with divinely inspired brushstrokes. Across six decades we can witness how internal and external pressures exerted themselves on this format until finally forcing open new vistas for exploration. This alone makes for lively intellectual and visual sport, but also worth watching is the retrenchment and reconsideration by recent members of this lineage who, circling back again, remind us of the losses and the gains from previous skirmishes.

The smoking guns of those early mid-century battles are very much in evidence in this group of paintings. Early works by Mark Rothko and Franz Kline show how these consummate abstractionists shed their attachments to the figure and recognizable forms. Kline's *Nijinsky* (c. 1942, plate 6), for instance—one of a group of works that trace the developments of Kline's career—suggests links to an earlier generation of American artists such as Walt Kuhn or to the Pierrots of Pablo Picasso. The graphic power of the decoration in the brim of the dancer's hat and the dynamic line in his costume now read as premonitions of the powerful paintings that would make Kline famous. Two such signature canvases are among this group, *Painting No. 11* from 1951 (plate 8) and *Cross Section* from 1956 (plate 9). These commanding paintings show Kline at his

6 **Franz Kline**
American, 1910–1962
Nijinsky, c. 1942
oil on canvas, 23 × 19 in.
Jane Lang Davis Collection

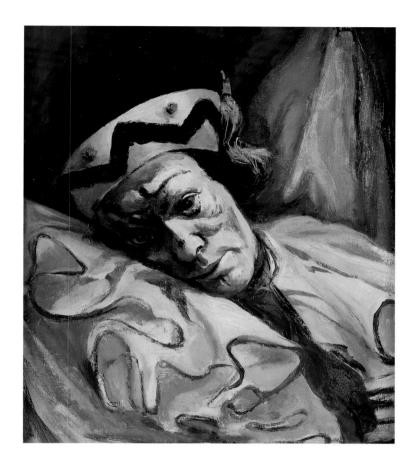

7 **Franz Kline**
American, 1910–1962
Untitled (study for *Cross Section*), 1956
ink on paper, 9 × 12 in.
Promised gift of the Virginia and Bagley Wright Collection,
in honor of the 75th Anniversary of the Seattle Art Museum,
T2006.65.73

(above)
8 Franz Kline
American, 1910–1962
Painting No. 11, 1951
oil on canvas, 61½ × 82¼ in.
Jane Lang Davis Collection

(left)
9 Franz Kline
American, 1910–1962
Cross Section, 1956
oil on canvas, 53½ × 63 in.
Promised gift of the Virginia and
Bagley Wright Collection, in honor
of the 75th Anniversary of the Seattle
Art Museum, T98.84.34

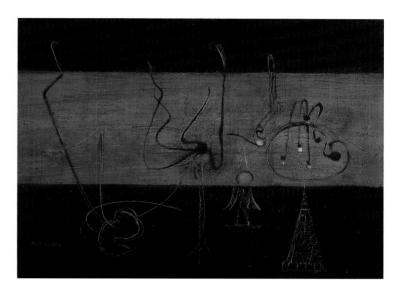

10 **Mark Rothko**
American, 1903–1970
Untitled, c. 1939–40
oil on canvas, 29¾ × 36 in.
Jane Lang Davis Collection

11 **Mark Rothko**
American, 1903–1970
Untitled, 1945
oil on canvas, 22 × 30 in.
Jane Lang Davis Collection

confident best, wrestling a large canvas into a tense whole with a starkly reduced compositional scheme in *Painting No. 11*, and muscling his way to an evocation of mighty industry in *Cross Section*. While the alluring myth of action painting would have us believe that artists such as Kline came to their compositions spontaneously, his works on paper reveal that his paintings were often pre-considered. We are now fortunate to have one such study (plate 7), for *Cross Section*, that shows this important but overlooked aspect of his practice.

Rothko's less-than-pure path to his mature style is also visible in the recent pledges and gifts, beginning with *Untitled* (c. 1939–40, plate 10), in which his preferred organizational scheme of horizontal bands, already in evidence, is filled with recognizable elements such as classical, even Picasso-esque faces, suggestions of water, and fragmented body parts. A handful of years later, in *Untitled* (1945, plate 11), vestiges of European influence continue to attend Rothko's stripes, as biomorphic hallucinations handed down from Joan Miró cavort across nocturnal striations. The universal and elemental language that Rothko was groping toward in these early canvases finds full expression in *Orange on Red* (1956, plate 12), a work

in which the artist balanced the earthbound and the transcendent in his refined, mature style. The margins he left between the edges of the canvas and his brushy blocks of color, as well as between the simple compositional elements, do not allow viewers to ever completely forget that they are looking at an object made by applying rosy hues to a stretched canvas support. The tonal and scalar harmony created by these elements, aided by the otherworldly glow of the colors, is transporting.

An increasingly intellectual conception of abstraction, as well as a growing melancholy, is evidenced in yet another marker from Rothko's incredible career, the large, horizontal *Untitled* from 1963 (plate 13). This painting, in its more regularly scaled bars and almost environmental scope, hints at a smoother transition from abstract expressionism to minimalism than most histories or even the bombastic rhetoric of the day would suggest, as it shows strong formal links to Frank Stella, Robert Ryman, and even Donald Judd. The brooding quality of the work, however, with its penumbral hues and deathly, insistent horizontality, reveals a personal darkness and skepticism. The museum now holds seven canvases, spanning the years 1939 to 1963, by this immensely influential artist.

12 **Mark Rothko**
American, 1903–1970
Orange on Red, 1956
oil on canvas, 69 × 38 in.
Partial and promised gift of Jon and Mary Shirley,
in honor of the 75th Anniversary of the Seattle Art
Museum, 2002.68

13 **Mark Rothko**
American, 1903–1970
Untitled, 1963
oil on canvas, 69 × 90 in.
Jane Lang Davis Collection

14 **Adolph Gottlieb**
American, 1903–1974
Follow the Red Line, 1946
oil on canvas, 34 × 26 in.
Promised gift of Ann P. Wyckoff, in honor of
the 75th Anniversary of the Seattle Art Museum,
T2006.126.2

Alongside Rothko, Adolph Gottlieb in the 1930s worked his way from archaic and primitive forms with rich but elusive associations to an even more ambiguous strain of abstraction in the 1950s. At the museum this transition can now be traced through paintings such as *Follow the Red Line* (1946, plate 14), a dynamic and accomplished example of Gottlieb's pictographic approach, and the signature *Crimson Spinning No. II* (1959, plate 15), a bold, echt abstract expressionist fusion of the primordial—glowing orb, dark explosion—and the base factuality of paint slathered on canvas.

15 **Adolph Gottlieb**
American, 1903–1974
Crimson Spinning No. II, 1959
oil on canvas, 90 × 72 in.
Jane Lang Davis Collection

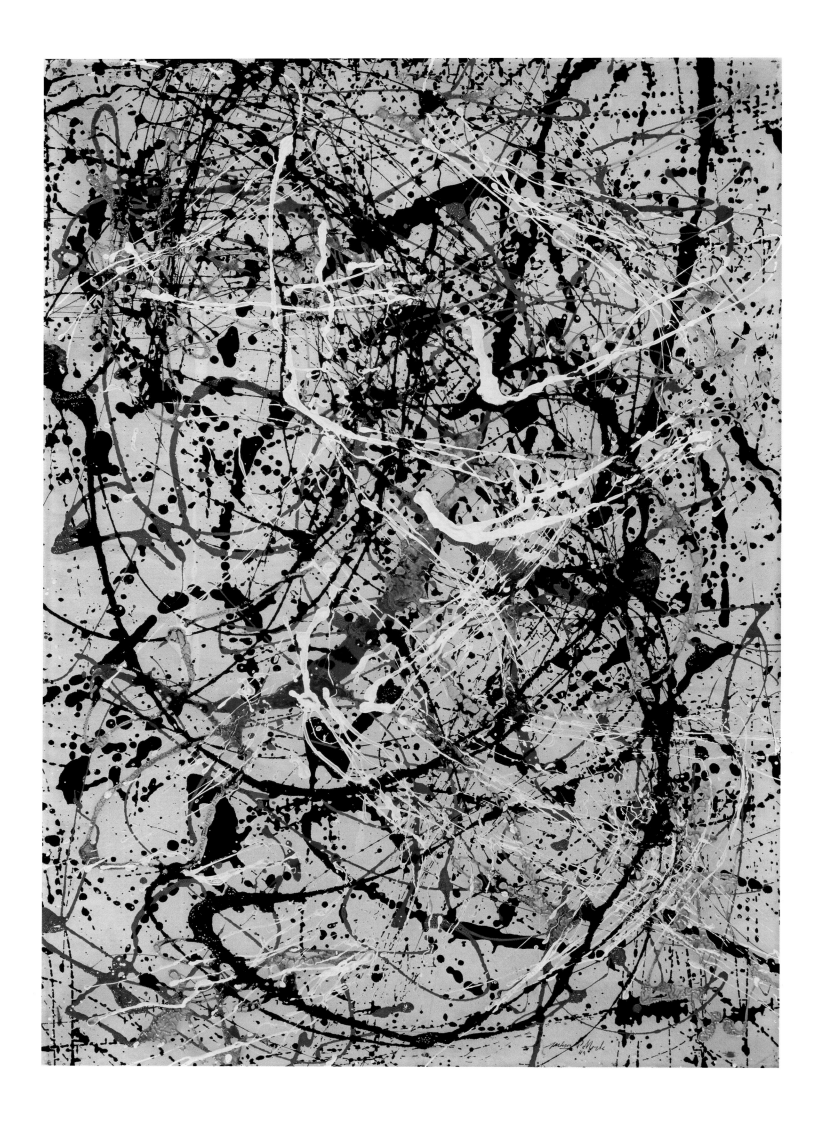

An interest in celebrating and revealing the materials and gestures that make up a painting and a simultaneous grappling with the ineffable course through other important abstract expressionist works from the seventy-fifth anniversary initiative. One of these touchstone paintings is the classic, multicolored drip painting *Number 20* (1949, plate 16) by Jackson Pollock, which carries forward the early experiments evident in the aptly named *Sea Change* (1947) in its evocation of microbiological or astrophysical structure. A wonderfully rhythmic and confident canvas by Lee Krasner titled *Easter Lilies* (1956, plate 17) finds its formal and metaphoric power in regenerative botanical allusions. Krasner's loose tangle of broad, adjacent brushstrokes and liberated drips anchors her fevered jungle vision in the here and now of a studio practice; in much the same way, Clyfford Still asserted the materiality of a work such as

(opposite)

16 **Jackson Pollock**
American, 1912–1956
Number 20, 1949
paint on paper mounted on board, 28 × 20 in.
Partial and promised gift of Jon and Mary Shirley, in honor
of the 75th Anniversary of the Seattle Art Museum, 2002.66

17 **Lee Krasner**
American, 1908–1984
Easter Lilies, 1956
oil on canvas, 48 × 60 in.
Jeffrey and Susan Brotman Collection, T2006.113.2

18 Clyfford Still
American, 1904–1980
Number 2, 1949, 1949
oil on canvas, 91¾ × 68⅞ in.
Jane Lang Davis Collection, T2006.103.1

19 **Paul Horiuchi**
American (born Japan), 1906–1999
Wintered by Nature (Survival of Sensitivity), 1965
casein and Japanese paper on canvas, 65½ × 53 in.
Promised gift of the Marshall and Helen Hatch Collection,
in honor of the 75th Anniversary of the Seattle Art Museum,
T2000.17

Number 2, 1949 (1949, plate 18) through a suffocating, scabbed surface of oil paint that is like the dry, craggy landscape of the West
or the inscrutable nebulae in the night sky. Paul Horiuchi crafted a
different approach to this dichotomy in his *Wintered by Nature (Survival of Sensitivity,* 1965; plate 19), in which he used torn Japanese

papers to make collages on canvas that are at once delicate and
imposing. Artists from this protean generation tilted toward big
themes and allowed their imaginations to run free, but they also
carefully maintained a self-awareness of their medium that ensured
an important criticality.

20 Willem de Kooning
American (born The Netherlands),
1904–1997
Town Square, 1948
oil on paper, 17 × 23½ in.
Jane Lang Davis Collection

One of the artists from this group, Willem de Kooning, embodied all the traits of abstract expressionism but resisted full abstraction throughout the heyday of the movement. De Kooning could not banish human bodies, primarily female ones, from his mental sourcebook, yet he was an emblematic and revered member of the New York coterie. The important *Town Square* (1948, plate 20), for instance, was included in de Kooning's first solo exhibition and is part of a group of his most influential works which also includes *Attic* (1949, Metropolitan Museum of Art, New York) and *Excavation* (1950, Art Institute of Chicago). This picture pointed the way toward the nonhierarchical, allover compositions that were crucial to the period, but the mostly white palette, broken up by overpainted lines and underlying recesses in black and occasionally ocher, holds back from the descriptiveness of the title. Only the hustle and bustle of its composition is comparable to an urban center. In fact, like other of the artist's works from this time, it is the fragmentary suggestion of human form that is most recognizable and keeps full abstraction at bay. Rather than buildings, this town square is made up of

21 **Willem de Kooning**
American (born The Netherlands),
1904–1997
Woman with Smile, 1967
oil on canvas, 23½ × 18½ in.
Jane Lang Davis Collection

distinctly female curves outlining breasts, hips, waists, shoulders, and buttocks (a catalogue of erogenous zones), with perhaps one mascara-laden eye in the top-left quarter of the composition. De Kooning would be less coy in the years immediately after this with the introduction of his extensive series of *Woman* paintings, a later example of which is *Woman with Smile* (1967, plate 21). Here the human form is again the intermediary between the artist's loaded, wristy brush and the passive, expectant canvas.

22 **Philip Guston**
American, 1913–1980
Untitled, 1954
oil on canvas, 51 × 48¾ in.
Promised gift of the Virginia and Bagley Wright Collection,
in honor of the 75th Anniversary of the Seattle Art Museum,
T98.84.22

Philip Guston's career mirrors that of his peers in many ways. He learned his craft through figuration, expanded his horizons by exposure to surrealism, and developed a luminous, deeply humane abstraction through direct and unabashed engagement with his medium. Paintings such as *Untitled* (1954, plate 22) established Guston's reputation and were unlike the works of any other artist at that time. As the world changed around him, however, Guston, like Rothko, became disillusioned by the art-for-art's-sake nature of abstract painting and thought his practice should engage weightier questions than "to adjust a red to a blue" (quoted in Robert Storr's 1986 monograph, p. 53). In one of the most storied stylistic breaks in art history, Guston exhibited a new body of work in 1970 that eschewed abstraction in favor of cartoonish figures that allowed him to address personal as well as social traumas, including the horrors of the Vietnam War. *The Painter* (1976, plate 23) is a monumental expression of this late style and embodies Guston's isolation from the art world as he peeks from behind a brick wall. These works also trace the artist's sincere reticence toward facing up to the complications of the real world, including the upheavals caused by the Watergate scandal. (Richard Nixon became one of Guston's most explicit characters, in addition to the artist himself.)

23 **Philip Guston**
American, 1913–1980
The Painter, 1976
oil on canvas, 74 in. × 9 ft. 8 in.
Jane Lang Davis Collection

24 **Philip Guston**
American, 1913–1980
Untitled, 1968
oil on canvas, 24 × 24 in.
Promised gift of Robert B. and Honey
Dootson Collection, in honor of the
75th Anniversary of the Seattle Art
Museum, T2008.54.6

25 **Francis Bacon**
British, 1909–1992
Study for a Head, 1952
oil on canvas, 25 × 22 in.
Jane Lang Davis Collection

On the other side of the Atlantic, Francis Bacon shared the overt painterliness of his American peers but made figuration the vehicle for his expressiveness with the brush and for his evocation of physical and psychological duress. Three paintings by Bacon promised to the collection give the museum the chance to compare his achievements with those of American artists working at the same time. *Study for a Head* (1952, plate 25), for instance, overtly calls attention to the brushwork and the structure and shape of the support with lines tracing the vertical edges of the canvas and crossing behind the figure. We also see illusionistic space sketched out from a single perspective and a deeply hierarchical composition with a sole figure placed in the middle. Only de Kooning among the leading Americans would have preserved such a central pictorial anchor, and his figures would have been flattened and abstracted such that they would merge with the support. Bacon, however, emits an emotional heat that can also be felt in the frenzied energy of his Yankee contemporaries. As Guston (as well as the next generation) would find out, figuration, especially the tortured sort practiced by Bacon in a work like *Study for a Portrait* (1967, plate 26), was perhaps a more direct way of engaging with a society undergoing turmoil and change.

26 Francis Bacon
British, 1909–1992
Study for a Portrait, 1967
oil on canvas, 61 × 55 in.
Jane Lang Davis Collection

41

27 **Jasper Johns**
American, born 1930
Thermometer, 1960
charcoal and pastel on paper, 22 × 15½ in.
Promised gift of the Virginia and Bagley Wright Collection,
in honor of the 75th Anniversary of the Seattle Art Museum,
T2006.65.70

By the late 1950s the pure expression of paint and abstracted states of nature had ossified in America into a rigid school of thought, and the melodrama of an artist like Bacon was not a common way out. Instead, a calculated, critical coolness began to emerge that through irony, absurdity, literalism, and an embrace of everyday images steered a new course for painting.

Jasper Johns was one of the sharpest critics of the generation that preceded him. He took tenets of abstract expressionism to absurd extremes as a means to both debunk some of its lofty (and perhaps no longer valid) aspirations and move forward some of its more intellectual positions. In Johns's *Thermometer* (1960, plate 27) we see just such a multipronged approach. This work on paper is based on a painting of the same title created one year earlier (also in SAM's collection). In reversing the common practice of making a drawing as preparation for a painting, Johns challenged notions of originality in this work (and several others from the same period) by repeating himself and reproducing an image he had already made. By creating the drawing in black and white (the painting is in garish colors), Johns crafted a deathly, bloodless facsimile, but the lack of color also reveals more clearly a reference embedded in his compositional scheme of two panels separated by a narrow vertical band: the "zips" of Barnett Newman.

The museum now has a classic Newman canvas, *The Three* (1962, plate 28), which though later than the works by Johns, nevertheless follows a scheme established much earlier. Newman's signature protominimalist compositions have been found lurking in other of Johns's works from this time (*Diver* from 1963, for instance), but whereas for Newman these vertical voids are a source of space, light, and possibly divinity ("the three" is not far from "trinity"), Johns in *Thermometer* fills the gap with an everyday, mundane object. Indicative of the searing commentary and lasting radicalism of the work, the thermometer mocks the vocabulary of contemporary color theory (hot, cool) and slyly introduces elements of accuracy and objectivity to the subjective practice of painting.

Another recent gift, by a figure from an earlier generation who made groundbreaking work deep into his career, also features a found thermometer. The esteemed surrealist Max Ernst, in his late *Spring, The Redeemer and the Redeemed* (1965, plate 29), painted a similarly "impure" abstraction, filling in rectangles of color (reminiscent of those of Josef Albers) with a birdcage, a thermometer, and other household ephemera. Ernst's composition might not be as barbed as that of Johns, but its characteristic and playful non sequiturs make for good comparison.

28 Barnett Newman
American, 1905–1970
The Three, 1962
oil on canvas, 76¼ × 72 in.
Promised gift of the Virginia and Bagley
Wright Collection, in honor of the 75th
Anniversary of the Seattle Art Museum,
T98.84.46

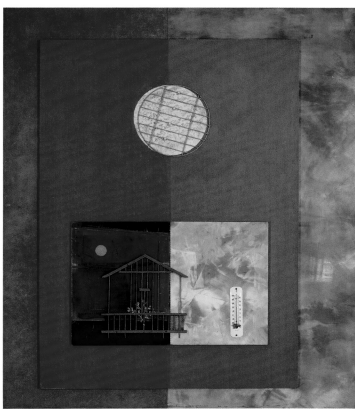

29 Max Ernst
German, 1891–1976
Spring, The Redeemer and the Redeemed, 1965
oil and objects on board, 45 × 39 in.
Gladys and Sam Rubinstein Collection, T2004.76.2

30 **Robert Rauschenberg**
American, 1925–2008
Octave, 1960
oil on canvas with assemblage,
77½ × 42¼ in.
Promised gift of the Virginia and
Bagley Wright Collection, in honor
of the 75th Anniversary of the Seattle
Art Museum, T2006.65.123

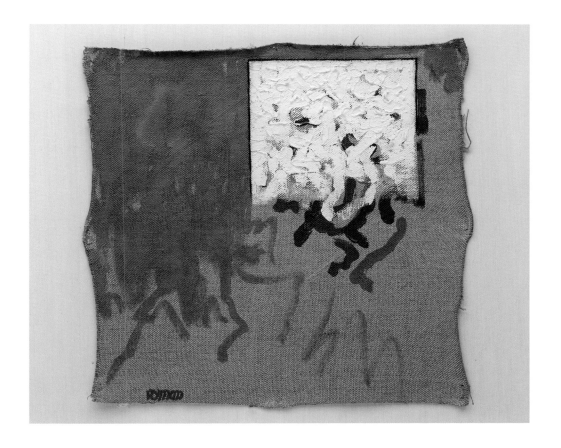

31 **Robert Ryman**
American, born 1930
Untitled #26, 1963
oil on linen, 10¾ × 10¾ in.
Promised gift of the Virginia and Bagley Wright
Collection, in honor of the 75th Anniversary of
the Seattle Art Museum, T2006.65.130

32 **Claes Oldenburg**
American (born Sweden), 1929
Giant Wedge of Pecan Pie, 1963
muslin soaked in plaster over wire frame, wood,
painted in enamel, 14⅜ × 50½ × 20¾ in.
Promised gift of the Virginia and Bagley Wright
Collection, in honor of the 75th Anniversary of
the Seattle Art Museum, T98.84.48

Robert Rauschenberg's *Octave* (1960, plate 30), one of his seminal group of "combine" paintings, is another pivotal work that interrogates the values of abstract expressionism. Here the spontaneity so cherished by champions of the New York school is lampooned in drips that originate from thumbtacks, men's ties that stand in for brushstrokes, and a geometric order (with allusions to Mondrian or Rothko) that derives not from Cartesian purity but from the broken-off uprights of a slat-back chair. The loud mix of materials and gestures—trousers, umbrella, torn posters, newspaper clippings, and an array of brushstrokes—makes the painting, infused as it is with the flotsam and jetsam of the street, as vigorous and as whole as any by his predecessors. Although without question works such as this or the found objects and motifs in Johns paved the way for the emergence of pop art, a certain systematic criticality also inspired newcomers such as Robert Ryman. In a manner that is visually distinct from Johns and Rauschenberg (although the latter made an infamous series of white paintings), Ryman, too, in a work such as *Untitled #26* (1963, plate 31), seemed to catalogue all the necessary components of painting—rectangle, canvas, paint, evidence of the hand, signature—and serve them up in a detached, basic, and undeniably humble way that both takes a noticeable step away from abstract expressionism and acknowledges its influence.

This fascinating transition from one dominant generation to an equally influential next is played out in a number of outstanding new additions to the collection. Claes Oldenburg's notorious installation of 1961–62, *The Store*, in which the blatantly commercial purposes of a shop and the perceived purity of an art gallery were promiscuously scrambled, also ribbed abstract expressionism in crudely made plaster replicas of household items that were then slathered with Pollock-like drips of paint. His *Giant Wedge of Pecan Pie* (1963, plate 32), a hybrid of painting and sculpture, is from this body of work. A lurid example of the segue from one art movement to another, it marks a shift from the sensibility of high culture to low.

33 Jim Dine
American, born 1935
Vise, 1962
oil on canvas with wooden table and metal vise,
80 × 36 × 30 in. overall
Promised gift of the artist, in honor of the 75th Anniversary
of the Seattle Art Museum, T2006.91

34 James Rosenquist
American, born 1933
Dishes, 1964
oil on canvas, 50 × 60 in.
Promised gift of the Virginia and Bagley Wright Collection,
in honor of the 75th Anniversary of the Seattle Art Museum,
T98.84.53

Jim Dine's seminal *Vise* (1962, plate 33) likewise intertwines painting
and sculpture, the sacred and profane. The vise of the title, a found
object that is both dumb hardware and an echo of Dada precedents,
extends the wall-mounted painting into the viewer's space through
the pipe held in its jaws and the table on which it rests. Moreover,
the vise is an accomplice in the desecration of the hallowed surface
of the painting, allowing the pipe to pierce the otherwise blank and
pure canvas amid a controlled thicket of brushwork.

In *Damage* (1964, plate 35), Ed Ruscha performed a similarly iconoclastic maneuver. Interrupting a beautiful blue monochrome with the word "damage," painted in commercial sign lettering as a further affront to the elevated status of the painter, he set the canvas "on fire" in an act of illusionism anathema to the previous generation. James Rosenquist enacted yet more patricide in *Dishes* (1964, plate 34), enlisting the skills he learned as a billboard painter to render one of the commonest household subjects, a rack full of drying dishes, in luminous Technicolor. Such raucous revolt was legion among this generation. The rectangular, wall-mounted canvas, filled with the deeply personal residue of the brush, was the locus of some of the most vehement agitation during the 1960s and 1970s.

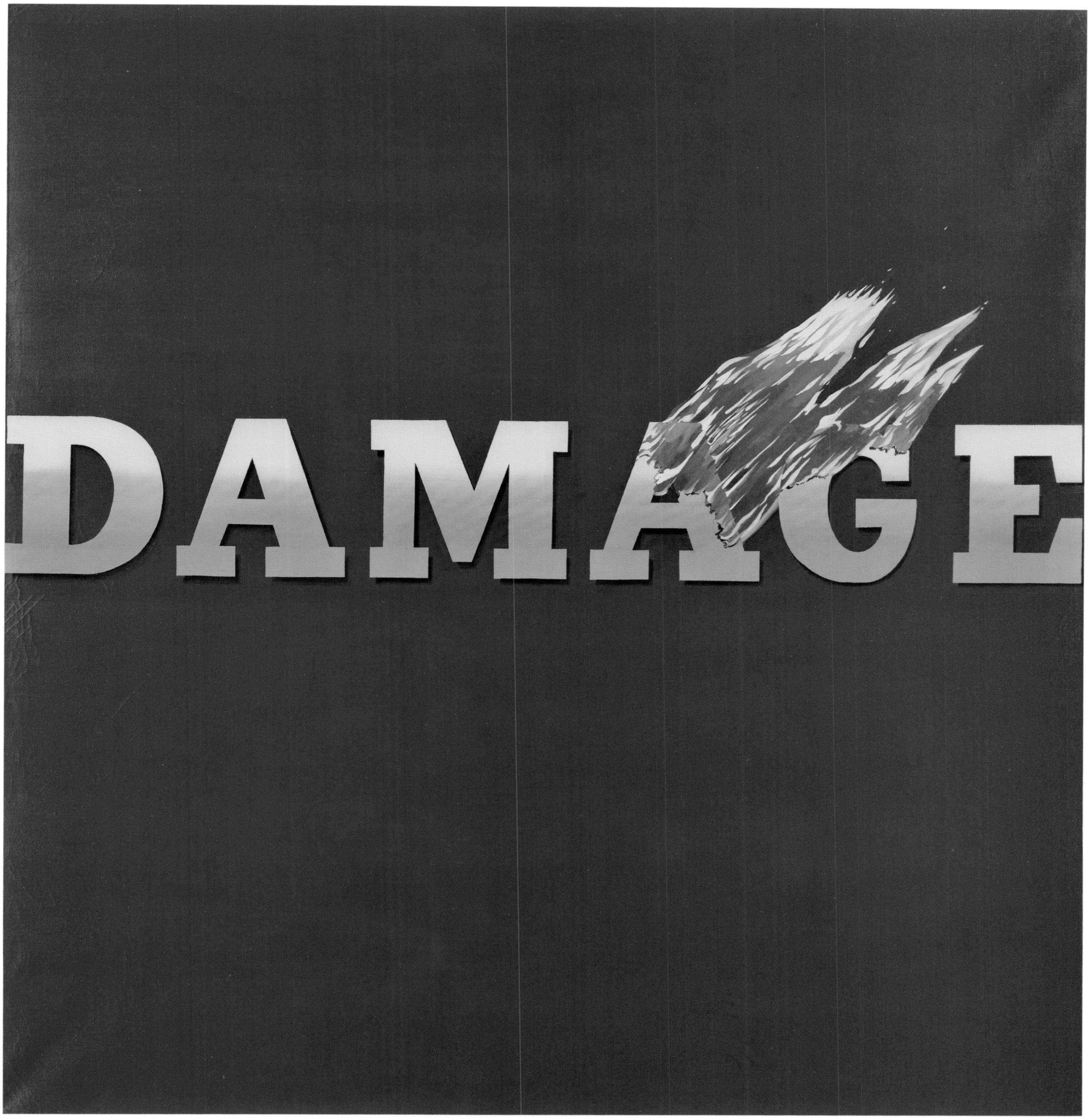
DAMAGE

36 **Jasper Johns**
American, born 1930
Harlem Light, 1967
oil and collage on unprimed canvas, 55 in. × 9 ft. 9 in.
Partial and promised gift of Jon and Mary Shirley, in honor
of the 75th Anniversary of the Seattle Art Museum, 2002.67

Restlessness and dissatisfaction of this sort are found in the paintings during this period of the ever-skeptical Jasper Johns. *Harlem Light* (1967, plate 36), for example, with its disparate elements and slipping and sliding planes (or perhaps panes), is to disjointedness what Pollock's work is to pictorial unity. The canvases of Frank Stella from the same time—*Sabra I* (1967, plate 37) is one—reveal a similar internal compositional struggle that led to decidedly nonsquare formats and a mathematical rigor that belies the coolness of the age. These qualities are also found in the works of formalist painters such as Kenneth Noland, in *And Again* (1964, plate 38), and Ellsworth Kelly, in *Blue, Green, Red II* (1965, plate 39).

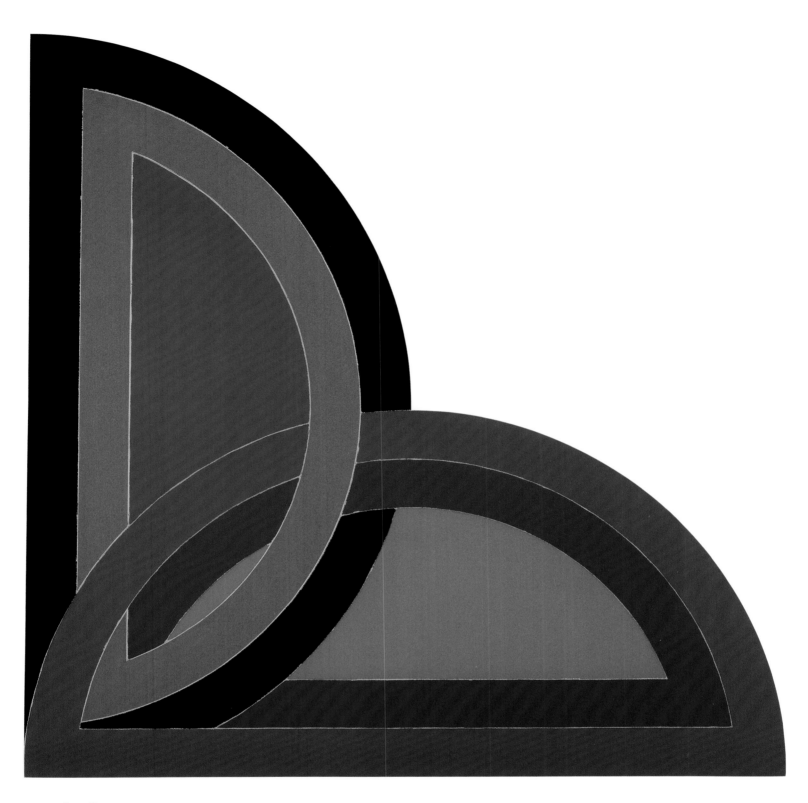

37 **Frank Stella**
American, born 1937
Sabra I, 1967
acrylic on shaped canvas, 10 ft. × 10 ft. × 3 in.
Gift of the Virginia and Bagley Wright Collection, in honor of
the 75th Anniversary of the Seattle Art Museum, T2006.65.142

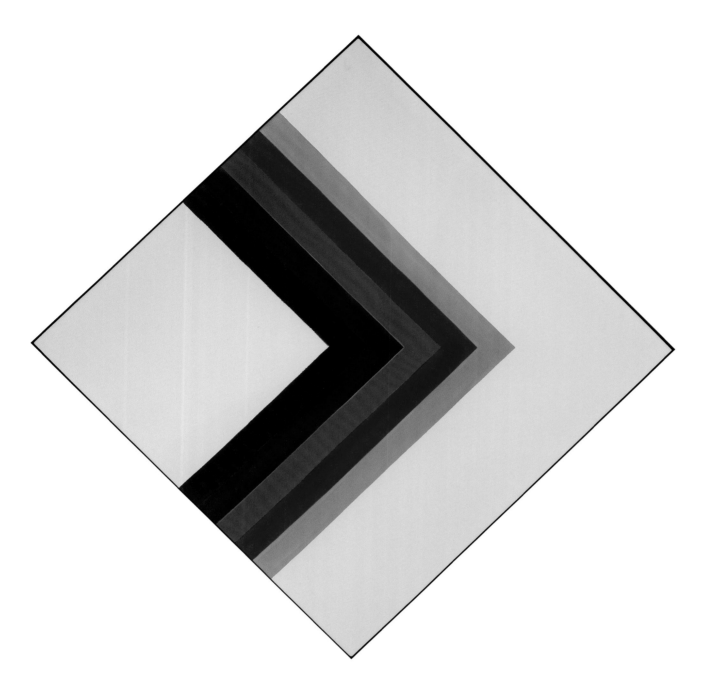

38 Kenneth Noland
American, born 1924
And Again, 1964
acrylic resin on canvas, 69½ × 69½ in.
Promised gift of the Virginia and Bagley Wright Collection,
in honor of the 75th Anniversary of the Seattle Art Museum,
T98.84.47

39 Ellsworth Kelly
American, born 1923
Blue, Green, Red II, 1965
oil on canvas, 88 in. × 8 ft. 6 in.
Gift of the Virginia and Bagley Wright Collection, in honor
of the 75th Anniversary of the Seattle Art Museum, 2007.119

Alex Katz was steadfast in his devotion to figuration during a time when abstraction almost always held sway, and his commanding portrait *Ada in White Hat* (1979, plate 40) has a similarly detached attitude while also suggesting that the rectangle cannot contain the energy of its composition—or perhaps the spirit of the sitter. This kind of internal combustion in American painting reaches the breaking point in a piece like *Why Painting (Traveler's Umbrella),* 1987, (plate 41) by Elizabeth Murray. As in *Ada,* we witness in Murray's work the full flowering of doubt (evidenced in her title), critique, rebellion, and new prerogatives that had been building over the preceding thirty years. In this masterpiece the banal subject matter of pop—a version of illusionism—the winking inclusion of dripping paint, and the physical deconstruction of the hallowed flat-bed picture plane make for a dramatic denouement in this chronology of American painting.

41 **Elizabeth Murray**
American, 1940–2007
Why Painting (Traveler's Umbrella), 1987
oil on canvas, 94 in. × 10 ft. 10 in. × 23½ in. overall
Promised gift of the Virginia and Bagley Wright Collection,
in honor of the 75th Anniversary of the Seattle Art Museum,
T2006.65.98

On another continent, Murray's peer, the German Anselm Kiefer, also packed his paintings with recognizable objects that pushed his surfaces into three dimensions. Yet Kiefer did not rely on paint and canvas alone to rewrite the history of painting as he saw it. In a monumental piece such as *Die Welle (The Wave*, 1990; plate 42), Kiefer's use of lead, ash, earth, and sentimental materials such as clothing was part of a sustained rumination on the tragic history of modern Germany, a subject that Kiefer has explored in various ways throughout his career. Kiefer's oeuvre has a consistency that can now be traced across multiple examples in the collection.

Two painters who directly preceded Kiefer in the slowly rebounding Germany of the 1960s chose multiplicity as their way forward. If the museum's new paintings suggest an internal agitation in American art from the late 1950s to the 1980s, the most dominant German painters of the past half century—Sigmar Polke and Gerhard Richter—were moved by external pressures toward fragmentation and destabilizing shifts of style. Both Polke and Richter used photographic images, whose endless supply pervades newspapers, magazines, books, and television, to open an awareness of the potential for contemporary painters to take on any number of guises or possibilities.

In two great paintings promised to the collection, Polke employed photographs to link painting to the modern mechanism of image proliferation. At the same time he asserted painting's diffidence through his experimentation with various media and surface treatments. In *Untitled* (1975, plate 43), the found image of a harem girl with a hookah becomes a vehicle for psychedelic updates on Pollock's splatter technique and Lucio Fontana's existential cuts in the canvas, which here help to define the serrated leaves of a marijuana plant. *Wachturm (Watchtower)* (1985, plate 44) could be by a different artist in its even cruder juxtaposition of elements, including Polke's favored rasters or coarsely pixilated images, a silhouetted tower, and an electrical storm of paint in which drips suggest the canvas was spun this way and that during its creation. The dissonance between elements and between canvases generates an ambiguous zone that defers quick readings and allows multiple interpretations, while also discouraging the myth of the painter in pursuit of a signature, synthesizing style.

43 Sigmar Polke
German, born 1941
Untitled, 1975
oil, gouache, graphite, and metallic paint
on canvas, 57⅛ × 59⅛ in.
Jeffrey and Susan Brotman Collection,
T2006.113.1

44 Sigmar Polke
German, born 1941
Wachturm (Watchtower), 1985
mixed media with acrylic on canvas,
10 ft. × 13 ft. 4 in.
Promised gift of the Virginia and Bagley Wright
Collection, in honor of the 75th Anniversary of
the Seattle Art Museum, T2006.65.118

45 **Gerhard Richter**
German, born 1932
2. *Schattenbild (Balken)* [*Second Shadow Painting (Bars)*], 1968
oil on canvas, 78½ in. × 9 ft. 10½ in.
Promised gift of the Virginia and Bagley Wright Collection,
in honor of the 75th Anniversary of the Seattle Art Museum,
T2003.155.2

46 **Gerhard Richter**
German, born 1932
Seestück (Seascape), 1975
oil on canvas, 78¾ × 9 ft. 10⅛ in.
Promised gift of Lyn and Jerry Grinstein, in honor of
the 75th Anniversary of the Seattle Art Museum, T98.45

Richter was even more coolly calculating in his debunking of the modern painter as master of a single, hard-won voice, paralleling, albeit through very different means, the gamesmanship of Johns and Rauschenberg. Richter's achievement cannot be measured in a single "masterpiece," a view that also chafes at convention but is evident across the range of modes he deployed, often within the same time period. Through a convergence of works from a handful of collections, Seattle audiences can now experience the breadth of Richter's output both chronologically and stylistically, moving from the hard-edged 2. *Schattenbild (Balken)* [*Second Shadow Painting (Bars)*, 1968, plate 45] to the soft-focus *Seestück (Seascape*, 1975; plate 46), the spatial gymnastics of *Abstraktes Bild (Abstract Picture*, 1984; plate 47), or the dazzling, surface-bound smears of *Abstraktes Bild (Abstract Picture*, 1993; plate 48). Few museums in the country are able to communicate the epochal import of Richter's experiments in such a visceral way.

47 **Gerhard Richter**
German, born 1932
Abstraktes Bild (Abstract Picture), 1984
acrylic on canvas, 47 × 39½ in.
Promised gift of Ann P. Wyckoff, in honor of the 75th
Anniversary of the Seattle Art Museum, T2006.126.1

48 Gerhard Richter
German, born 1932
Abstraktes Bild (Abstract Picture), 1993
oil on canvas, 94½ × 94½ in.
Promised gift of the Virginia and Bagley Wright Collection,
in honor of the 75th Anniversary of the Seattle Art Museum,
T2006.65.125

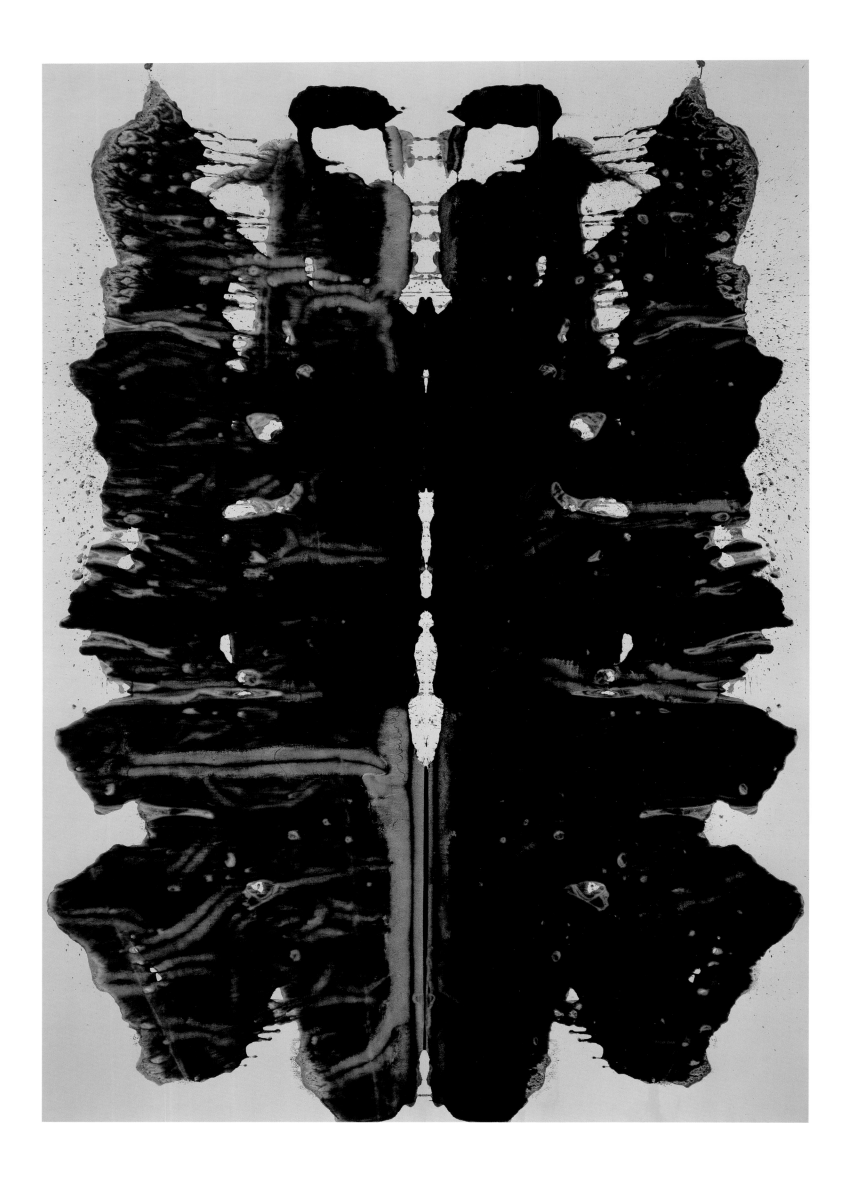

(opposite)
49 Andy Warhol
American, 1928–1987
Rorschach, 1984
acrylic on canvas, 13 ft. 8 in. × 9 ft. 7 in.
Promised gift of the Virginia and Bagley Wright Collection,
in honor of the 75th Anniversary of the Seattle Art Museum,
T2006.65.155

50 Damien Hirst
British, born 1965
Beautiful Christmas Constellation, 2001
household gloss and glitter on canvas, diam. 84 in.
Promised gift of the Virginia and Bagley Wright Collection,
in honor of the 75th Anniversary of the Seattle Art Museum,
T2006.65.64

Richter's challenge is daunting. Both craft and concept are elevated to such breathtaking heights in his work that, in the wake of his almost imperialistic claims on seemingly all subgenres of painting, counterreactions were bound to occur. The response in Germany came in the form of merry pranksters such as Martin Kippenberger, beginning in the 1980s, but reactions also occurred in the United States and Britain in the 1990s, in the legacy of the über-prankster Andy Warhol, for instance. In works such as his late, great Rorschach paintings (plate 49), Warhol spoofed the splattering abstract expressions of id in Pollock, Kline, and others by taking a tool of psychoanalysis and putting the New York school on the couch. A similar kind of intergenerational ribbing takes place in Damien Hirst's spin paintings, such as *Beautiful Christmas Constellation* (2001, plate 50), in which carnival crafts are aggrandized into majestic, if goofy, riffs on nonobjective painting. The struggle with historical precedents is made even more manifest in *On the Wall Above* (2001, plate 51), in which Sean Landers reallegorizes as fan mail the debt American artists have paid to Picasso and in the process reveals his bald ambition, crushing doubt, and perhaps redemption through Oprah-style catharsis.

51 **Sean Landers**
American, born 1962
On the Wall Above, 2001
oil on canvas, 92 × 68 in.
Promised gift of the Virginia and Bagley Wright
Collection, in honor of the 75th Anniversary of
the Seattle Art Museum, T2006.65.77

52 **David Smith**
American, 1906–1965
Untitled (The Billiard Players), 1936
oil on canvas, 47 × 52 in.
Barney A. Ebsworth Collection

53 **John Currin**
American, born 1962
Rachel and Butterflies, 1999
oil on canvas, 68 × 38 in.
Promised gift of the Virginia and Bagley Wright
Collection, in honor of the 75th Anniversary of
the Seattle Art Museum, T2001.40

Landers's work returns painting to a somewhat painful past, a time when pieces such as David Smith's early *Untitled* (*The Billiard Players,* 1936; plate 52) showed a nascent American art working its way through the shadows of Picasso's towering triumphs before finding its own path in abstract expressionism. To that generation, abstraction was a weapon against convention, stasis, and history, and to be truly modern, painters shed all vestiges of classical mastery and gave rein to their individual visions. A lot of the rhetoric of modernism has stayed with us, enough that the Renaissance revisionism of John Currin is still seen as heretical by many and is divisive among most quarters of the art world. Currin, too, is now part of the story of painting that Seattle can tell. His great, Botticelli-esque *Rachel and Butterflies* (1999, plate 53) throws down a new gauntlet, one that marries exquisite craft with Sunday-painter sentimentality and the mannerism of Ingres with a physiognomic shorthand learned from cartoons. At this juncture Currin's brand of in-your-face traditionalism can be read as a bold affront to the last half-century of progress. What a story to tell!

Pamela McClusky

Building with Cloth Blocks

rtists occasionally put unexpected materials on a pedestal. Northwest artist Marie Watt takes piles of used, often worn, blankets with tattered satin trim or frayed tassels and carefully folds them to form a tall column. The quilter Annie Mae Young cuts up used clothes and leftover scraps of corduroy and stitches them into a rectangle. Years before them, the conceptual artist Joseph Beuys hid a tape recording in an orderly stack of felt squares. While the materials seem mundane, reactions swirl around the galleries where these compositions reside. How does an artist trigger new associations from understated cloth?

Like most of the art Joseph Beuys created, the cube of stacked, wool felt squares titled *Ja ja ja ja ja, Nee nee nee nee nee* (fig. 1) confounds immediate recognition of what it is or why it is important. Beuys preferred to provoke viewers into learning about his philosophic tenets through the objects he made. In this case, the felt stack encloses a sound recording of the artist slowly incanting the words "yes" and "no" over and over again during a concert in Dusseldorf in 1968; he gave this hypnotic recitation the action title "I Try to Make You Free." Beuys set up several conundrums for audiences to consider. How can a repetitive action be liberating? If his words are enclosed in felt, how can they be effective? For viewers familiar with Beuys, these are conundrums to savor. For those who are not, a few hints can help.

Felt, often gray and drab, was a signature material for Beuys, who embraced it as a reminder of an epic accident in his life. While serving as a Nazi pilot during World War II, he was shot down over

Crimea and almost froze to death before he was saved by Tartar nomads, who used felt and fat to insulate his body. Forever after, Beuys turned to felt as a unique medium that is both protective and permeable. He used it in many actions that widened the definition of what art can do, even as that art caught viewers off guard. By slowly repeating "yes" and "no," Beuys produced sound vibrations, akin to a mantra or spiritual tool, that could make cosmic forces resonate through the listener's body. Yet this resonance is encased in felt, and thereby silenced. Setting up incongruities was a mainstay of Beuys's many public performances as well. He strove for active involvement in art, saying that "from the way people today . . . face pictures, one can see that they have, from their education, an encounter with the work of art which is nothing more than a peepshow. . . . This situation in which one faces an object without taking part must finally cease."[1]

Marie Watt invites audiences to face her art and take part in inventive ways. The interaction begins when a person comes across one of her tall columns of folded blankets. The title establishes an orientation to the work: *Three Sisters: Cousin Rose, Sky Woman, Four Pelts, and All My Relations* (plate 54). Three Sisters and Sky Woman are characters in the primary creation story of the Seneca Nation, of which Marie is a member. The "sisters" are corn, beans, and squash, the staple foods that thrive when grown together: corn stalks grow tall, beans send their vines to climb up the stalks, and when both decompose, they fertilize the soil for squash to spread across the land. Sky Woman is based on a mythic character whose life connects

Figure 1. Joseph Beuys (German, 1921–1986), *Ja ja ja ja ja, Nee nee nee nee nee*, 1969, wool felt and recording tape, 9⅝ × 6 × 7 in. Anne Gerber, Drs. R. Joseph and Elaine R. Monsen, and the Margaret E. Fuller Purchase Fund, 97.51

54 **Marie Watt**
American, born 1967
Three Sisters: Cousin Rose, Sky Woman, Four Pelts, and All My Relations, 2007
wool and satin with cedar base, 12 ft. 6 in. × 40 in. × 40 in.
General Acquisitions Fund, in honor of the 75th Anniversary of the Seattle Art Museum, 2007.41

55 **Annie Mae Young**
American, born 1928
Blocks, 2003
cotton, polyester, and corduroy, 90½ × 74 in.
General Acquisitions Fund, in honor of the
75th Anniversary of the Seattle Art Museum, 2005.199

sky and ground. Cousin Rose's blanket was added to the stack specifically for Seattle. A dark, striped patchwork sitting in the middle of the stack was once taken by Rose Niguma to Camp Minidoka in Idaho, one of the ten sites at which Japanese Americans were interned during World War II. Assembled by Rose's father from samples of woolen suiting cloth, the blanket fixes the memory of a family episode that haunted twentieth-century life in the Northwest. "Four Pelts" refers to the point system that was a standard of trade with Native people, with one point being equal to the value of one pelt. It can be seen in a four-point blanket like those which the Hudson's Bay Company used in exchanges.

Another type of participation is prompted by the tags attached to the blankets, which sometimes dangle down for inspection. They recount the names and stories of the people who donated the blankets to the artist. Enacting yet another variation of trade, Watt in return gives donors a print that she has created. The stack is defined as twelve feet of blankets, but it contains countless associations.

Through the title and the form, the blanket stack is established as both a mythic and a personal endeavor. Watt has put a spotlight on blankets but the experience does not end there. On a shelf nearby, a hand-bound book extends an invitation to anyone present to respond to the assemblage with memories of their own use of blankets. Audiences participate with a sense of elevated pride in remembering how blankets marked parts of their past. Just a few testimonies hint at the way Watt's blanket stack conjures emotional reactions from her audience. The premise of active involvement in art that Joseph Beuys's small stack implied is hereby realized.

"Both of my daughters have carried, slept with, snuggled, cried into, and adored their 'blankies' since birth. My husband and I joke about the sacred blankies, but there is truth in that adjective when applied to something that provides such comfort and a sense of protection."

"When I see this stack of blankets, I have an overwhelming compulsion to charge it, like a bull to the matador. I imagine that when I make contact, I will scream 'Yeeearrgh!' and throw my arms upward like the wings of a triumphant War Bird, flinging blankets in all directions and giving the surrounding land a fuzzy-warm feeling."—Sincerely, the unknown Guard.

"I remember the satin edging of warm wool blankets against my cheek while sleeping as a little girl at grandma's. Very comforting and it lessened the homesickness. I'm a child of divorce—6-week visitations every summer from age 4 on. And at my grandma's the soft satin edging reminded me of my soft, loving mom. That I'd be able to return to her once I did my time."

"We have a similar pile of blankets in the corner of our very cold bedroom. I didn't know my wife was an artist."

Using blocks instead of stacks, Annie Mae Young also loads cloth with messages. The center of her quilt offers the first hint about her choice of image and material (plate 55). It is a tan rectangle framed with black at top and bottom, and red on either side. Looking across the entire quilt, this basic form is repeated with many variations in color and shape. No two blocks are exactly alike; each is invented anew, tumbling into place without aligning into a standard pattern. At the core of this dynamic graphic is a very basic quilting block known as the Log Cabin. Fabric logs surround a center square, simulating the arrangement of rough-hewn logs as they are laid out to construct a dwelling type that often housed slaves (and a highly influential president). Mud mortared, usually with one window, log cabins were the most common form of housing when Annie Mae Young was born in Gees Bend, Alabama, in 1928. The Log Cabin block is still a popular choice for quilters all over America, but it took the women of Gees Bend to jostle the pattern with an arresting asymmetry.

Annie Mae Young is a master of the distinct quilting style developed in this community. She does not like silk, crepe, or wool, nor designs with "little itty bitty pieces."[2] Instead, she cuts up old worn clothes of family members and incorporates them into elegant compositions of faded denim. In this quilt, she worked more extensively with corduroy, a type of cloth with its own history for her. Derived from the seventeenth-century French material called *cord du roi*, or "king's cloth," corduroy became common in Young's household after a local sewing cooperative signed a contract to produce pillow covers for Sears and Roebuck Company. Although Young was rejected as a seamstress because her stitching and cutting weren't straight enough, her sister participated and stockpiled corduroy scraps.

Young originally made quilts as warm coverings for her family to sleep under. By blanketing them in a mesmerizing graphic, the quilt offered a layer of protection from wayward spirits who might come into the house at night. In *Blocks*, Young sharply contrasted the nap of the corduroy with flat bright slivers of cotton. The shifting rhythms give the eyes no rest, creating almost a visual equivalent to Joseph Beuys's hypnotic pulsation of sounds.

Few might expect stacks of wool felt, retired blankets, and corduroy scraps to have such compelling potential. By harnessing the tactile sensations of cloth, and recognizing its subtle associations, these artists make us take a second look at the soft surfaces that offer us comfort.

NOTES
1. Joseph Beuys, *Par la présente, je n'appartiens plus à l'art* (Paris: Editions l'Arche, 1988), 171.
2. Paul Arnett, Joanne Cubbs, and Eugene W. Metcalf Jr., eds., *Gees Bend: The Architecture of the Quilt* (Atlanta: Tinwood Press, 2006), 132.

Pamela McClusky

Performing with Shadows

56 **Nick Cave**
American, born 1954
Soundsuit, 2006
human hair, fencing mask, and thrift store sweaters,
h. approx. 6 ft.
Gift of Josef Vascovitz, in honor of the 75th Anniversary
of the Seattle Art Museum, 2007.70

Extracting Nick Cave's *Soundsuit* (plate 56) from a wooden crate was an unnerving experience. Unlike a conventional suit, its parts were not clearly defined; it emerged as an amorphous body with bizarre appendages. When the last of the protective bubble wrap was pulled away, instead of a face, there was flaming metal; legs and hips were lumpy masses of old sweaters, and arms covered in long human hair were connected to a winged spike out the back. *Soundsuit* has the air of a fashion Frankenstein, making one question whether to run from it or hug it. Is it a dangerous deviant or a sympathetic oddity? Or both? There was no doubt, however, that the suit was worth getting to know in a gallery setting where these same issues of character assessment are under consideration.

Soundsuit is placed in the gallery so that it is constantly "viewing" the video *Shadow Procession* (plate 57) by William Kentridge. Both works reinforce the sense that each person needs to establish his or her own definition of what is going on in this space, where suits are perplexing, scissors walk, and occasional buffoons are on display. Appearances are deceiving as masks, fully costumed masqueraders, and moving projections disrupt normal routines of dressing and acting in public. For his part, Nick Cave creates suits for the unknown performer in us all. He says, "It's a suit, but for whom?" He encourages audiences to daydream about possible uses: "I believe that the familiar must move toward the fantastic. I want to evoke feelings that are unnamed, that aren't realized except in dreams."[1]

Soundsuits offer an altered personality a chance to emerge. If the suit now in the museum were to come to life, what might it do? Conduct workshops on strange dance movements? Enter the surrealist gallery and take up residence in a Joseph Cornell box? Turn the textile gallery into a free-for-all costume-making center? Turn pirouettes in the boardroom? Or open the doors for a posse of other Nick Cave–suited personalities to stage an invasion?

Besides unleashing imaginary encounters, Cave's suits are a triumph in the reshaping of the ordinary. This suit is made of a fencing mask, metal, human hair, and sweaters from thrift stores. It is exquisitely constructed, with couture finishes even on those parts of the suit that no one but the wearer might see. Toggled closures and closed seams are signatures of an artist who also serves as a professor and chairman of the Fashion Department at the School of the Art Institute of Chicago. Cave does not stand alone when he stitches suits together, however. He works with students, associates, and dancers who collaborate with his other identity as a performer trained at the Alvin Ailey American Dance Theater. A multitude of hands make the suits in sewing circles in his studio, enveloped in music, discussion, and a visual opulence derived from scavenged sources. Secondhand dresses, socks, sweaters, afghans, and commonplace elements are collected, disassembled, and reconfigured in endlessly inventive suits.

One of Nick Cave's first suits was inspired by brutality in 1991. The Los Angeles police beating of Rodney King made the artist think about how King was made into a monster or bogeyman. Cave created a suit in which the wearer was immersed entirely in twigs, a suit that offered complete camouflage and subtle sounds. When Cave moved, the suit scraped and rustled, and allowed him to approach people in a new way. He says, "The suits confront you. There's a live person in them who you cannot see—you have a little fear and are attracted too."[2] Cave has gone on to create more than one hundred

57 **William Kentridge**
South African, born 1955
Shadow Procession, 1999
video with music by Alfred Makgalemele
Purchased with funds from the 1999 Maryatt Gala, William and Ruth True, Rebecca and Alexander Stewart, General Acquisition Fund, and Christina and James Lockwood, in honor of the 75th Anniversary of the Seattle Art Museum, 2002.51

unique suits and has staged a multitude of performances to disrupt the false security of conventional suits.

William Kentridge first used torn and cut paper to create figures for *Shadow Procession* (plate 57), a seven-minute black-and-white video that is projected to life-size proportions. Black silhouettes struggle to get from the left to the right side of a featureless landscape. Many are moving against impossible odds, with crutches, stacks of chairs, donkeys, enormous sacks, or even entire cities on their backs. Some figures appear to be miners stumbling toward the light, while a pair of scissors jerks forward with ungainly momentum. Whether they are fleeing a disaster or hurrying to safety is unknown. This incongruity is underlined by a South African voice singing the hymn "What a Friend I Have in Jesus."

The next scene of *Shadow Procession* opens with a grotesque buffoon who climbs up into view and enacts a menacing dictation with gestures. He struts around awkwardly, cracking a whip with his finger and laughing at his bullying power. Kentridge cites this as his version of Ubu Roi (a character invented by the French surrealist writer Alfred Jarry), a despot who may have inspired the discordant nature of the procession. It is again sound that identifies the scene as South African, when *toyi toyi* chants of insurrection, an integral part of apartheid-era protest, respond to Ubu Roi. In many minds, Kentridge is classified as an anti-apartheid artist. Indeed, as the son of a distinguished attorney whose clients included Nelson Mandela and the family of Stephen Biko, it would be hard not to be influenced by South African politics. Kentridge has described his country as an exemplary moral fairy tale of the late twentieth century. While doing theater work related to the Truth and Reconciliation Commission, the government body that documented human rights abuses under apartheid, he deemed the proceedings to be a battle between the paper shredders and the photocopiers. But he also asserts that the moment of apartheid has passed, and he wants to create his own versions of the broader moral fairy tales of our time.

While *Shadow Procession* is full of possible references to the forced migrations of laborers in South Africa, it also presents two universal dilemmas. One is the absurdity of an authority figure who does not realize how bumbling his brute force seems to those around him. Ubu Roi is the everyman dictator who is blind to the consequences of his actions. Another is the sad fate of those who move ahead while carrying unwieldy burdens, epitomized by a person who stumbles while supporting an entire cityscape on his shoulders. How many of us carry too much of the world in our minds and let it stifle our ability to act?

Like Nick Cave, Kentridge offers art full of ambiguity that rebels against convention. The imaginative trappings of Cave's suits allow the provocative nature of hidden characters to come to life. Kentridge challenges Disney and Pixar animation with its Technicolor realism, seductive special effects, and happily-ever-after endings. Instead, Kentridge prefers what he calls a "stone age" filmmaking technique that is deliberately raw and better suited to his intent: "I am interested in a political art, that is to say an art that is full of ambiguity, contradiction, uncompleted gestures and uncertain endings. An art and a politics in which my optimism is kept in check and my nihilism at bay."[3] Both artists cast new shadows—and manage to make them alluring but elusive—keeping us guessing where they are going and what they might do next.

NOTES
1. Nick Cave, www.JackShaiman.com (accessed 2006).
2. Nick Cave, quoted in Fred Camper, "What's That Sound You're Wearing?" *Chicago Reader*, June 2, 2006.
3. Quoted in Eddie Chambers, "The Main Complaint," *Art Monthly* (June 1999).

Pamela McClusky

Completing the Map

Fly vast distances; consult with an art adviser. Charter a bus, fill it with people and food, and ride for hours on bumpy roads. Get to a sacred site. Walk the ground. Sit down. Watch as primed canvases and tubes of acrylic paints are handed out. Listen to an elder sing. Observe hours of discussion, and see how a composition unfolds. Chew on a charred kangaroo tail. Watch a dog walk across the painting. Wait for the paint to dry, and the story to be written up. Buy the painting.

These are just a few of the steps necessary to purchase a painting at the source of the Aboriginal art movement, in places far outside the cities of the Australian continent. Spinifex, Utopia, Balgo, Yuen-demu, Yirrkala, and Tiwi are communities with active artists whose names roll off the tongues of only a few Americans. In Seattle, one couple has relentlessly pursued for two decades the finest art to come out of these places. Margaret Levi and Robert Kaplan have visited with artists, art advisers, and curators involved with this movement, and their dedication has resulted in a growing collection that allows the Seattle Art Museum to push for international equity in this area of art. Not many Americans have had the opportunity to watch such paintings be created, but they now can see this contemporary art whose time has come in museums.

White pastoralists who settled a central Australian desert outpost in the 1920s gave it the name "Utopia." Emily Kame Kngwarreye, an Aboriginal woman who grew up there, became an artistic sensation when she began painting canvases around the age of seventy-eight. With a natural bravado and with years of experience in painting women's bodies for ceremony, she became a prolific artist. Most of the time, her fingers flew stridently, without hesitation, forcefully stabbing a brush to build up layers of paint. She established a style all her own, and in six years, she produced hundreds of canvases that opened many Australian eyes to the boldness of an elder who would not stop painting. Her approach has been called "gestural expressionism" and echoes American artists such as Jackson Pollock and Mark Tobey. Painting on the ground in her own country, however, Emily Kame Kngwarreye had a very different picture in mind—one that pointed out features of a landscape, the knowledge of which she carefully guarded. In *Anooralya* (*Wild Yam Dreaming*; plate 58), she takes viewers underground to see long "pencil yam" roots crossing over one another in a tumbling matrix.

Kngwarreye was the first of a family of women from Utopia to become distinctive artists. Kathleen Petyarre witnessed her aunt's rapid rise to success and went on to devise her own unique style of applying tiny dots of paint in patterns. She has paid homage to a creature that no one had painted before, a mountain devil lizard. Its meandering path through sandstorms results in a maze of pointillism in *Mountain Devil Lizard Dreaming—Winter Storm* (plate 60). Admired as a model of adaptation, this lizard insists on never moving in a straight line and can traverse land no matter what kind of storms arise. Gloria Petyarre, Kathleen's sister, takes the Utopia penchant for mesmerizing detailed abstraction even further. Using only strokes of white paint, she covers a large canvas in a pattern that has been read as fur or water, but is known to the artist as a study of leaves swirling through space (plate 59). As the guardian of knowledge about the medicinal properties of certain plants, she takes it upon herself to focus attention on the moment that the leaves fly. Through attentively observant canvases, Utopia's women

58 **Emily Kame Kngwarreye**
Australian Aborigine, Utopia Station,
c. 1910–1996
Anooralya (Wild Yam Dreaming), 1995
acrylic on linen, 59⅞ × 48¼ in.
Gift of Margaret Levi and Robert Kaplan, 2000.157

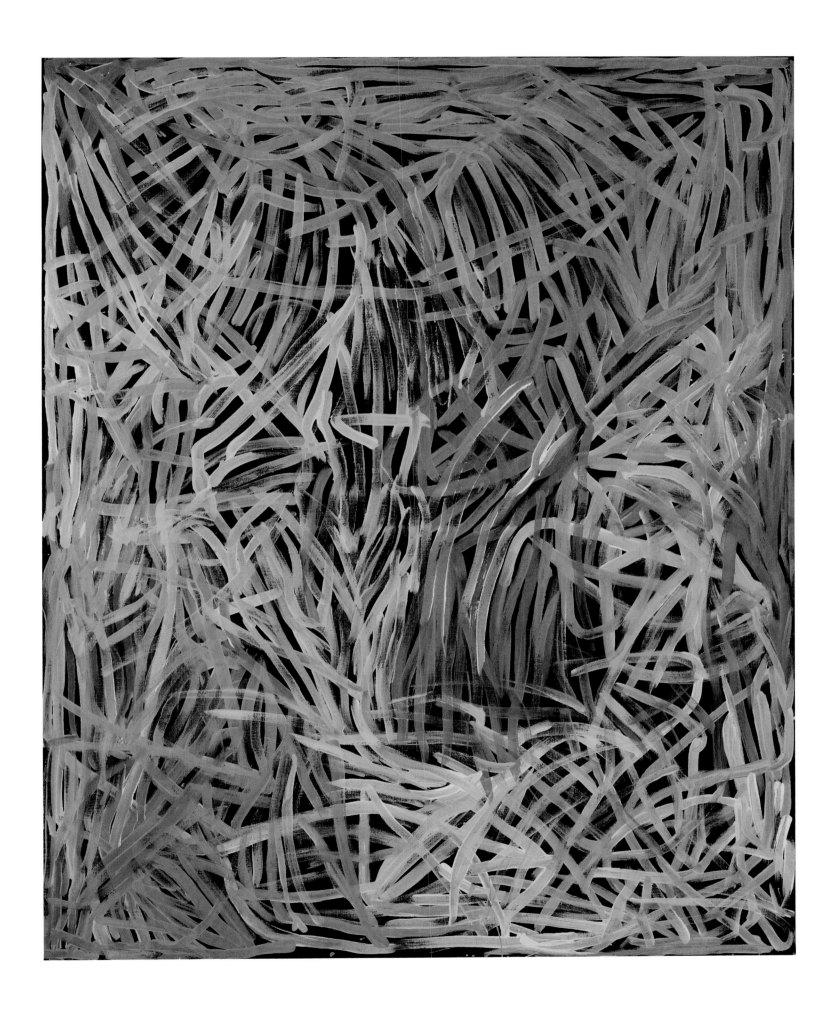

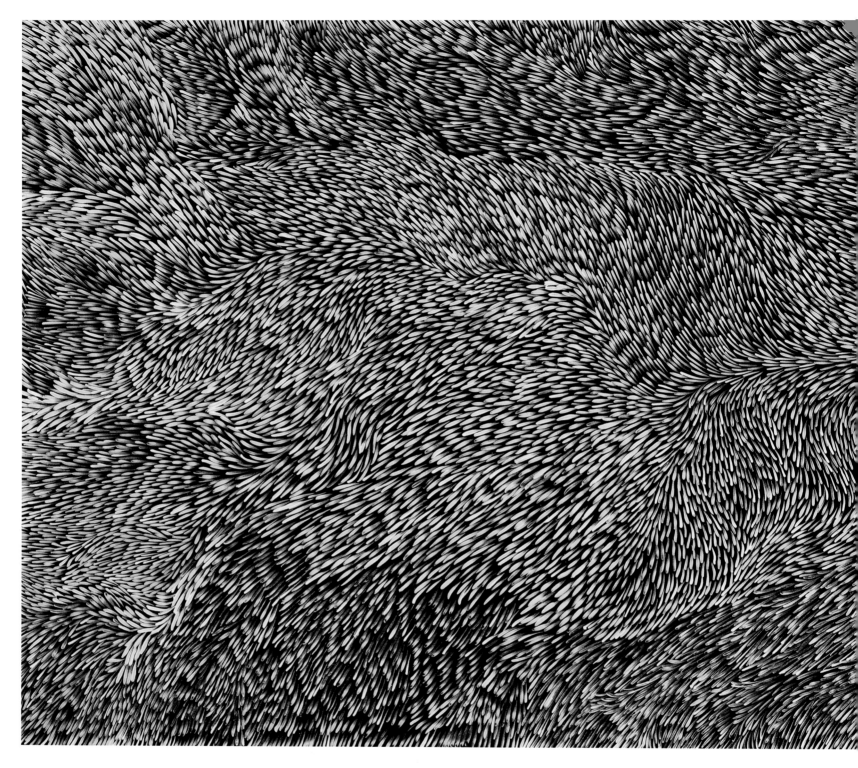

59 Gloria Petyarre
Australian Aborigine, Utopia Station,
born c. 1938
Leaves, 2002
acrylic on linen, 70¾ × 157½ in.
Promised gift of Margaret Levi and Robert Kaplan,
in honor of Bagley and Virginia Wright, and in honor
of the 75th Anniversary of the Seattle Art Museum,
T2006.64.1

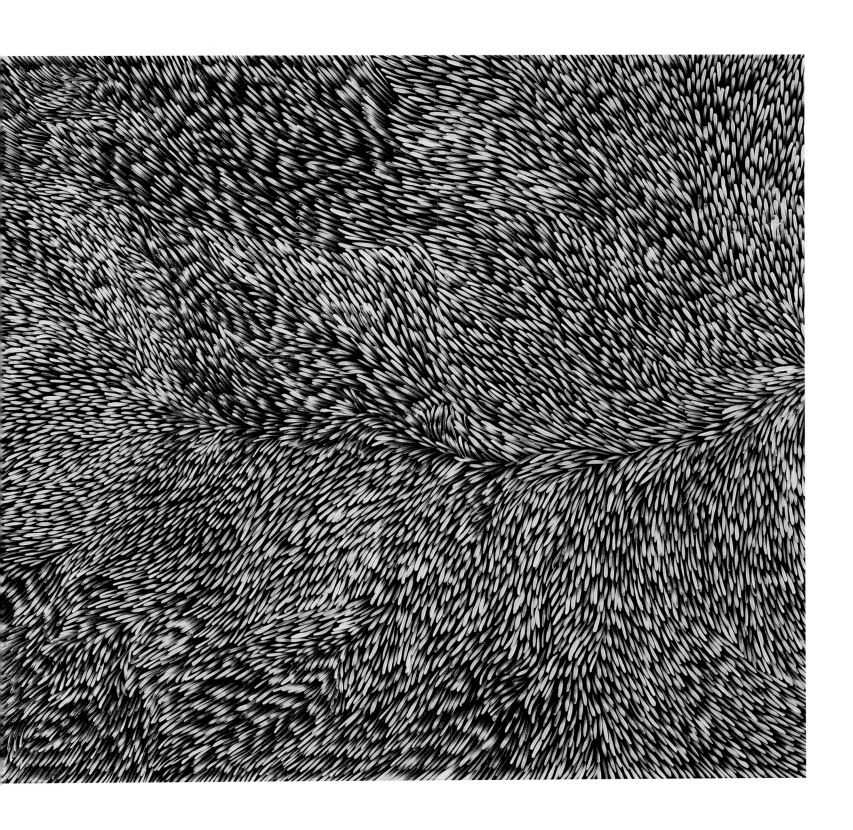

60 **Kathleen Petyarre**
Australian Aborigine, Utopia Station,
born c. 1940
Mountain Devil Lizard Dreaming–Winter Storm, 1999
acrylic on linen, 59⅞ × 59⅞ in.
Gift of Margaret Levi and Robert Kaplan, in honor of the
75th Anniversary of the Seattle Art Museum, T99.62.8

have made champions out of leaves, lizards, and yams. Creating their own methods, they have become renowned for painting with a distinctive fluidity.

Getting to the Spinifex community requires traveling across the Great Victoria Desert to the eastern margin of Western Australia. This hard environment, requiring a careful strategy for subsistence and tenure, has fostered reliance on an intricate religious philosophy. Rain is rare, there is no flowing water and not much game, and the land is extremely infertile. Spinifex is far from Seattle, but this is where Robert Kaplan and Margaret Levi traveled to enact a commission whose details were engineered by advisers in the network of Australian art administrators who play a unique role in Aboriginal communities. Seventeen Spinifex men and ten women loaded buses and journeyed together to a sacred site to paint two canvases. The features that each man would enact were discussed, marked, and addressed with ritual singing to build attachment to the country into their painting. A central position is given to two serpents, a father and son, whose bodies curve around each other. The long story of their relationship is recounted, including the wicked turn taken by the son, who begins devouring people and has to be stopped by his father (plate 61). To document the intensely emotional and spiritual knowledge embedded in the painting, an art adviser wrote a lengthy account of it titled *Wati Kutjara (Two Men Story)*. In addition, the collectors asked a videographer to follow the process and edit a synopsis for outsiders. This video gives museum audiences glimpses of how creation of the paintings unfolded and introduces a few of the elders who guide the community.

Among the seventeen men, Simon Hogan is an elder who also paints canvases on his own. Hogan is surrounded with respect and has been called a walking encyclopedia of traditional knowledge. He was born at a site associated with many significant creation stories that feature the Bush Turkey Man, a Wild Cat, and Dingo. Hogan first saw white men as a young man. When frightened by the electric lights of their settlements, he stayed out in the bush for a long time. He has witnessed numerous difficult encounters with outside authorities. Most notably, in the 1950s Spinifex lands were the site of atomic-bomb testing, which began a series of displacements. By the 1990s Simon Hogan was elected by members of his community to represent their needs and assert ways for the Australian government to recognize Aboriginal laws and land rights. He fulfilled these duties through attending meetings, testifying, and painting. His painting *Papuri* (plate 63) depicts several rock holes and the tracks of Nyiru, a mischievous old man who pursues seven sisters. The sisters are subjected to the relentless tricks of this cheeky man, who lurks just out of sight, waiting for his chance to grab one of them. Chased all over the Western Desert, the sisters finally end up as stars in the cluster known to Westerners as the Pleiades, of which seven are visible in the southern sky.

Epic encounters guide the art of many elders, whose references are based on what is well defined in each community and can be roughly described as Dreamings, or "sacred law." Stories of ancestral actions, including punishments, murder, intrigue, and deceit, are known well by senior men who paint those sections that pertain to the lands they own. A visit to meet the artist Tjumpo Tjapanangka required a far trek to Balgo, a community at the edge of the Great

61 **Spinifex Men's Collaborative**
Australian Aborigine, Spinifex
Wati Kutjara (Two Men Story), 2003
acrylic on linen, 82¾ × 74⅞ in.
Gift of Margaret Levi and Robert Kaplan, in
honor of the 75th Anniversary of the Seattle
Art Museum, T2006.64.3

Sandy Desert with a very active art center. Sporting stylish sunglasses and known for his gifts of humor and healing, Tjapanangka often welcomed visitors. He spoke with fondness of being raised in the desert, hunting for goanna, porcupine, and wallaby, and constructing shelters for the wet season. Tjapanangka chose yellow and white lines to paint a vibrating maze of lines to tell the story of two ancestral brothers who traveled to a vast salt lake in *Wati Kutjara (Two Brothers Dreaming*, plate 62). Vertical lines in the center show where the brothers made camp and slept. A long horizontal line is the windbreak they made to protect themselves, and parallel lines radiate out to represent the water of the lake. When asked about his art, Tjapanangka insisted on finding a map to point out Lake Mac-Kay, a salt lake south of Balgo, as the leading site he was dedicated to painting.

An old woman's mythic journeys are retold in the painting *Kutungka Napanangka (Old Woman Dreaming)* by George Ward Tjungurrayi (plate 64). The woman stops to drink at a rock hole, gathers seeds for bread, and is accosted by one of a group of boys. Outraged by their behavior, she catches them all, except the leading offender, and proceeds to kill and cook them in a fire. It is hard to reconcile this nasty story with the painting, a subtle contour map with meticulous dotting. Tjungurrayi paints dense patterns that chart ancestral movements in minute detail. Some observers equate the patient painting of this sacred geometry with the labor-intensive work required for the ceremonial sandpaintings enacted by Aboriginal people in earlier days. Painting for ceremony involved marking bodies with ocher pigments and dotting the earth with white flecks of bush cotton in patterned sequences. Tjungurrayi was raised near the desert Papunya community, whose members first transferred ceremonial sandpaintings onto small canvas rectangles in 1971. He waited a few years before trying to paint canvases but quickly settled into his austere framework for depicting creation

62 **Tjumpo Tjapanangka**
Australian Aborigine, Balgo, 1929–2007
Wati Kutjara (Two Brothers Dreaming), 2004
acrylic on linen, 70⅞ × 59⅛ in.
Gift of Margaret Levi and Robert Kaplan, in honor of
the 75th Anniversary of the Seattle Art Museum, T2006.64.6

63 **Simon Hogan**
Australian Aborigine, Spinifex, born c. 1935
Papuri, 2002
acrylic on linen, 60¼ × 48¼ in.
Gift of Margaret Levi and Robert Kaplan, in honor of
the 75th Anniversary of the Seattle Art Museum, T2006.64.4

64 **George Ward Tjungurrayi**
Australian Aborigine, Pintupi, born c. 1945
Kutungka Napanangka (Old Woman Dreaming), 2004
acrylic on linen, 96⅛ × 72⅛ in.
Gift of Margaret Levi and Robert Kaplan, in honor of the
75th Anniversary of the Seattle Art Museum, T2006.64.7

journeys. This highly admired painter remains reticent, not willing to speak English or to travel to Alice Springs, where his paintings are sold at the gallery for Papunya Tula artists.

One art adviser who worked with artists of the Yirrkala region described his surroundings in northern Australia as "paradise." Indigenous owners still manage magnificent stretches of land and sea that sustain an abundant diversity of life, from dugongs (sea cows) to turtles, emus to wandering whistling ducks. An art form strikingly adapted to this environment is the tall column that signifies a place of "sorry business," dedicated to mourning and ritually acknowledging the death of a community member. The hollow column serves as a coffin for the deceased, whose bones are placed inside the log during grieving ceremonies and eventually decompose. In recent years, hollow log coffins have been painted for collectors who see them as columnar sculptures that can carry images of northern Australia to outsiders.

Hollow log coffins are covered in geometrical clan designs and features from the landscape. Artists in this region aspire to create a shimmering surface through careful cross-hatching and line work. Matrixes of white and yellow ocher paint can transform a dull surface into a brilliant one, encoding sacred insights. The patterns used revisit the lessons imparted during initiations, when matrixes are painted on initiates' bodies. These patterns also honor the special visual effects that occur in nature: light refracting on the surface of water, in bubbles of freshwater, in sea foam, or in ribbons of tide. Such moments suggest the magnificence that the ancestors created for their descendants to see.

Galuma Maymuru, Baluka Maymuru, Wanyubi Marika, Jimmy Augungana, and Nawurapu Wumunmurra paint hollow log coffins that take one to paradise to see how abundant life there can be (plate 65). Fish and turtles, birds and clouds, rocks and mangrove trees are matched with song cycles that recount the reverence artists have for interactions in and around water. Yirrkala artists often pay particular attention to the places where freshwater streams mix with the saltwater of the ocean. White lines evoke sea foam but also represent deep knowledge of this country. How the waters mix, as tides ebb and flow, is seen as a special lesson. Djon Mundine, an Australian curator, has written that in this region people "use water as a tool, a model for philosophizing. . . . Where fresh- and saltwater mix and return is known as *ganma*. This is used as a metaphor to describe a different kind of mixing: mixing Balanda [outsider] thought from overseas (saltwater) and indigenous wisdom from the land (freshwater) to create new life and ways of thinking."[1]

Among the many creatures depicted on log coffins is the parrotfish, seen on the example painted by Galuma Maymuru (plate 65, second from left). In narrating this scene, Maymuru speaks about the life cycle of the parrotfish: an ancestral woman buries the remains of the parrotfish on the beach; its remains are eaten by maggots, scavenged by crabs, and further picked apart by birds. Before long, all traces of it are washed away into the sea. The parrotfish's fate, a metaphor for what happens when a human dies, is placed on the coffin to encourage the living to come to terms with death and to see hope in the cleansing actions of ancestral processes.

65 (left to right):

Nawurapu Wununmurra
Australian Aborigine, Yirrkala, born 1952
Garraparra, 2001
earth pigments on hollow log, h. 85 in.

Galuma Maymuru
Australian Aborigine, Yirrkala, born 1951
Manggalili Larakitj, 2001
earth pigments on hollow log, h. 83 in.

Wanyubi Marika
Australian Aborigine, Yirrkala, born 1967
Rirratingu Larrakitj, 2003
earth pigments on hollow log, h. 114 in.

Jimmy Augungana
Australian Aborigine, Blyth River, born 1935
Hollow Log, 1995
earth pigments on hollow log, h. 64 in.

Baluka Maymuru
Australian Aborigine, Yirrkala, born 1947
Djarrakpi, 2001
earth pigments on hollow log, h. 89 in.

Gifts of Margaret Levi and Robert Kaplan, in honor
of the 75th Anniversary of the Seattle Art Museum,
2005.151, .150, .158, .152, .149

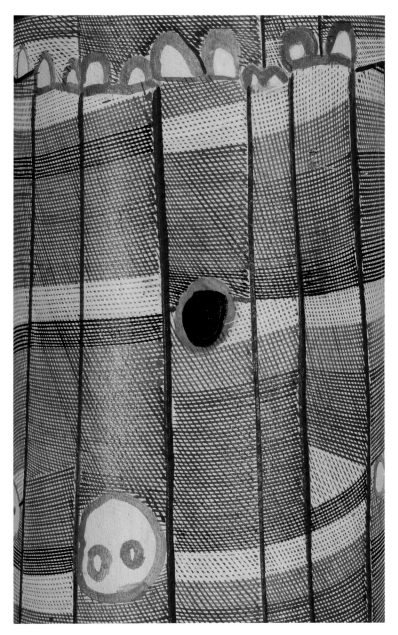

66. **John Mawurndjul**
Australian Aborigine, Maningrida, born 1952
detail of *Lorrkon*, 2005
earth pigments on hollow log, h. 86⅝ in.
Gift of Margaret Levi and Robert Kaplan, in honor of
the 75th Anniversary of the Seattle Art Museum, T2006.64.9

mythic Rainbow Serpent believed to be manifest in the landscape. This serpent legendarily once traveled through the region, making rivers as she slithered along, before settling into remote water holes to await a chance to trap transgressors. Removed from his land during government assimilation in 1960, Mawurndjul returned after a land rights law was passed in 1976. He became a prominent ceremonial leader and often paints series about the Rainbow Serpent, the first being and mother of all species and clan lands. She personifies the notion of a vast inchoate femininity at work, but her abundance can turn to wrath when her creations are damaged. Freshwater mangrove lilies are attached to her back, and if anyone dares to pollute or disturb her water holes, the lilies' movement sends shock waves down to alert her. Full of ferocity, she might unleash destructive downpours, or in her gentle guise, she might send forth a water spirit who is friendly to humans.

For many years, Mawurndjul painted images of this serpent as she coiled and curled up upon herself. Eventually, however, he pulled away from literal visions and preferred to paint the complex world of her water holes (plate 66). Reflections, transparencies, surfaces, and deep pools became metaphysical indicators of his country. In paint, he has used layers of linear patterns to convey iridescence and the color variations that occur when the surface of water is ruffled.

Aboriginal art from Australia adds new dimensions to consider in contemporary art and life. It often provides a different version of abstraction. Meanings implied by patterns and gestures transport viewers underground to look at yams, to the surface of shimmering water, and on journeys with forceful ancestors. The perception of painting as a sacred action, carrying laws with it, is given visual evidence in this art. As an elder artist, Dula Nurruwuthun from Yirrkala asserts, "Do you know what we are doing? We are working our Law. This is interpreting our wisdom, our foundation, and the sinews of Yolnu [the Aboriginal people]. This is a true story, not lies. And this hair on my head is true. The truth comes out of this hair brush."[3]

The artist John Mawurndjul from the Northern Territory has removed figures from his paintings. He distinguishes between restricted designs used for ceremonies and the bark paintings that offer a public view of his work: "People can look at the designs, but they won't know what they mean. . . . but buried inside are secret meanings that others don't need to know. Other senior Aboriginal men will look at the painting and know what those deeper levels of meaning are and understand them."[2] Painted with a human-hair brush, Mawurndjul's eucalyptus log is coated with a repertoire of fine geometric lines applied with extreme discipline to the slight variations of its surface. Born in western Arnhemland, Mawurndjul grew up in a region filled with billabongs, swamps, and huge river systems. Rock faces were his art galleries. There he often found the

NOTES
1. Buku-Larrngay Mulka Centre, *Saltwater: Yirrkala Bark Paintings of Sea Country, Recognising Indigenous Sea Rights* (Sydney: Jennifer Isaacs Publishing, 1999), 20.
2. *"Rarrk" John Mawurndjul: Journey through Time in Northern Australia*, exh. cat. (Basel: Museum Tinguely, 2006), 46.
3. Buku-Larrngay Mulka Centre, *Saltwater*, 1, 12.

Yukiko Shirahara

Contemporary Korean Art and Cultural Identity

For many decades, discussion of the arts of Korea fell under the umbrella of Chinese culture because of Korea's close and at times complicated relationship with China. Art historians are still sorting out the place of origin of some ancient sculptures and paintings.

The Korean people began to assert their own philosophical tradition in the Chosŏn (Joseon) period (1392–1910), when they adopted Confucian dogma as the backbone of their social order. Inspired by the Neo-Confucianism of eleventh-century Chinese philosophers and favored by the Chosŏn rulers, Korean Neo-Confucianism eventually supplanted Buddhism as the touchstone of intellectual life. Its emphasis on self-control, humility, and the conduct of various rituals honoring ancestors had an overwhelming influence on the visual arts which continues to the present.

In a set of four hanging scrolls, the contemporary calligrapher Son Man-jin 孫晚鎮 transcribed the famous annotations to a Confucian proverb composed by Chinese philosopher Cheng Yi 程頤 (also known as 程正淑, 1033–1107). Cheng Yi (and his brother Cheng Hao) contributed to the establishment of Neo-Confucianism as a philosophical school of study during the Song period. The original Confucian proverb (四勿箴) mentions four practices essential to perfect virtue:

> To look at nothing in defiance of ritual, to listen to nothing in defiance of ritual, to speak of nothing in defiance of ritual, never to stir hand or foot in defiance of ritual.[1]

In his so-called Look Admonishment, Cheng Yi gave a philosophical reading of the proverb:

> The mind-and-heart is originally unprejudiced, responding to things without trace. There is an essence to holding it fast, which may be found in the example of looking. Clouded by contact with the outside, what is within changes. Regulate it in its dealing with the external in order to still it internally. Subdue the self and return to ritual, and in time one will become true to one's nature.[2]

Son Man-jin boldly brushed Chinese characters for "look," "listen," "speak," and "act" on four hanging scrolls in abstract splashes of ink (plate 68). On the left scroll, an ideogram for "look" jumps off the paper in its large scale; at the lower right Cheng Yi's interpretation is given in small characters. The prominent square shape, with a splashed dot inside, must represent a human eye and is just one example of Son Man-jin's talent for expressing traditional texts and poems in dynamic calligraphy. The delicate balance he maintains between ink and paper, abstract drawing and calligraphy, is possible only by someone who has learned the history and styles of Chinese ideograms. The characters of his calligraphy breathe with vitality as they admonish contemporary viewers.

White was regarded as the supreme color in the Chosŏn period. Referring to integrity, innocence, truth, purity, and life, it represented the essence of Korean Neo-Confucianism. Undecorated white porcelain in particular became a symbol for austereness and was used at the court, nobles' residences, and scholars' libraries. It is not an exaggeration to say that 95 percent of Chosŏn porcelain is plain white ware. The bulbous moon jar 滿月壺 was praised as the epitome of Chosŏn porcelain, displaying a beautiful snowy whiteness in its spherical body. Its allure comes in part from its imperfect form, a subtle reminder of the human hand that shaped it, which resonated with the Chosŏn people's deep response to unaffected beauty over intentional showiness. High quality white porcelain was produced in the official kilns located in Kwangju (Gwangju), southeast of Seoul. Japanese invasions in the late sixteenth century devastated the Korean ceramic industry, but even so, moon jars were created up to the eighteenth century. The technique for making such jars was lost completely in the early twentieth century as the court declined in power.

The contemporary Korean ceramist Park Young-sook 朴英淑 is acclaimed for her white porcelain ware. In 2001 she set herself the challenge of creating moon jars on a larger scale than the vintage ones. A tiny deposit of porcelain clay from her hometown in Kyongju province produced the white she desired. Although simple in appearance, this moon jar was preceded by countless others that split, warped, or collapsed during firing because of the difficulty of making such a large vessel. Park experimented for two years before achieving the desired shape. With its delicate whiteness and natural unevenness, this jar is an exquisite contemporary revision of the traditional original (plate 67).

Although Korea in recent decades has been undergoing a remarkable metamorphosis as an industrialized nation, adherence

to Neo-Confucian concepts and aesthetics is deep-rooted, as these beautiful and meaningful contemporary works indicate. They remind viewers of the power of cultural identity. Through their forceful shape and brushwork, such works may bring a warning for the consumer society of today. More important, they bridge the past and the present in their beauty, color, shape, and profound meaning. These recent gifts are now at the core of the Seattle Art Museum's collection of Korean art.

67 **Park Young-sook**
Korean, born 1947
Moon Jar, 2007
Porcelain with pale blue glaze, h. 20 × max. diam. 19½ in.
Gift of Frank S. Bayley III, in honor of the 75th Anniversary of the Seattle Art Museum, 2007.86

(following pages)
68 **Son Man-jin**
Korean, born 1964
Four Admonishments by Cheng Yi, 2005
four hanging scrolls, ink on paper, 85½ × 31½ in. each
Gift of Frank S. Bayley III, in honor of the 75th Anniversary of the Seattle Art Museum, 2007.93.1–4

NOTES
1. Arthur Waley, trans., *The Analects of Confucius* (New York: Vintage Books, 1989), book 12, 162.
2. Daniel K. Gardner, *Zhu Xi's Reading of the Analects: Canon, Commentary, and the Classical Tradition* (New York: Columbia University Press, 2003), 81.

Marisa C. Sánchez

More than an Object

Early in the twentieth century, the Romanian-born artist Constantin Brancusi reenvisioned sculpture and its relationship to the pedestal in elegant, highly abstracted monuments. By mid-century, minimalist artists were radically stretching the genre with objects made from industrial materials whose form and meaning depended on the specific site in which they were located. These sweeping changes initiated a sense of urgency among artists, critics, and curators toward establishing a new common language for contemporary sculpture. Artists today have inherited this legacy and an awareness of how a sculptural object functions within a specific context and, further, in relation to a community. In turn, their practices continue to broaden the very notion of sculpture by extending the object into social space.

An expression of the radical redefinition of sculpture came as early as 1926, when Brancusi articulated his vision for a monumental version of his sculpture *Endless Column*. It would take the form of an apartment house on Central Park: "It would be greater than any building, three times higher than your obelisk in Washington, with a base correspondingly wide—sixty meters or more. It would be made of metal. In each pyramid there would be apartments and people would live there, and on the very top I would have my Bird—a great bird poised on the tip of my infinite column."[1] Brancusi envisioned his habitable endless (infinite) column, crowned with a bird, at such a tremendous height and scale that it would have become "one of the wonders of the world."[2] The project never came to fruition, but Brancusi's notion of dwelling within the space of a sculpture or its environment would become important to the minimalists and further explored by contemporary artists.

Brancusi explored the idea and form of the bird over four decades in more than thirty versions. He made the first *Bird in Space* in 1923 of carved white marble. A year later, he formed his first bird in bronze, exploiting the reflective, highly polished surface to create a viewing experience that had no precedent. In its simplicity and in Brancusi's insistence on the reduction of form, the Seattle Art Museum's soaring bronze *Bird in Space* (1926, plate 69) establishes for the permanent collection a foundation for the history of abstraction within modernist sculpture.

69 **Constantin Brancusi**
French, born Romania, 1876–1957
Bird in Space, 1926
bronze with wood and marble base, h. 9 ft. 7¼ in.
Partial and promised gift of Jon and Mary Shirley, in honor of
the 75th Anniversary of the Seattle Art Museum, 2000.221

70 **Alexander Calder**
American, 1898–1976
Eagle, 1971
painted steel, 38 ft. 9 in. × 32 ft. 6 in. × 32 ft. 6 in.
Gift of Jon and Mary Shirley, in honor of the 75th Anniversary
of the Seattle Art Museum, 2000.69

Alexander Calder's iconic *Eagle* (1971, plate 70), an abstract, stabile bird in flight, although not formally similar to Brancusi's sculpture, proposes another conception of a bird in space—one that is stationary and grounded, yet soars against the backdrop of the sky. Calder situated his outdoor constructions directly on the ground, taking the questioning of the pedestal-bound sculpture to an extreme conclusion. By mid-century, in fact, thanks to artists such as Calder and David Smith, the pedestal was no longer the norm in sculptural practice.

Nearly forty-five years after *Bird in Space*, the minimalist Carl Andre acknowledged that Brancusi was essential to his artistic process: "All I'm doing is putting Brancusi's *Endless Column* on the ground instead of in the sky."[3] Andre's *12th Copper Corner, New York* (1975, plate 71) operates literally at floor level and rejects the dramatic thrust toward verticality embodied in traditional sculpture. Refusing historical monumentality, Andre pursues instead the potential toward infinity, albeit on a flattened plane, that Brancusi had initiated. Sharing the structural logic of Brancusi's *Endless Column*, Andre's work is never arbitrary. He establishes a rational system of form based on the serial repetition of a single, modular unit, as in *12th Copper Corner, New York*, which comprises 78 copper plates each measuring 19⅝ × 19⅝ inches. The work is an example of the minimalist's use of industrial materials, geometric shapes, and repeated forms, as well as his desire to claim a distinctive space in a site for his sculpture. In *12th Copper Corner, New York*, the structure's dependence on the corner further accentuates the intersection of two walls and the floor, reinforcing how the corner functions as the sculpture's base while drawing the viewer's attention to the edge, not the center, of the gallery. As he intended for this corner piece, Andre challenges the viewer to interact with his sculpture by walking across its surface. This radical step transforms the viewer's perception of his or her relationship to the work and the site.

72 **Beverly Pepper**
American, born 1924
Perre's Ventaglio III, 1967
stainless steel and enamel, 94 × 80 × 96 in.
Gift of Jon and Mary Shirley, in honor of the
75th Anniversary of the Seattle Art Museum,
2005.200

(opposite)
71 Carl Andre
American, born 1935
12th Copper Corner, New York, 1975
copper, ¼ in. × 19 ft. 8 in. × 19 ft. 8 in. overall
Promised gift of the Virginia and Bagley Wright Collection,
in honor of the 75th Anniversary of the Seattle Art Museum,
T2008.42

73 Donald Judd
American, 1928–1994
Untitled, 1967
stainless steel and Plexiglas, 6 × 24 × 27 in. each unit
Promised gift of the Virginia and Bagley Wright Collection,
in honor of the 75th Anniversary of the Seattle Art Museum,
T98.84.30

Like Andre, Beverly Pepper encourages the viewer to engage with a work from multiple perspectives. In the 1960s she began making geometric sculpture from industrial materials which change in response to specific sites and the position of the viewer. The stainless steel surface of Pepper's minimalist *Perre's Ventaglio III* (1967, plate 72) reflects its context, and the viewer walking around the object discovers multiple vantages of one stationary structure unfolding in space. If the sculpture were moved and placed at another site, it would reflect its new context and the viewer's experience of it would change, further accentuating the mutual dependency of the sculpture and its surroundings.

A commitment to the infinite repetition of form begun by Brancusi and continued by Andre is apparent in the work of Donald Judd. He turned to industrially produced sculpture in the mid-1960s and made his first geometrically repeating "stack"—seven units of galvanized iron—in 1965. A year later he produced a second stack, but this time of ten units, which became the standard count for his structures installed from floor to ceiling. By 1967 Judd had introduced color into wall stacks of stainless steel by inserting Plexiglas at the top and bottom of each unit. The incorporation of Plexiglas—sometimes green, blue, purple, or yellow—produces a stunning effect, with color emanating from within the sculptural body and further heightening the physical presence of the pillar, radiating and containing color and light in space. A prime example from this period, *Untitled* (1967, plate 73) is a vertical stack of ten units in stainless steel and light blue Plexiglas. Each single unit is identical in size, measuring 6 by 26 by 24 inches. The work rises vertically, one unit above the other at 6-inch intervals.[4] Like Andre, Judd devised an order for his structures that was systematic, measured, and, potentially, endlessly repeatable.

(opposite)
74 **Richard Serra**
American, born 1939
Wake, 2004
weatherproof steel,
14 ft. ¼ in. × 125 ft. × 46 ft. overall
Purchased in part with funds from Susan
and Jeffrey Brotman, Virginia and Bagley
Wright, Ann Wyckoff, and the Modern Art
Acquisition Fund, in honor of the 75th
Anniversary of the Seattle Art Museum,
2004.94

Figure 1. Tony Smith (American,
1912–1980), *Stinger*, 1967–68 /1999,
painted steel, 6 ft. 6 in. × 33 ft.
4¼ in. × 33 ft. 4¼ in. Gift of Jane
Smith, 2004.117

Richard Serra explores the relationship between sculpture, architecture, and site in a body of work that dramatically defines space. His titanic *Wake* (2004, plate 74) is composed of five identical, curvilinear volumes of weatherproof steel that tower over the viewer at 14 feet high and 48 feet wide. In their current site at the museum's Olympic Sculpture Park, these monumental elements visually echo cargo ships passing in the distance on Puget Sound. Colossal yet lyrical, *Wake* occupies space in ways both inviting yet intimidating. For Serra, space itself is tangible, a material that can be shaped and controlled by way of the sculpture and its form.

Serra's approach resonates with an equally compelling work by Tony Smith. In a manner similar to Serra, Smith envisioned his forms both as sculptures and as architectural monuments. He impressively achieved this aim in *Stinger* (1967–68/1999, fig. 1). With three closed sides, *Stinger* has a hard-edged, fortresslike exterior. But through its one open side, the viewer can enter its interior, where the delicate edge on which the massive structure rests becomes apparent.[5] The visual and experiential tension of the work overwhelms the viewer even as he or she is invited into the space of the object. The effect is at once imposing and comforting, sheltering and aggressive.

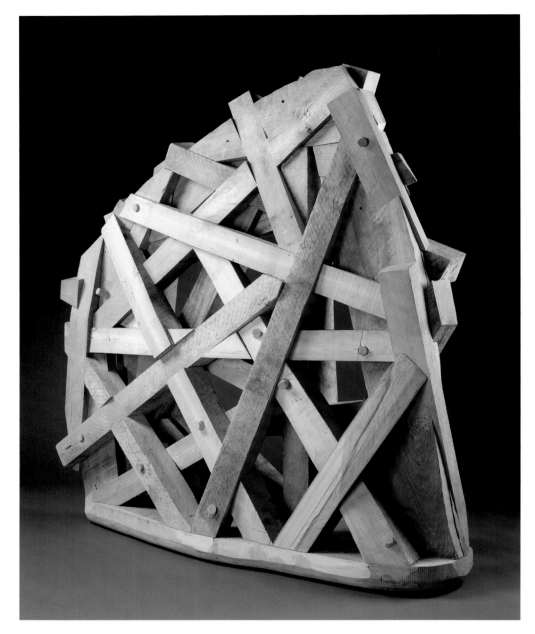

Figure 2. Martin Puryear (American, born 1941), *Thicket*, 1990, basswood and cypress, 67 × 62 × 17 in. Gift of Agnes Gund, 90.32

(opposite)
75 Martin Puryear
American, born 1941
Noatak, 1989
red cedar, 66¼ × 62 × 18 in.
Jeffrey and Susan Brotman Collection

Unlike the minimalist artists of the 1960s who emphasized literalism over illusionism, Martin Puryear permits metaphorical associations in his sculptures. Although confident in the use of pure, reductive forms, Puryear rejected minimalism's cool manufactured aesthetic for handcrafted and natural materials. The artist's abstract, sometimes anthropomorphic, sculptures have a commanding physical presence and visual weight. Two works, *Noatak* (1989, plate 75) and *Thicket* (1990, fig. 2), demonstrate Puryear's concern with the dualities of inside and outside, mass and form, and transparency and opacity. Their titles refer to the landscape Puryear experienced during a trip to Alaska in the 1980s. *Noatak* gains its name from the Noatak National Reserve and river, and the shape of *Thicket* can be traced to a rock he found on the trip.[6] The natural environment is also evoked in Puryear's choice of materials—basswood, cypress, and cedar. *Thicket* is the hollowed-out skeletal form of *Noatak*, and this correspondence in shape and size prompts a dialogue about structure, form, and space that is especially rich when the works are viewed together. *Thicket* tends toward the chaotic with its lines of wood pushing and pulling through space, whereas *Noatak* has a weightlessness subtly achieved by a closed, seductive form and a refined surface.

76 **Roxy Paine**
American, born 1966
Split, 2003
polished stainless steel, h. 50 ft.
Promised gift of the Virginia and Bagley Wright Collection,
in honor of the 75th Anniversary of the Seattle Art Museum,
T2004.106

More recently, Roxy Paine has explored the relationship between nature, sculpture, and artifice in works that disguise the very elements of their fabrication by dissolving into their environment. *Split* (2003, plate 76) is an intricate network of polished, stainless-steel pipe that stands 50 feet high. Placed in an outdoor, public setting, it is a striking example of the artist's ability to blur the boundary between the artificial and the organic. The form mimics a tree, but Paine has subverted natural processes by creating a never-changing, stationary object that refuses to be altered by the forces of nature. Paine installed his first metal tree in a forest in Sweden: "I was really seeking to explore ideas of permanence and impermanence and death and decay."[7] His delicate and uncanny monuments to nature borrow from minimalism's insistence on the use of industrial materials as well as site-specificity while pushing the sculptural object further into a dialogue with its environment. The unnatural imposition of the artificial tree that seeks to mimic a natural form while disguising its artifice reinforces the complexity of the relationship the artist seeks between the object and its context.

77 **Alberto Giacometti**
Swiss, 1901–1966
Le Couple (Homme et Femme), 1926
bronze, h. 23¾ in.
Jane Lang Davis Collection, T93.43

78 **Alberto Giacometti**
Swiss, 1901–1966
The Dog, 1951
bronze, 18⅛ × 38¼ × 6 in.
Partial and promised gift of Jon and Mary Shirley,
in honor of the 75th Anniversary of the
Seattle Art Museum, 2000.220

(opposite)
79 **Alberto Giacometti**
Swiss, 1901–1966
Femme de Venise II, 1956
bronze (edition 6 of 6), h. 48 in.
Jane Lang Davis Collection

Abstraction was just one pursuit among many for sculptors in the twentieth century. A number of artists firmly believed in the narrative potential and humanizing effect of their work, which often makes use of the figure. Although inherently linked to reality, these sculptures are often symbolic expressions possessing a poignant psychological intimacy. They are rooted in surrealism and a belief in a reality informed by dreams and the collective imagination.

Three bronze sculptures by the Swiss-born Alberto Giacometti embody this idea. The earliest work, *Le Couple (Homme et Femme*, 1926; plate 77), straddles abstraction and figuration. Giacometti made it during his early days in Paris, shortly after he began moving away from purely figurative sculpture to explore the creative potential of an abstract language. As the title suggests, the artist represented two figures, male and female. He presented the two forms frontally, side by side, on individual pedestals that rest on a larger base. Giacometti applied geometric shapes to each "body" to indicate its sexuality. This subtle recognition of male and female locates the real in the abstract form.

However tempted he was by abstraction, Giacometti never abandoned his interest in the figure. In the early 1930s, after seeing the work of Joan Miró and Alexander Calder, he began to make sculptures that were in line with the dreamlike qualities of surrealism. As

his ideas developed, his renderings of the figure began to express certain states of mind or qualities of experience. *The Dog* (plate 78) poignantly conveys the fragility of existence. The almost skeletal animal with bowed head and emaciated body generates a sympathetic reading as a malnourished, wandering creature. The narrowness of the sculpture and the simplicity of its exaggerated form, silhouetted in space like a drawn line, accentuate the near disappearance of the animal's strength and life.

Giacometti gave gestural and densely textured finishes to *The Dog* and *Femme de Venise II* (1956, plate 79). The latter is one of approximately fifteen standing female figures that Giacometti created for the 1956 Venice Biennale. There he exhibited the plaster casts, of which nine were made into bronzes. Each sculpture in this series (known as Women of Venice) is different, although they share a sloping base and frontal stance reminiscent of Egyptian sculpture. In this example, the woman takes a severe form, with angular facial features, closely held arms, which seem to melt into her torso and thighs, and minuscule head. Giacometti built up each sculpture on the same armature from virtually the same clay. After shaping a figure, he had a plaster cast made of the form and then reworked the clay to produce the next *femme*. In these solitary, anonymous figures, Giacometti produced a delicate and striking exaggeration of the human form abstracted from reality.

80 **David Smith**
American, 1906–1965
Royal Incubator, 1949
steel, bronze, and silver, 37 × 38⅝ × 9⅞ in.
Promised gift of the Virginia and Bagley Wright Collection,
in honor of the 75th Anniversary of the Seattle Art Museum,
T98.84.64

Informed by the work of Giacometti and grounded in surrealism, David Smith's early works of the 1940s are filled with symbolic content. For *Royal Incubator* (1949, plate 80) Smith relied on primal forms to convey the subconscious realm. The sculptural language suggests both the natural world (two fetuslike creatures embracing in the center) and the spiritual sphere (the angel-like form letting out a primordial scream). "Incubation" in the title can refer to time, enclosure, containment, and periods of healing and illness as well as psychological states. In its extreme linearity and flatness, with spearlike welded lines thrusting and jutting out from the central, architectural structure, *Royal Incubator* takes shape as a drawn outline more than as a three-dimensional mass in space. *Untitled* (1949, plate 81), Smith's drawing for this work, shows his initial working-out of the central dominating figure and demonstrates his negotiation between figuration and abstraction.

81 **David Smith**
American, 1906–1965
Untitled, 1949
egg ink on paper, 20¼ × 26¼ in.
Gift of Virginia and Bagley Wright, in honor of the
75th Anniversary of the Seattle Art Museum, 2006.136

82 **David Smith**
American, 1906–1965
Cubi XXV, 1965
stainless steel, 9 ft. 11¼ in. × 10 ft. ¾ in. × 31¼ in.
Jane Lang Davis Collection

As Smith's work moved closer to pure abstraction, the scale of his sculpture became more dramatic. In the *Cubi* series, begun in the early 1960s, he assembled stainless steel sculptures from the basic elements of cubes, beams, and cylinders. Burnished in circular movements, the steel attained a textural surface. In this mature work, of which *Cubi XXV* (1965, plate 82) is a prime example, the forms are in proportional harmony; Smith delicately balanced the individual parts to make a visual whole. Reductive and highly sophisticated, the *Cubi* series relates more to the aesthetic and conceptual concerns of minimalism than to abstract expressionism. Even so, one can read Smith's decision to grind the surface as an indication of his insistence on reaffirming the hand of the artist.

With interests similar to those of Giacometti and Smith, Louise Bourgeois sought to express symbolic meaning and to create psychological impact in her work. Her *Winged Figure* (1948, plate 83)

articulates the language of abstraction and is suggestive of the figure as well. From 1946 to 1953 Bourgeois developed *Personages*, a series of vertical forms that represent the body or the relationships of bodies in space. She saw these forms as people but did not assign specific identities to them: "For that first show [of *Personages* in 1949], I made a social gathering of people. I tried to make them relate to each other, so that they would have a dialogue in their different forms and personalities."[8] The sculptures are typically slender, singular forms, sometimes clustered or grouped in conversation with one another. Each is precariously balanced on a support that is thinner at its base than its top. The totemic *Winged Figure* from this series is reduced to an elemental form and yet, through the narrative associations Bourgeois created, the series intimately relates to human existence and personal relationships.

83 **Louise Bourgeois**
American (born France), 1911
Winged Figure, 1948
bronze, paint, and stainless steel
70½ × 37½ × 12 in.
Promised gift of Herman and Faye
Sarkowsky, in honor of the 75th
Anniversary of the Seattle Art
Museum, T2005.38

84 **Robert Gober**
American, born 1954
Urinal, 1984
wood, wire, plaster, and enamel paint, 30 × 20 × 20 in.
Promised gift of the Virginia and Bagley Wright Collection,
in honor of the 75th Anniversary of the Seattle Art Museum,
T98.84.20

Owing more to the influence of Bourgeois than to Giacometti or Smith, the psychologically driven sculptures of Robert Gober and Katharina Fritsch rework the surrealist interest in the body by using the figure or fragments of the human form to express often conflicting emotions of desire, pleasure, loss, and fear. Gober and Fritsch were among a number of artists working in the 1980s and 1990s who blurred the boundaries between fantasy and reality. Gober's anthropomorphic sculptures are strangely disarming, their familiarity overridden by the artist's subversion of forms and their ordinary functions. Gober has repeatedly investigated sinks, drains, and pipelines. For the 1984 *Urinal* (plate 84), he removed the drainage system, transforming an object of utility into one of dysfunction. Silenced through the absence of the drain and water, the sculpture is disorienting. Although this work immediately calls to mind Duchamp's Readymades, specifically his iconic *Fountain* (1917), Gober intended to stimulate a fresh response rather than simply restage his predecessor's concerns with the art object and modes of display and context. Gober's urinal is a surrogate or analogue for the human body, which is strongly evoked by its mere absence but also by its bulbous form, suggestive of a womb or abdomen. Through this gesture of transformation and fragmentation, the known is made unknown by the artist.

The disquiet caused by Gober's ambiguous sculptural objects is also experienced by the viewer of Katharina Fritsch's *Mann und Maus* (*Man and Mouse*, 1991–92; plate 85). Fritsch conjures the real and symbolic in this work, which is expressed in the "vision" of a sleeping man whose breath is slowly consumed by a gigantic mouse perched on his body. Fritsch probes the realm of the imagination, asking the viewer to search the borderline between the reality of an object and our perception of it. "I find the play between reality and apparition very interesting," Fritsch says. "I think my work moves back and forth between these two poles."[9] The fantasy implicit in Fritsch's work draws on the psychological notions of pleasure and fear while probing the fundamental question of truth and fiction.

85 **Katharina Fritsch**
German, born 1956
Mann und Maus, 1991–92
polyester resin and paint, 90½ × 51½ × 94½ in.
Gift of the Virginia and Bagley Wright Collection, in honor
of the 75th Anniversary of the Seattle Art Museum, 2007.118

86 **Pedro Reyes**
Mexican, born 1972
Capula XVI (obolo a) and *Capula XVIII (obolo b),* 2006
stainless steel and woven vinyl, approx. 98 × 98 × 78 in. each
Olympic Sculpture Park Art Acquisition Fund and the Modern
Art Acquisition Fund, in honor of the 75th Anniversary of the
Seattle Art Museum, 2007.3–.4

Some contemporary artists use the language of sculpture to invent dynamic situations that require participation before a work can be considered complete. These artists create dialogues within environments which themselves become extensions of the sculptural object. Because of this, the work inevitably changes over time depending on its location and the interactions that occur with its viewers. To be fully realized, these "living" sculptures depend on either the object's transformation over time or the viewer's involvement. The works of Pedro Reyes and Roy McMakin, for instance, invite audience participation. Their sculptures can be appreciated simply as objects, but full aesthetic experience is best achieved through tactile engagement or other interaction. When this happens, the viewer shares in producing the meaning of the work.

Born in Mexico City in 1972, Pedro Reyes belongs to a younger generation of conceptual artists interested in social or participatory sculpture. In 2001, with the help of Mexican basket weavers, he began designing and making large hanging baskets woven in vinyl. The artist calls the baskets "capulas," a composite term that merges the words "cupola," "cupule," "capsule," "couple," "copulate," and "capillary." Reyes creates his interactive capulas in response to particular sites; two dynamic examples from 2006 (plate 86) are *Capula XVI (obolo a)* and *Capula XVIII (obolo b).* Reyes drew up a list of conditions to establish the form of each capula relative to the architectural environment, such as "If a room has square walls, the capula shall be round," or "If a room creates a fixed field of vision, the capula shall be kinetic," or "If a room is grounded, the capula shall hover." Because they depend on preexisting architecture, the sculptures, whose forms suggest otherworldly, futuristic spacecraft, can be understood as site-specific.

In *Love & Loss* (2005–6, plate 87) Roy McMakin promotes social interaction with sculptural elements placed in a natural environment. Combining a living tree, benches and a table, and a revolving neon ampersand, this work responds to place and, by extension, community. The cleverly arranged seating spells out the name of the work letter by letter. In the process of sorting out the overall "image," the viewer becomes physically absorbed into the work itself. Each letter reveals its placement within a landscape of text, in which individual components or letters depend on the other elements to complete the title phrase. Each experience of *Love & Loss* is affected by the choices the viewer makes—the direction of approach, whether to sit or stand, staying near or far. In this shifting between clarity and confusion, the work begins to mimic its title: the nature of love and loss offers the ideas of beholding and separation. Through language, McMakin suggests two mutually dependent moods or conditions—love, which comes with the fear of eventual loss, and loss, which can only spring from some level of fondness. It is left to the viewer to choose whether to sit on the side of love, around a communal table whose circular top is painted to form the letter *E,* or to walk on the side of loss, along the fragmented pavement of the second letter *S.* The nexus of the work is the letter *O* uniting the words "love" and "loss." The hollow interior of the *O* itself becomes a container to collect rainwater and at times functions as a reflecting pool and wishing well. McMakin typically surprises his audience with the unexpected, and here in a playful touch he incorporated a V-shaped tree, its two trunks painted white to form the third letter of "love." Standing freely, the rotating illuminated ampersand—a vibrant neon red—connects and animates the still words.

87 **Roy McMakin**
American, born 1956
Love & Loss, 2005–6
mixed-media installation, 40 × 24 ft.
Olympic Sculpture Park Art Acquisition Fund and gift of Paul G. Allen Family Foundation, in honor of the 75th Anniversary of the Seattle Art Museum, 2007.2

(opposite and above)
88 Mark Dion
American, born 1961
Neukom Vivarium, 2006
mixed-media installation, greenhouse structure: l. 80 ft.
Gift of Sally and William Neukom, American Express
Company, Seattle Garden Club, Mark Torrance Foundation,
and Committee of 33, in honor of the 75th Anniversary of
the Seattle Art Museum, 2007.1

Interaction with Mark Dion's *Neukom Vivarium* (2006, plate 88) is ever-changing because the work itself is in a constant state of transformation. For this installation Dion built a greenhouse that sustains and nurtures a 60-foot nurse log—a fallen tree that in decay "nurses" other vegetation, in this case, a log from the Duwamish/Green River watershed and a victim of a 1996 winter storm. In this and other works, Dion critiques systems or institutions of display, most often natural history museums: "Historically . . . things that lived at a distance were brought into one's own environment to be studied as specimens. Which is to say, what was thought to be [the] observation of life was actually the study of death. Then came the breakthrough when naturalists became field scientists, not only observing nature's operations in its own context, but discovering nature as a system of relationships, an ecology."[10] Dion's thoughts are fully realized in this work for which a living object (the perfect specimen) was removed from nature in order to be housed, maintained, displayed, and observed in a controlled environment. The phenomenon of simultaneously observing life while studying death, as the artist remarked, is perfectly demonstrated by the nurse log in the natural process of decay and rebirth. As it decomposes, it supports other plants and becomes a nursery for seedlings, which find nutrients in the rotting tree. New life—ferns, mosses, mushrooms—comes forth on the log. The "composition" of the nurse log is impermanent and will eventually deteriorate, but the system of relationships it exemplifies is expressed in this embodiment of art as a laboratory or field study.

Whiting Tennis has explored the notion of sculptural transformation. He initially intended *Bovine* (2006, plate 89), a large, hollow structure of found plywood and outfitted with various tools and household objects, to deteriorate over time as its form was challenged by the natural conditions of a specific climate. In an interview the artist stated: "I had thought that I . . . would put it in . . . an empty lot in Seattle. . . . I actually got offered a field up on Lopez [Island] . . . and I was going to put it up there and let it fall into the earth."[11] Placing this object in a neglected urban space or a rural field would challenge the notion of permanence; the artwork would be subjected to a natural process of decay much like Robert Smithson's 1970 *Partially Buried Woodshed* (Kent State University, Ohio). For *Bovine*, the process of decay is conceptual, its death an imagined state, which is heightened by the work's preservation or presence over its deterioration or absence.[12] This impressive sculpture memorializes the romantic dream of westward expansion. But

here the adventurous traveler is not offered a place to dwell or to prosper. Instead, the windows are boarded up, and the wheels of the camper have become the four, stationary legs of this mammoth beast. The sculpture is cumbersome but also elegant and fantastical, and encountering it draws out a melancholic awareness of the passing of time, which is further accentuated by the soulful sound of country music legend Hank Williams, whose forlorn tunes can be heard playing within the belly of *Bovine*.

The cyclical nature of time, experience, artistic impulses, and the dialogue between objects made during different historical periods is wonderfully revealed in a work by the British artist Simon Starling. His 2004 *Bird in Space* (plate 90) is inspired by and directly related to Brancusi's 1926 *Bird in Space* (see plate 69), which was entangled in a famous court case over what constitutes a work of art. The influential modernist photographer Edward Steichen, the original owner of Brancusi's *Bird in Space*, purchased the sculpture directly from the artist in Paris and shipped it to the United States in October 1926. But custom officials, who did not think the sculpture looked like a bird, refused to exempt it from duty as a work of art. Steichen appealed the decision on Brancusi's behalf, and in a 1927–28 trial, a judge eventually ruled in favor of the artist, tacitly endorsing the concept of abstract art. Starling used this incident as a departure point for his *Bird in Space*, a 4,900-pound steel plate that hovers effortlessly above the ground thanks to the support of helium-filled rubber jacks. The steel, imported from Romania,

89 Whiting Tennis
American, born 1959
Bovine, 2006
lumber, found plywood, found objects, and compact disk,
8 ft. 6 in. × 14 ft. × 90 in.
Gift of Greg Kucera and Larry Yocom, friends of Whiting
Tennis, and the Mark Tobey Fund, in honor of the
75th Anniversary of the Seattle Art Museum, 2006.134

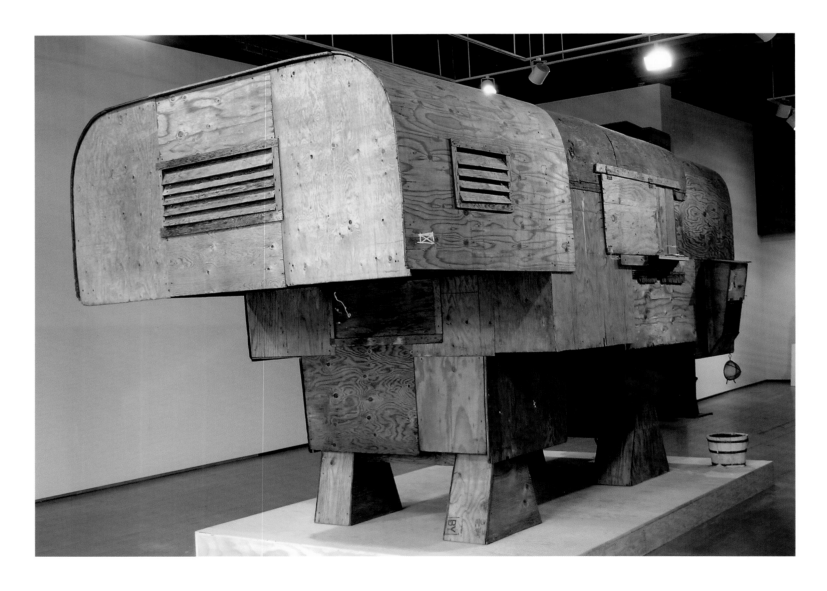

references Brancusi's birthplace as well as the stiff steel tariffs imposed by the United States in 2002 (later ruled illegal by the World Trade Organization). Starling's work powerfully conflates the *Bird in Space* case and definitions of art with contemporary global economics.

The artists highlighted in this essay have all expressed concern for scale, materiality, subjectivity, and engagement with an object in space. Over time, they have moved toward abstraction, explored architecture and environment, and tackled a concern for the body and mind. A new group of contemporary artists continues to expand sculptural practice, giving rise to the innovative approaches seen in the genre today. Together and as a complex pageant of change, these seminal works allow the Seattle Art Museum to offer a dynamic reading of the past while offering a better understanding of more recent art histories. The single, remarkable infusion of objects that comprise the gifts made in honor of the museum's seventy-fifth anniversary document the most significant impulses within sculptural practice over the course of a century.

90 **Simon Starling**
British, born 1967
Bird in Space, 2004
imported Romanian steel plate, inflatable jackets, and helium, 72 in. × 20 ft. × 12 in.
Margaret E. Fuller Fund and gift of Jeffrey and Susan Brotman, Jeff and Judy Greenstein, Lyn and Jerry Grinstein, and Virginia and Bagley Wright in honor of Jon and Mary Shirley, and in honor of the 75th Anniversary of the Seattle Art Museum, 2007.264

NOTES
1. Friedrich Teja Bach, "Brancusi: The Reality of Sculpture," in Bach, Margit Rowell, and Ann Temkin, *Constantin Brancusi, 1876–1957,* exh. cat. (Philadelphia: Philadelphia Museum of Art, 1995), 29n48.
2. Margit Rowell, "Catalogue: Sculptures," in *Constantin Brancusi, 1876–1957,* 248.
3. David Bourdon, "The Razed Sites of Carl Andre: A Sculptor Laid Low by the Brancusi Syndrome," *Artforum,* no. 2 (October 1966): 15.
4. The vertical stacks were made in two sizes: small, measuring 6 by 27 by 24 inches (each unit) and large, measuring 9 by 40 by 31 inches. Judd's systematic method required that each unit be installed on a wall one above the other at a distance equal to the height of each unit.
5. Although the sculpture was posthumously fabricated in 1999, Smith made a life-size maquette of *Stinger* for the 1968 exhibition *Art of the Real* at the Museum of Modern Art, New York.
6. See the entry on Puryear's *Thicket* by Patterson Sims in *Selected Works* (Seattle: Seattle Art Museum, 1991), 134.

7. "Conversation/Roxy Paine and Allan McCollum," in *Roxy Paine/Bluff* (New York: Public Art Fund, 2002), 23.
8. Robert Pincus-Witten, *Louise Bourgeois: The Personages* (New York: C&M Arts, 2001), 1.
9. "Katharina Fritsch," Tate Modern, Past Exhibitions, http://www.tate.org.uk/modern/exhibitions/fritsch/default.htm (accessed November 2007).
10. Miwon Kwon, "Interview: Miwon Kwon in Conversation with Mark Dion," in Lisa Graziose Corrin, Miwon Kwon, and Norman Bryson, *Mark Dion* (London: Phaidon Press, 1997), 22.
11. Quoted from a podcast interview with Jen Graves, "Invisible," *The Stranger* [Seattle], June 23, 2007.
12. The actual display of *Bovine* within the controlled and stable environment of a gallery denies the object's deterioration and reinforces its monumentality.

Michael Darling

Caught on Film

The field of photography is one of the most vital in contemporary art, its offerings ranging from direct visual documentation, communicated through the language of "straight" photography, to experimental techniques that disrupt the conventions and purposes of the camera to bring us new insights into the mechanics of perception and the genre itself. The much younger arena of video art is also dependent on photographic processes and rules, but with the added dimension of movement and sometimes sound. The Seattle Art Museum is committed to documenting the best work from past and present in these areas, and thankfully, recent gifts in honor of the museum's seventy-fifth anniversary have shored up our holdings in critical areas.

The museum's laudable photography collection, extending from the nineteenth century to the sharpest edges of the most contemporary, has been built up over the years through strategic acquisitions and important gifts. Despite having iconic works by some of the twentieth century's greatest practitioners, greater

depth is always sought. For example, the museum had four fine works of the great colorist William Eggleston, three of which reflect his complex view of nature. To that was added *Black Bayou Plantation, Near Glendora, Mississippi* (1970, not illustrated). Here, a welcoming, lush rural landscape opens up before the lens, only to be compromised ecologically (but not compositionally) by scattered bleach bottles and cardboard boxes. In classic Eggleston fashion, the scene looks entirely casual, but it is structured by extremely subtle framing and brims with simmering content. The unflappable English duo Gilbert and George were likewise represented within the museum's collection by but a single great piece, *Coloured Shouting* (1982). Their complicated and far-reaching career could only be hinted at with a solitary work. With the promise of *Son of a God* (2005, plate 92), a monumental, multipanel piece dealing with the doubly inflammatory subjects of religion and sex, the museum can begin to sketch the outlines of their provocative concerns.

91 **Nan Goldin**
American, born 1953
Self-portrait on the Train, Germany, 1992
Cibachrome print, 28½ × 41⅛ in.
Promised gift of William H. Gates, in honor of
the 75th Anniversary of the Seattle Art Museum,
T2001.100

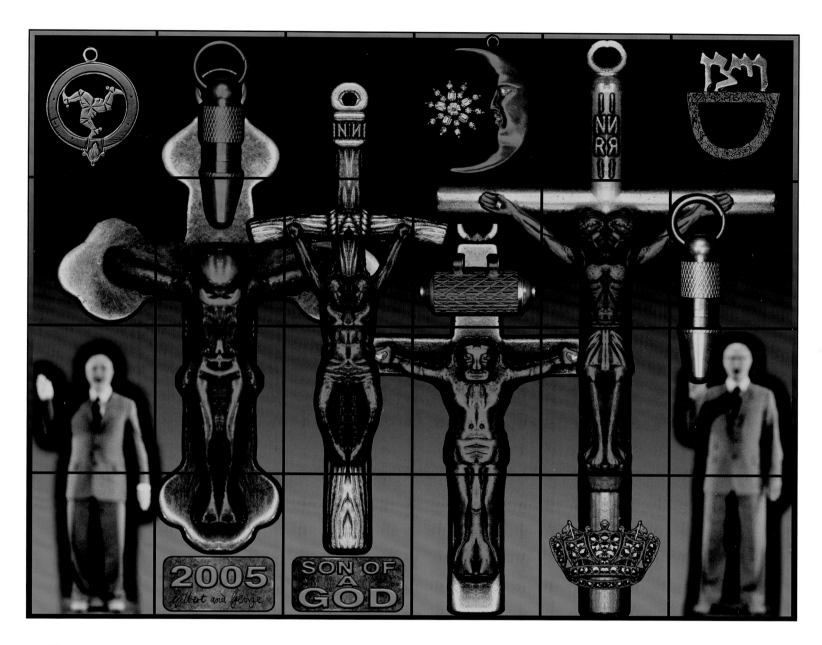

92 **Gilbert and George**
British (born Italy), 1943; British, 1942
Son of a God, 2005
mixed media, 9 ft. 10 in. × 12 ft. 6 in.
Promised gift of Merrill Wright, in honor of the 75th
Anniversary of the Seattle Art Museum, T2006.131.1

93 **Edward Burtynsky**
Canadian, born 1955
Shipyard #7, Qili Port, Zhejiang Province, 2005
chromogenic print, 48 × 60 in.
Gift of Charles Cowles, in honor of the 75th Anniversary
of the Seattle Art Museum, 2007.59

94 **Candida Höfer**
German, born 1944
Neue Nationalgalerie, Berlin VI, 2001
Cibachrome print, 47¼ × 47¼ in.
Promised gift of James and Christina Lockwood, in
honor of the 75th Anniversary of the Seattle Art Museum,
T2006.130.2

Another recent pledge of two iconic Cindy Sherman works (see plate 4) fills a significant gap, giving the museum a toehold in representing one of the most influential photographers of the past thirty years. Similarly, the much-imitated Nan Goldin was not represented until three works came in under the aegis of the seventy-fifth anniversary, the wonderfully pensive *Self-portrait on the Train, Germany* (plate 91) and two other moody portraits. A characteristic and moving work by the Canadian Edward Burtynsky, *Shipyard #7, Qili Port, Zhejiang Province* (2005, plate 93), is also the first to enter the collection by this important artist, whose fascinating oeuvre chronicles the vast scale of globalized commerce and industry. Burtynsky provides a North American analogue to the German photographer Andreas Gursky, whose work is in the museum's collection, but others from the so-called Dusseldorf school had been conspicuously absent until the addition of Candida Höfer's breathtakingly empty *Neue Nationalgalerie, Berlin VI* (2001, plate 94).

 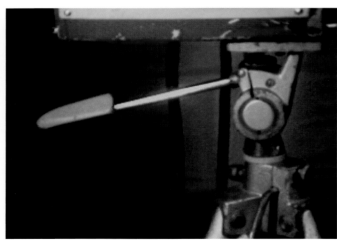

A LINE OF REASON

THE
SOUND
OF ONE HAND
CLAPPING IN
ONE MANS MIND

(opposite, top to bottom)
Gary Hill
American, born 1951

95 Stills from *Why Do Things Get in a Muddle?*
(Come on Petunia), 1984
single-channel video, running time 32 min.

96 Stills from *Incidence of Catastrophe,* 1987–88
single-channel video, running time 43 min. 51 sec.

97 Stills from *Around & About,* 1980
single-channel video, running time 4 min. 45 sec.

98 Stills from *Happenstance (part one of many*
parts), 1982–83
single-channel video, running time 6 min. 30 sec.

Gift of the artist, in honor of the 75th Anniversary
of the Seattle Art Museum, 2007.90, .89, .91, .92

99 **Hirsch Perlman**
American, born 1960
Stills from *Two Affect Studies,* 2001
single-channel video installation with sound, edition 1/3,
running time 15 min.
Promised gift of William and Ruth True, in honor of the
75th Anniversary of the Seattle Art Museum, T2007.90

Seattle is the home of Gary Hill, one of the most influential artists to wield video as a medium. The artist has acknowledged his close relationship with the museum by donating four important early works (plates 95–98). In each, his interests in the fascinating pitfalls and pleasures of language are explored, paired with imagery that holds the eye while provoking the mind into action. Hirsch Perlman and Sterling Ruby take up Hill's mantle, in differing ways, to exploit the codependency of image and sound. In Perlman's *Two Affect Studies* (2001, plate 99), the viewer comes upon one of two projected images and inevitably makes a judgment about it without other stimulation. But when accompanying headphones are put on and the evocative soundtrack is experienced with the visuals, a new, highly manipulated perception is formed. Similarly, the droning voice in Ruby's *Dihedral* (2006, not illustrated) alternates between providing insights about the amorphous blobs of color on the screen and remaining obstinately unhelpful. Such critical ambivalence is a hallmark of the best recent work in both video and photography, and these watershed gifts keep the Seattle Art Museum's collection refreshingly relevant.

Pamela McClusky

To Mask or Not to Mask

Can masks be modern art? If modernity requires moving into more progressive lanes of life, isn't masquerade an anachronism whose time has passed? In many parts of the world, masquerades have already been edited out of contemporary life, except for children at Halloween, horror films, or an occasional theme party. What is lost when masks fade from use? The gift to the Seattle Art Museum of a suite of masks provides one answer from a community that still uses masquerade to usher in a season of transformation and to stage encounters with spirited beings. Because of the distinguished career of the collector, who investigated this phenomenon for fifty years, the museum is able to stage a reenactment of a play and parade that combines masks from the 1950s with recent recordings and costumes. To do so accurately required assistance from an association of men whose professional lives are fully modern and yet find inspiration from the songs and insights of those who perform exuberant masquerades on a regular basis.

Few gifts of African art have been as thoroughly documented and extensively published as this one. Simon Ottenberg began collecting the masks as part of his research among the Afikpo, an Igbo group, in southeast Nigeria in the 1950s. Trained as a cultural anthropologist by William Bascom and Melville Herskovits, two of the academic leaders of the twentieth century, he carried out field-work with a relish for detailed observation, obtaining interviews and photographs, and all the while carefully separating his viewpoints as an outsider from those of his Afikpo informants. It did not take long for him to recognize the significance of masquerades to everyone in the village he studied. This dedication to what he termed "an aesthetic that emphasizes action" was to become a central subject of his life's work.

This group of masks is distinguished by the fact that most are dated and credited to a known artist. These simple details are anomalies in African art since early collecting often was not carefully documented. Simon Ottenberg got to know the carver Chukwu Okoro and commissioned many masks from him as part of his study of the artist's role and process. This was just one of many ways in which Ottenberg accumulated a repository of data for deeper consideration of this art form. His landmark *The Masked Rituals of Afikpo: The Context of an African Art* (1975), a synthesis of years of observation, explored masquerades through photographs and a step-by-step analysis of mask types, uses, song texts, and dialogues.

Masks from the Afikpo are not among the most shocking, aggressive, or even inventive in the corpus of African art. They have tightly defined faces, often rather small in scale with delicate features in white or sometimes with grotesque features in black (plate 100). Quiet and still, they hardly suggest the complexity of the satirical theater and vivid encounters of which they were once a part.

When the masks arrived at the museum in 2005, a plan to enact a more thorough display of the special effects of masquerading was soon devised. Ottenberg was returning to Nigeria in 2006 for the launch of a book on Igbo life. As a respected elder and honorary Igbo chief, he was escorted to Nigeria by the president of the Afikpo Association of America, Sam Irem. The gift of the Afikpo masks to the museum was a valuable catalyst for collecting what usually is left behind: the costumes, sounds, dancing, music, acting, and speeches that are part of a masquerade. Two dozen masking characters were identified for revival, and a deal was struck whereby the details of each character would be provided as long as the sources for masquerade elements remained a secret, most especially from women.

Many confidential conversations and negotiations were undertaken as single masks were reunited with their complex characters. Just a month after the trip was completed, an abundant shipment of costume parts arrived at the museum. Recognizable accessories were mixed in with some that challenged identification. Straps of red velvet and lace turned out to be a "breast holder" or bra for a maiden character. Striped stocking caps were identified as essential headgear for certain male players. Piles of raffia ruffs dyed a vibrant rust orange tumbled out of boxes along with deerskins, strands of plastic beads, a wide-brimmed woven hat, a black cloth "50 cent" hat, and handwoven towels and cloths with metallic dots. From this assortment, it became evident that the 1950s masks were still well known and enacted, albeit updated with 2006 accents.

In the new gallery installation, two young masked children walking close together greet visitors. They are the harbingers of a unique Afikpo parade called Njenje (walkabout), Act 1 of the Dry Season Festival, which Afikpo say is their "Christmas," a time of rich meals, visits with friends and family, and ceremony. A village's entire population can become involved in this season of highly charged personalized theater. Men in their twenties are organized in age-grades and required to orchestrate the parade. For months beforehand, they assemble elaborate costumes that often involve loans of cloth and jewelry from sisters, wives, lovers, and friends

100 **Chukwu Okoro**
Nigerian, Afikpo, 1910–1987
Mask: Beke (White Person), 1953
wood and pigment with raffia, 9 × 5 × 6 in.
Gift of Simon Ottenberg, in honor of the 75th Anniversary
of the Seattle Art Museum, 2005.32

101 Okumkpa players: Opa Nwa (Queen)
and Omankwo (Woodpecker) with the pot
of foolishness in the foreground

who eagerly await the finished ensemble. Secrecy excludes women and boys from the dressing process, adding to the suspense of the audience that awaits the players.

It is a parade of imposters. No one is in his normal role, but everyone takes another identity to try on. Ushers wearing netted disguises appear as players known as "path clearers." They stride forcefully and dance grotesquely to maintain control of the parade. They may be accompanied by maskers known as "youthful exuberance" or "madness" who also protect the line of players, especially from curious young boys who tend to swarm in their way. Ultra-feminine players are the stars of the parade. They dress in layers of sweet accessories—headdresses with mirrors and feathers, shimmery shirts with metallic inserts, and loads of waist beads. Embodying the essence of unmarried girls, the players walk with fine posture and do their best to take long strides that draw attention to their presence. After the female stars pass by, a mix of village characters follows.

In Seattle's mix are two couples, one Afikpo and one foreign. The Afikpo man wears a leader's shirt and hat with an embroidered roaring lion, while his wife is dressed in a stylish outfit of wax-printed cotton accessorized with bold jewelry. He walks with a cane, while she has a jaunty step. The foreign man wears a suit coat and carries a cane; his wife appears to be a British matron with a slightly outdated sense of fashion in a green flowery dress and bright red parasol. A Muslim man in a somber embroidered outfit strides confidently, while a final usher lurks at the end of the parade sequence. His darkly twisted face mask is matched with a grotesque costume weighted down with netting, a gun, and mismatched garments. In Afikpo villages, this procession would meander though neighborhoods in a line for everyone to review. In Seattle, the parade surrounds Act 2—a stage that is set for the most popular masquerade, called Okumpka (see plates 101–105).

It is in the faces and reactions of the audience for the play that its effect is most clearly seen. Glee, concern, delight, and laughter are evident. Above all, it is an audience extremely alert to all that is going on. No one sits back comfortably, ready to absorb the play without being involved. As Simon Ottenberg states, "The Afikpo aesthetic carries with it the idea of participation." This is true of the players, of course, but this theater is distinctly different from Western productions in that it is customized to fit the audience of each day. Without written scripts or elaborate staging, the Okumpka play is of the moment. Part of its intensity is due to its specificity, and for this reason in the museum galleries a screen carries a projection of the audience members, whose faces record their nervous

102 Okumkpa players: Okpesu Umuruma
(Frighten Children), Nne Mgbo (Mother of
Mgbo), and Obaraja (Goat)

energy in watching a play that at any moment might throw a veiled spotlight on them.

After finding their seats, the exclusively male audience is ready for the powerful opening of the play, during which an impressive mass of costumed spirits surges into view. Often as many as a hundred characters dance in, waving fly whisks, swirling raffia ruffs, shaking rattles, and singing as they come. All the players wear masks and are known as *mma*, a type of spirit with the freedom to criticize all they have seen going on in any village during the course of the year. Eventually the spirits take their seats on the ground in the center of the village. The audience adjusts in its place, crowds in to listen, and watches for hours.

Between the audience and the players, two spirited moderators appear in masks, one of whom carries a microphone. This senior leader, known as the "father of the Okumkpa play," is a conductor who offers commentary on the skits and songs that follow. His face is covered in eggshell, not a consequence of bad reviews but because eggs are not a typical Afikpo food. Often reserved for devotional acts, eggs are given to diviners and shrines as offerings when requesting spiritual insight. To be an Okumkpa leader is akin to being the event's producer, and the men best suited for this task are said to be those "who have buried their own non-

sense." Circling in and out of the action of the play, the leaders maintain the order of the afternoon's performance and ensures that the play stays critical without insulting anyone to excess.

What Okumpka offers is a showcase for sophisticated humor. Devised by men in the community specifically for their peers, it brings dilemmas into the open. In just one play, up to fourteen short original songs and skits might turn attention to people who have not handled situations very well. Common troubles that songs address include men who are stingy, leaders who should speak up about issues but do not, leaders who take advantage of others, people who drink too much palm wine, men who behave as if they are "rabbits of the night," henpecked husbands, women who cannot sit still long enough to hear the songs, and women who demand entirely too much independence. Skits can take many forms, appearing almost vaudevillian, with disasters ensuing from not understanding which pill to take for which illness or not knowing how to handle someone who is much too foolish.

Foolishness is, in fact, a constant subject in the play and appears in explicit form in a skit in which a soup or water pot is deemed to be "the pot of foolishness." It becomes the centerpiece in a highly unusual competition that begins when a masked player comes out to explain why he is the most foolish of them all. Others vie

(opposite)
103 Njenje Parader: Nwaoke Mba (Male Leader) with a group of seated Okumkpa players in the background

104 Nnade Okumkpa (Junior Leader) in foreground; Njenje paraders in background

105 Njenje Parade Couple: Beke (White Person) and Mma Ji (Yam Knife Male)

106　**Chukwu Okoro**
Nigerian, Afikpo, 1910–1987
Leader Mask: Nnade Okumpka, 1960
wood and pigment with raffia, 13 × 6 × 5½ in.
Gift of Simon Ottenberg, in honor of the 75th Anniversary
of the Seattle Art Museum, 2005.42

107　**Chukwu Okoro**
Nigerian, Afikpo, 1910–1987
Mask: Mma Ji (Yam Knife), 1952–53
wood and pigment with raffia, 17 × 5 × 6½ in.
Gift of Simon Ottenberg, in honor of the 75th Anniversary
of the Seattle Art Museum, 2005.41

for the chance to step forward and offer their case for why they
deserve to be known as the most foolish. Stories about stupidity
abound and can evolve into long, chanted accounts. One such
story offers the tale of a man completely obsessed with growing
and harvesting yams (see plate 107). This farmer works so hard accumulating yams that he refuses to take the time to eat and keeps
fainting from lack of food. No one can figure out what is wrong
with him except his wife, who, knowing how foolish he is, deter-
mines that he needs to eat. Once she offers him a meal, he eats
greedily with both hands. Hours pass as songs with explicit lyrics
call out the foibles of those in the audience for all to review, and
highly skilled players enact their exacting parodies. Humor keeps
everyone tuned in as they watch for the reactions of the persons
mentioned in the songs. Stoic acknowledgment is said to be the
best response.

A group of players sits on a platform in the museum, dressed
and ready for Okumpka. At the center is a player known as the
"queen" or "maiden," who wears a white polo shirt and a "breast

holder," carries a handkerchief, and sits with her legs straight in
front of her (see plate 109). Imitating a woman who rejects suitor
after suitor until finally relenting, she commands attention when-
ever she gets up to dance. Male performers do their best to be as
graceful and delicate as possible when portraying her. Beside her, a
musician wearing a black goat mask sits in the midst of the players
to help lead the singing with drumming. Nearby is a player called
"frighten children" whose mask has grotesque features—bulging
cheeks, crooked mouth, and twisted nose—designed to be upset-
ting (plate 108). Such a mask immediately signals greediness and
self-interest, and is worn by a player who appears to have evil inten-
tions. From the sublime maiden to the working drummer to the
ridiculously awful, the players assume a range of personality types
in a morality play that reviews secrets and misfortunes for all to
witness and gossip about during the festival season.

When talking with Simon Ottenberg about his carving process, Chukwu Okoro cautioned how careful carvers should be with
masks. The divide between what was public and what was secret

108 Chukwu Okoro
Nigerian, Afikpo, 1910–1987
*Mask: Okpesu Umuruma
(Frighten Children)*, 1952
wood and pigment, 11 × 5½ × 5½ in.
Gift of Simon Ottenberg, in honor of
the 75th Anniversary of the Seattle Art
Museum, 2005.46

109 Chukwu Okoro
Nigerian, Afikpo, 1910–1987
Mask: Opa Nwa (Queen), 1953
wood and pigment, 23 × 4½ × 6 in.
Gift of Simon Ottenberg, in honor of
the 75th Anniversary of the Seattle Art
Museum, 2005.51

was impenetrable in the 1950s. Okoro also expressed dismay about
a story he had heard of a "rascal" man who dared to hang a mask
on a wall in his house. He said it was wrong to hang a mask on
the wall—no mask, even a foreign one, deserved to be treated so
poorly. To be able to display so much of Chukwu Okoro's carving
in 2007 has required stretching the boundaries between public and
secret knowledge, and between American and Afikpo expectations
of what masks can do and how they should be displayed. Without
Simon Ottenberg's exacting work, it would not have been possible.
Equally, it required the assistance of many unnamed Igbo men who
invested in the potential of spirited exchanges to change human
behavior. These men—professors, pharmacists, and artists among
them—participated in preparing this display so that American audiences could gain an idea of the value such masks hold for their culture. Afikpo masquerades look at the foolishness, greed, deceit, and
despair that build up in communities. Perhaps masqueraders who
use humor to defuse such difficulties can inspire new notions for
the next parade or play in our midst.

131

Pamela McClusky

Repeat, Repeat

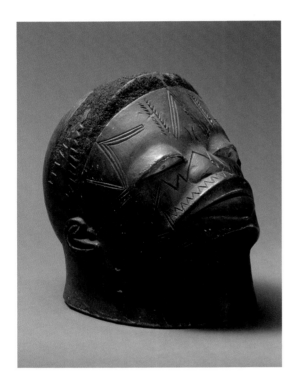

Figure 1. *Lipiko Mask*, Mozambique, Makonde, 20th century, wood and human hair, 9 × 6⅞ × 6⅛ in. Gift of Katherine White and the Boeing Company, 81.17.1220

Figure 2. *Bush Cow Crest Mask*, Nigeria, Mama/Katana, 20th century, wood, 5½ × 13⅛ × 18½ in. Gift of Katherine White and the Boeing Company, 81.17.544

Contrary to the quest for a single masterpiece, many cultures search for excellence by making multiples. Looking at a single mask, sculpture, apron, or cloth often does not make aesthetic sense, and for museum-goers, the pairing of objects can offer a strategy for seeing. The pairs newly formed by recent additions to the African art collection proclaim the value of comparison, sorting out when it is important to refine convention or, occasionally, to let the sparks of innovation fly.

An eerie realism is expected in Makonde masks, where human features are frozen in their expressions. Coiffures of real hair are affixed with beeswax; eyes are downcast; and open lips seem capable of speaking. The mask is worn with the head tilted back so that the performer can look out through the mouth or chin. The impression of an ancestor who has returned for a visit becomes ominous when masqueraders rush in forcefully, but then stop and nod slightly. The incongruity between the vigorous action of the masquerader and a face that never moves is unnerving. In the pair of Lipiko masks, the one with a darker face with indications of incised scar tattoos is likely the older example (fig. 1). Scarification, once the physical crucible for leaving childhood, has not been practiced on the face in this way for several decades. A circle of hair sets off the forehead of the mask with a reddish face, whose sleepy countenance may have been meant to satirize a foolish individual (plate 110).

Blunt formal shapes create two mask heads of the powerful and unpredictable cape buffalo (plate 111, fig. 2). The horns curl into a broken circle, and the mouth extends out in a balancing muzzle. Flat planes give a geometric crispness to one mask, while the other subtly curves in all directions. When worn, both masks were affixed to the head and carried horizontally in actions that emulated the frenzy of a charging buffalo. An ominous suit of tufted raffia would completely conceal the wearer, who was called upon to witness appeals for vigorous crop fertility and childbirth.

One historic and one contemporary cloth from Ghana are imbedded with meaning. A textile reserved for chiefs and kings, whose title translates as "Cloth of the Great," suggests the pervasiveness of proverbs in Asante oral and visual vocabularies (plate 9.3). A menagerie of creatures and symbols embroidered on the cloth alludes to proverbs and sayings that surround a leader when he appears during public functions. On this example, delicate wavering lines convey the images of a peacock, butterfly, fish, cocoa tree, armadillo, porcupine, and royal stool.

110 *Lipiko Mask*
Mozambique, Makonde, 20th century
wood and human hair, 10 × 11 × 8 in.
Gift of Dr. Oliver E. and Pamela F. Cobb, in honor of
the 75th Anniversary of the Seattle Art Museum, 2004.106

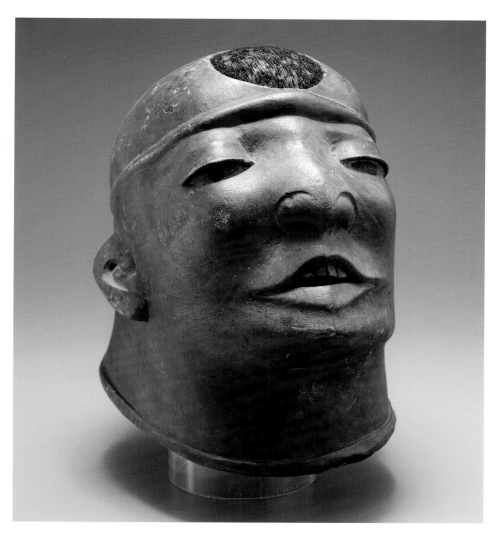

111 *Mama Mask*
Nigeria, Mama, late 19th–20th century
wood, 13 × 6 × 21½ in.
Gift of Mark Groudine and Cynthia Putnam, in honor of
the 75th Anniversary of the Seattle Art Museum, 2003.102

112 detail of *Akunitan (Cloth of the Great)*
Ghana, Asante, 20th century
wool cloth and yarn, 132 × 81 in.
African Art Purchase Fund, in honor of the 75th
Anniversary of the Seattle Art Museum, 2005.28

(opposite)
113 **Gilbert Bobbo Ahiagble**
Ghanaian, Ewe, born 1944
detail of *Atifofoe Susuavor Adanudo (A Cloth of
Multiple Designs and Much Skill, or Even Difference
Can Be Unified)*, 2004
cotton, 106 × 85¼ in.
African Art Purchase Fund, 2005.29

Among the proverbs suggested by the imagery are:

"Peacocks will not spare a cockroach that falls in their midst."
"One should never rub bottoms with a porcupine."
"There is no tree that cannot be felled by an axe."
"A lone tree will fall against the force of wind."
"The royal stool is no log long enough to seat two at a time."
"A small armadillo recoils when it sees its bigger counterpart."

Weaving among the Ghanaian Ewe is adapting to the twenty-first century. A cloth woven in 2004 (plate 114) originated at a flourishing community of artists led by Gilbert Bobbo Ahiagble. Twenty-four weavers provide the strips of cloth that he assembles into finished compositions. When asked to choose a cloth that exemplified the highest quality weaving attained by this workshop, Ahiagble selected this one. For him, the widely scattered, small inlay motifs are accents that suggest the strength to be gained by uniting differences, as reflected in the title he assigned to the finished cloth: "Even Difference Can Be Unified."

114 *Isicholo* (Woman's Hat)
South Africa, Zulu, 20th century
bast fiber and ocher, 17 × 12 in.
Gift of Dr. Oliver E. and Pamela F. Cobb, in honor of the
75th Anniversary of the Seattle Art Museum, 2005.147

115 *Msinga* (Headdress)
South Africa, Zulu, 20th century
grass, bast fiber, human hair, fat, and ocher, diam. 18½ in.
Gift of Dr. Oliver E. and Pamela F. Cobb, 2003.64

The evolution of two hundred years of hairdressing led to the design of two hats in a style once essential for women in Zulu cultures. In the early nineteenth century, married women regularly shaved their heads, leaving only a small tuft of hair on the crown which they smeared with a mixture of fat and ocher. Later in the century, they let the tuft grow into a truncated cone. Grass or false hair was eventually woven in, and by the end of the nineteenth century, the cone-shaped coiffure became detachable as a woven hat. These two examples showcase the textural difference between a hat of woven grass fiber and one incorporating human hair (plates 114, 115). The hat on the right (above) has a complex texture whose depth is hard to define until you know that it holds one woman's hair in an eternal circle.

Little is known about the reasons behind the mazes of geometry that women of northern Cameroon worked into small rectangular skirts of distinctive patterns. Placing the skirts side by side, however, allows a visual conversation to take place (plates 116, 117). Subtle variations emerge and showcase the value of looking carefully at pairs. At first the patterns seem to repeat, repeat, but they actually talk back and forth about the value of mastering an art form in unison.

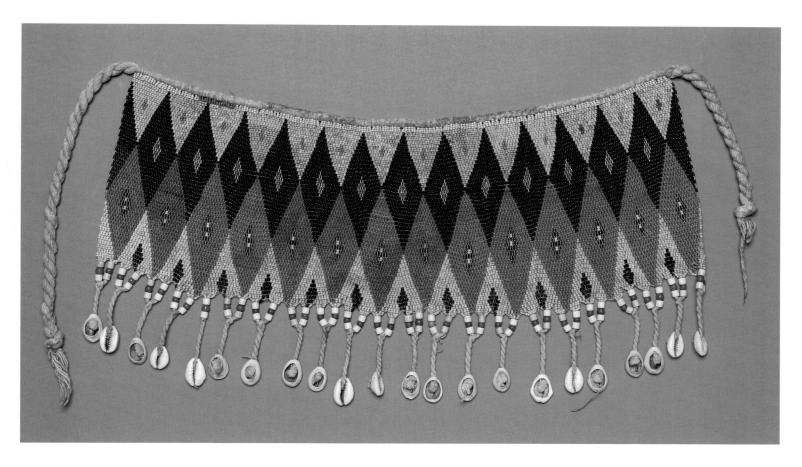

116 *Women's Skirt*
Cameroon, Kirdi, 20th century
cotton, beads, and cowrie shells, 8 × 17 in.
Gift of Oliver E. and Pamela F. Cobb, in honor of the
75th Anniversary of the Seattle Art Museum, 2004.109

117 *Women's Skirt*
Cameroon, Kirdi, 20th century
cotton, beads, and cowrie shells, 7 × 18½ in.
Gift of Oliver E. and Pamela F. Cobb, in honor of the
75th Anniversary of the Seattle Art Museum, 2004.112

Pamela McClusky

The Art of War

We all pick our battles and the weapons with which to fight them. When several shields from the Asmat people of New Guinea were given to the Seattle Art Museum, they instigated a battle of perception. In a stereotypical fashion, they could easily be regarded as evidence of another culture's fixation with violence. Head-hunting, a missing Rockefeller, and unfamiliar symbols all set an imaginary stage for a disturbing discussion. But looking at these shields in the midst of others in the collection offers another route. It leads through the mythic battles of Greek gods, to a tournament fought over love in medieval France, and onto the savannah of East Africa to confront a lion. It highlights the captivating force of shields, which embody a strength of purpose and showcase imagery that is carried with conviction, and gives a truer effect to the Asmat reliance upon them.

Gods and mortals clash constantly in Greek myths and in vase painting, where daggers and swords point, bows are drawn, and arrows fly. A defensive weapon, a large round shield, is seen on an amphora in the museum's collection (fig. 1). Three of them punctuate the expressive postures of their bearers. Athena is in all her protective garb—helmet, goatskin breastplate, lion pelt, and shield, its face turned away from us. Given Athena's affinities, the shield face might have carried the ultimate female battle ally, Medusa, whose serpentine hair was always terrifying to confront. On the far right, Athena's opponent, Heracles, holds a shield with a single serpent slithering across the face as a defensive emblem. Serpents are often associated with Heracles, the great heroic son of Zeus, who was born to a mortal woman. Heracles inspired the wrath of Hera, Zeus's wife, so she sent two snakes to kill him in his crib. He was later found playing with a strangled serpent in each hand as if they were toys, the first of his many acts of superhuman strength. As Athena and Heracles face off, Zeus raises his hands as if to give them room to go at their fight. Such scenes on Greek vases are a reminder that ancient historians stressed war as a glorious undertaking, a way to fame and immortality, as modeled by Homer in the epic poems the Iliad and the Odyssey. Shields with confrontational symbols were essential for Greek men and gods.

Centuries later, four extremely sleepy wyverns (a type of dragon) nap around the edges of a French mirror back that comes from an era of tournaments and ostentatious combat (fig. 2). Ivory's ability to retain detail is taken to maximum effect in this miniature composition that transports the viewer to an allegorical siege on a castle with two turrets. At the bottom, a knight on horseback

Figure 1. *Black Figure Amphora with Athena in Battle*, Greek, Attica, c. 530 BC, ceramic, 12¾ × 8¾ in. Gift of the Norman and Amelia Davis Classical Collection, 82.83

Figure 2. *Mirror Back: Siege of the Castle of Love*, France, Ile-de-France School, c. 1320–50, ivory, 4½ × 4¼ × ½ in. Donald E. Frederick Memorial Collection, 49.37

118 *Jamasji* (War Shields) New Guinea, Asmat, early 20th century
wood, lime, clay, and charcoal, 86 × 25 in. overall
Gift of Dr. and Mrs. Thomas W. Griffin, Mark Groudine, and Cynthia Putnam, in honor of the 75th Anniversary of the Seattle Art Museum, 97.60, 94.113, 2004.236–.241

holds a shield high to defend himself. Roses cover the front of the shield and issue a strong signal that perhaps this battle is not for blood. A careful look at the inhabitants of the castle reveals a group of women, whose main defensive action is to pummel their invaders with roses. Several do not even protest but are helping their attackers over the ramparts. The medieval lady who once owned this mirror case would have known this as the "castle of love," the attack as "courtship," and the rose as both the weapon and the symbol of surrender. There are accounts of actual sieges of castles of love being enacted in medieval festivals. One description of a mock battle seems very close to this scene: "The garrison of ladies was armed with flowers, and the knights, using all the appurtenances of siege warfare, but for ammunition roses, lilies, and violets, or more fantastically, vases of balsam and ambergris, had to scale the walls and remove the defenders. The resistance was symbolic, and after the usual phases of battle, the attackers always won."[1]

Shields may be hoisted in legends and in mock battles, but two shields that recently left Kenya and Sudan were put to use in actual defense. For a young Maasai male, a shield is essential for participating in activities with his peers. Painted designs on the surface designate the age-grade to which he belongs (plate 119). Shields are carried daily as groups of young warriors travel all over Maasai country. Before becoming a proven warrior (*moran*), he is required to assist his age-grade in hunting a lion. Kakuta Hamisi, a Maasai junior elder who experienced this rite of passage and collected the shield for the museum, describes a beautifully symbiotic relationship between buffalos, lions, and humans: "The shield is made from buffalo hide, the lion hunts the buffalo, then we come and skin the buffalo to make the shields to hunt the lion. . . . Lion hunting is part of a rite of passage. When a lion jumps onto you, you have to hold the shield and let it slide over your head. Sometimes the lion weighs about 400 pounds. So you really have to slide him over your head. You do that a few times, about three or four times, and you will confuse the lion. Then you have a chance to hunt. That is what the shield is used for."[2]

The shields of young Dinka men stretch the definition of the term. The museum's example, a long sliver of wood, seems hardly effective for defense (plate 120). The center of the pole thickens at the middle to accommodate a handle. It would have been used in parrying battle, with the pole ends spiraling from the center where only the hands were covered by the wood. Fighting with such poles tested a warrior's strength and stamina. They serve as a reminder of a time when Sudanese men faced each other without the possibility of the quick death of imported guns, which have now overtaken their country.

Asmat shields can help avoid a cloud of arrows or a stabbing attack of spears (plate 118). Like other shields, however, they create more than a physical barrier. Shields can project a psychological advantage based on the signs and symbols they carry. Among the Asmat, shields are precious and powerful allies throughout a man's life. They bring into view a number of the hidden forces that shape combat and cooperation with other men as well as with spirits of the dead and those of the environment.

Bursting out of a forest, a warrior prepared for battle would chant, swiftly leap, zigzag, and dart around while trying to assess the countering force. As the foes maneuvered and chanted, the bright designs on their shields stood out against the forest behind. The shields gained in energy as they massed together, investing the warriors with surging confidence. Battles were not uncommon since head-hunting was considered a sacred duty laid down by a mythical hero, Fumeripits, who also established a deep connection between trees and human beings. The Asmat myth of creation credits him as being the first to carve humans out of wood. He envisioned arms in tree branches, legs in roots, and the fruit of the tree as a skull. In creation logic, just as an animal eats the fruit of the tree to survive, so a human being takes the head of another human to survive. Every death had to be avenged to enable the spirit of the deceased to move on to the realm of ancestors.

War shields were usually made at a festival that preceded a raid to avenge death. Each new shield was named and imbued with a spirit who made demands of its owner and in return offered immense courage and protection. Master woodcarvers used hard woods from the flat buttress roots of swamp trees to compose the shields. In earlier times, shields were chiseled with the thighbone

119 *Shield*
Kenya, Maasai, Merrueshi community,
Kaputiei section, late 20th century
buffalo hide, pigment, goat sinew, and wood,
41½ × 28 × 4½ in.
General Acquisition Fund, 2000.4

of a cassowary bird or with other animal bones and shells. Later, iron tools made carving easier but resulted in facile surfaces.

In battle, shields present a who's who of signs, most harboring menace, with the flying fox (bat), wild boar, praying mantis, hornbill, whirlpools, and black palm cockatoo among them. Praying mantis females are known to eat the male's head during mating, so they certainly deserve a place in the roster of terror. Hornbills and cockatoos are ominous because they eat fruit which the Asmat equate with a tree's head. Curling boar's tusks bounce across one shield, while another shows off the ultimate symbol of head-hunting called *ainor*—a headless human torso with arms curled up at the sides. The right combination of a strong ancestral presence and symbols of deadly assault has the potential to shock an enemy into retreating or becoming paralyzed in fright.

Asmat shields are potent even when still. When stood upright in doorways or laid down to block an entrance, the ancestors in them guarded the house while the family was away. Though sturdy, the shields are surprisingly lightweight, ready to be carried for long distances, and could even protect owners against rain. It is said that a warrior is never alone if he has his shield.

In their stationary stance in the museum, the shields are denied their effect as weapons. As vibrant painted surfaces, they offer a study in flat earthy tones with relief outlines. Recognizing that it often took the thighbone of a bird to carve the symbols on a shield,

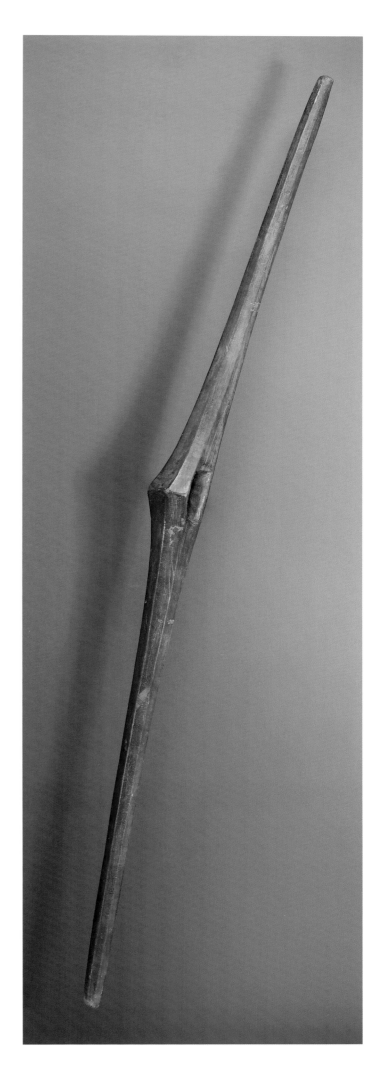

120 *Shield*
Sudan, Dinka, 20th century
wood, 4½ × 3¾ × 65 in.
Gift of Mark Groudine and Cynthia Putnam, in honor of
the 75th Anniversary of the Seattle Art Museum, 2003.100

a festival of head-hunting to complete it, and numerous battles to
season it, one tends to admire the conviction of the warrior who
once carried it. Violence comes in many forms and is met by shields
appropriate to the attack. When Athena is about to hurl a spear in
your direction, a shield with a writhing serpent should be readied.
If roses are flying off a castle turret with snoozing wyverns nearby,
a shield of complementary roses is the best defense. A leaping lion
requires a shield of breadth and structural strength, but also the
signs of alliance with other warriors. Seen in the context of other
battles, Asmat shields share many features with other cultures,
such as confrontational symbols and terrifying associations that
bolster the warrior's intensity as he faces his enemy. Such weapons
merge the psychological and physical reactions to war in a way that
underlines their consideration as art. They remind us that we all
prepare for conflict in different ways.

NOTES
1. A. McLaren Young, "A French Medieval Ivory Casket at the Barber
Institute of Fine Arts," *The Connoisseur* (September 1947): 18.
2. Kakuta Ole Maimai Hamisi, interviews recorded at the Seattle
Art Museum in 2001 as part of the exhibition *African Art: Long Steps
Never Broke a Back.*

Barbara Brotherton

Native Art of
the Northwest Coast

Like most museums, the Seattle Art Museum relies on generous gifts from patrons who believe that great art should be accessible to all and not sequestered in private homes. Objects once chosen by individual collectors according to their own tastes take on new meaning when they enter the museum, and with them come their often timely and heartfelt stories. In this essay I will recount just a few of the stories related to recent gifts to the museum's collection of Northwest Coast Native art.

Nearly two hundred gifts from longtime museum supporter John H. Hauberg (1916–2002) established the museum's collection of Northwest Coast Native and First Nations art as one of the finest in the country. Through Hauberg's magnanimous contributions between the years 1983 and 1991, Seattle residents, as well as visitors from far-flung places, can experience the aesthetic beauty and cultural depth of coastal traditions.

Hauberg's exuberance for material culture and history was nurtured in Rock Island, Illinois, by his father, John Henry Hauberg

Sr., a prominent attorney, businessman, and local historian. In 1927 the senior Hauberg was instrumental in creating Black Hawk State Park, which was named after a famed Sauk and Fox chief. John Henry Hauberg's collection of Sauk artifacts formed the core of the park's collection, and he wrote extensive treatises on the Native history of the region. For a time, the young Hauberg worked at the museum, building replicas of traditional houses under the direction of two Sauk chiefs. This abiding interest in Native history followed Hauberg to Seattle in 1946. After his studies at the University of Washington, he launched an illustrious career in forest resource management and the lumber industry. His innovative Pilchuck Tree Farm later became the site of the famed Pilchuck Glass School through his generous support and that of his first wife, Anne Gould Hauberg. Hauberg was passionate about the studio glass movement that was taking hold in Seattle, the art of the ancient peoples of Mesoamerica (pre-Columbian art), and later the art of Northwest Coast Native Americans and First Nations. Using

Figure 1. Attributed to Kadyisdu.axch' (Tlingit, active late 18th–early 19th century), *Yéil X̱'eenh* (Raven Screen), c. 1810, spruce and paint, 8 ft. 9¾ in. × 10 ft. 9 in. Gift of John H. Hauberg, 79.98

(opposite)
Figure 2. Preston Singletary (Tlingit, born 1963), *Keet Shagoon (Killer Whale)*, 2003, fused and sand-carved glass, 72 × 92 × ⅜ in. Purchased in honor of John H. Hauberg with funds from the Mark Tobey Estate Fund, John and Joyce Price, the Native American Art Support Fund, Don W. Axworthy, Susan and Jeffrey Brotman, Marshall Hatch, C. Calvert Knudsen, Christine and Assen Nicolov, Charles and Gayle Pancerzewski, Sam and Gladys Rubinstein, SAM Docents, SAMS Supporters, Frederick and Susan Titcomb, and Bagley and Virginia Wright, 2003.12

a clever mix of collecting directly from Native owners, from dealers, and at auctions, he amassed a brilliant assemblage of monumental sculpture, masks, headdresses, dance paraphernalia, and weavings. Believing that he was only a temporary custodian of these rare treasures, he generously lent pieces to exhibitions before making his last gift when the museum's downtown building opened in 1991. An array of those works is on permanent display in the John H. Hauberg galleries.

Given in 1979, *Yéil X̱'eenh* (Raven Screen) was acquired from the Frog House at the village of Klukwan Łlingit (or Tlingit), near Haines, Alaska (fig. 1). Interior house screens are among the most important of clan holdings, and many were still in Native hands when Hauberg purchased this one in 1979. The function of these esteemed works is twofold: they partition the chief's quarters in the communal cedar-plank dwelling from the rest of the house, and they display the painted and carved images (called "crests") of clan ancestors and benefactors. Scholar and artist Steve Brown has attributed this rare screen to the hand of an artist whose name appears in anthropologists' field notes as Kadyisdu.axch', a well-known carver from Wrangell, Alaska, who worked at the turn of the nineteenth century. The stylized raven painted on the joined spruce planks displays the elegant symmetry of design, the balance and proportion of individual forms, and the facile flow of design elements across the surface that characterize this master's work.

It is no wonder that this work's graceful, stately presence in the museum's gallery inspired a young Tlingit artist, Preston Singletary, who was raised in Seattle far from his family's roots in southeastern Alaska. Like many Native artists of his generation, Singletary turned to established Native artists, such as Joe David, and to important old Tlingit works in museum collections to kindle an understanding of the unique properties of traditional designs and their meanings. Singletary's experience, viewing and making sketches of traditional works like the raven screen, nudged his art deco–inspired vessels toward the tradition-based works in glass that have established his international reputation. In these complex forms, the artist uses revolutionary etching techniques to create designs that have affinities to Tlingit woven hats, carved screens, and delicate masks. Singletary created his monumental glass screen *Keet Shagoon* (Killer Whale) for the museum in honor of John Hauberg (fig. 2). Many of Hauberg's friends and fellow collectors contributed the funds to commission this significant work that elegantly reflects Hauberg's love of Northwest Coast Native art as well as glass. This is but one story of how the lives of many can be touched by a passion for art incited by an indelible childhood experience.

121 **Calvin Hunt**
Kwakw<u>a</u>ka'wakw, Kwagu'ł, Fort Rupert,
born 1956
Thunderbird Mask and Regalia, 2006
wood, paint, ostrich and turkey feathers, rabbit fur,
and cloth, 87 × 54 × 32 in.
Gift of the Native Arts of the Americas and Oceania Council,
friends of Native American Art, and the Ancient and Native
American Endowment, in honor of the 75th Anniversary of
the Seattle Art Museum, 2006.6

122 **Sonny Assu**
Kwakwaka'wakw, Laich-kwil-tach, Wei Wai Kai,
born 1975
Breakfast Series, 2006
five boxes digitally printed with Fome-Cor, 12 × 7 × 3 in. each
Gift of Rebecca and Alexander Stewart, in honor of the 75th
Anniversary of the Seattle Art Museum, 2006.93

The Hauberg collection is also rich in dramatic examples of Kwakwaka'wakw ceremonial art, including masks and dance regalia, and has a spectacular set of interior house posts acquired by Hauberg from John Scow's family longhouse on Gilford Island, British Columbia. Ceremonial regalia in the collection is represented by important works from the hands of early twentieth-century masters like Arthur Shaughnessy, Mungo Martin, Charlie James, and Willie Seaweed, who continued to create potlatch pieces in defiance of laws that prohibited such ceremonies. The unbroken thread of expression of traditional beliefs is alive in the modern potlatch and in the arts of contemporary practitioners like Calvin Hunt (Mungo's grandson) and the politically charged digital work of Sonny Assu.

As an adviser to the museum's new permanent collection display, Calvin Hunt lamented that although many collections have spectacular masks, the attendant costumes are rarely acquired. This condition was remedied with the commission of Hunt's thunderbird transformation mask and regalia (plate 121), made possible by donations of all sizes from the museum's supporters of Northwest Coast Native art. Museum staff were invited to Fort Rupert, British Columbia, to witness the thunderbird dance at a potlatch hosted by Hunt and his family before the work was presented to the museum. Today its prominent placement among the works of Hunt's ancestors and relatives provides museum visitors with the opportunity to understand that these traditions continue as a vital part of the lives of the First Nations. Of interest is the remarkable video footage that was taken at the potlatch and the taping of a

lengthy interview with this master carver. The interview includes a recitation of the ancient story of the thunderbird transformation, in which the thunderbird gathers the survivors of a great flood to have a feast. The event is represented by the human image inside the bird's head, made visible by maneuvering a sequence of strings that open the mask during a dramatic moment in the dance. Accompanying the story are a song and dance that are "owned" by Hunt's family and which Calvin Hunt will pass on to his son with a newly created costume and mask.

In *Breakfast Series* (plate 122), Vancouver-based artist Sonny Assu captures aspects of traditional Kwakwaka'wakw forms and then uses digital technologies to place each in a contemporary format on a cereal box, an object of popular culture. Strident commentaries about the loss of Native American lands and foods, poor health care, lack of educational opportunities, and other issues insinuate themselves onto the surfaces of the boxes, replacing information about questionable nutritional content with a mix of irony and humor. While maintaining a certain cultural ethos, Assu purposefully interrogates the status quo, reminding us that traditions can thrive only under conditions of economic, political, and social well-being. The work, donated by Alexander and Rebecca Stewart, helps update the museum's collection with contemporary forms that convey the vitality and meaning of First Nations art today.

Breakfast Series complements the museum's growing collection of Northwest Coast prints which spans the early years of Native printmaking in the 1970s to the experiments in graphic media today. This growth marks a new direction for Northwest Coast Native art at the

123 **Susan (Sparrow) Point**
Coast Salish, Musqueam, born 1951
The Wolf People, 1983
serigraph, 16 × 15 in.
Gift of Simon Ottenberg, in honor of the
75th Anniversary of the Seattle Art Museum,
2005.126

Seattle Art Museum, one which gives greater visibility to living artists. In addition to a small group of prints donated by John Hauberg, the museum acquired a selection of prints from Simon Ottenberg, a distinguished professor emeritus of anthropology at the University of Washington and the donor of a spectacular range of Afikpo masks and masquerade items obtained on his many research trips to Nigeria (see the essay by Pamela McClusky in this volume). Inveterate lovers of art, Simon Ottenberg and his wife, Carol Barnard, assembled an impressive collection of graphic works from the Northwest Coast and the Great Lakes Native peoples. When asked why, as an expert on African art, he turned his interest to Northwest Coast art, Ottenberg replied that he sought out and befriended local Native artists because of his desire to have a historical picture of this region and because he was drawn to the bold totemic designs and narratives embedded in the imagery.

Two gifts of works by eminent Salish artist Susan Point add depth to our collection of print media, which sometimes includes only a single work by a particular artist. While visiting the museum to consult about a major commission, Point noticed that we had installed one of her earliest prints (plate 123), made when she was experimenting with the traditional circular form of the spindle whorl. She has worked intensively in printmaking for nearly twenty-five years, in addition to her work in carved cedar and cast-glass and polymer sculptures, many of which are monumental commissions for public and private collections. Her gift includes

a complete portfolio of intimate, small-scale etchings and twelve large prints (plate 124); together they document Point's profound growth as an artist over the last ten years. It is always a special moment when an artist donates favorite works and provides insight into the intellectual and technical processes involved in their creation.

Traditionally, weaving has been the domain of Native women artists. The vagaries of collecting Northwest Coast art in the late nineteenth and early twentieth centuries gave the carving arts (masks, rattles, feast dishes) and technologies (such as cedar houses, poles, and canoes) more esteem than basketry and woven clothing. We know far fewer female artists' names and less about the particulars of their work. This state is quite a paradox given the high status afforded to mountain-goat wool robes, shirts, dresses, aprons, and headgear—all prized items that proclaimed the rank and ancestry of the wearer. For the Coast Salish, time-intensive wool weaving dwindled after contact with Euro-Americans, while basketry continued, using new materials and forms desired by non-Native buyers.

Until now, and the generous gift of Charles and Gayle Pancerzewski, the museum held several older Chilkat-style weavings and one early twentieth-century Salish robe in the collection but had no contemporary wool weavings. Susan Pavel, an apprentice of the late Skokomish artist Bruce subiyay Miller, an adviser to the museum, created *du'kWXaXa'?t3w3l* (Sacred Change for Each Other, plate 125).

124 **Susan Point**
Coast Salish, Musqueam, born 1951
Symphony of Butterflies, 2006
serigraph, 37 × 30 in.
The Point Family, Musqueam, in honor of the
75th Anniversary of the Seattle Art Museum, 2007.49

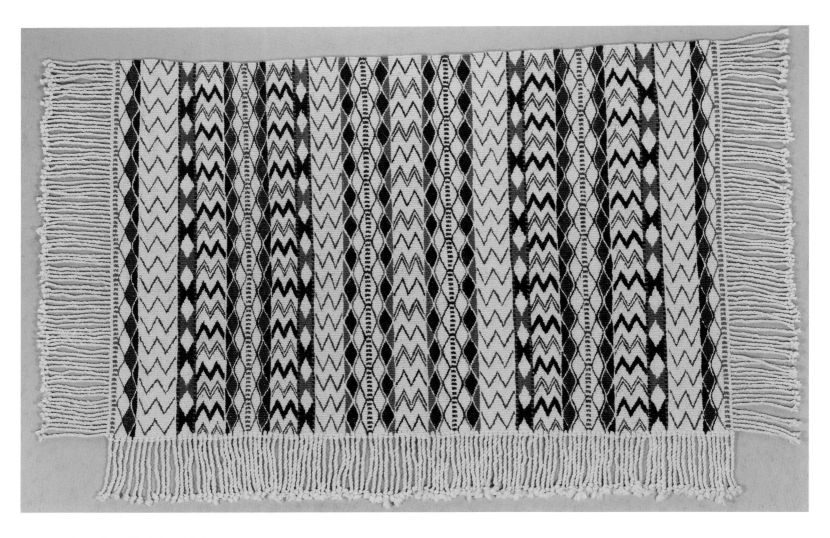

125 **Susan Pavel (sa'hLa mitSa)**
American, born 1968
du'kWXaXa'?t3w3l (Sacred Change for Each Other),
2007
mountain goat wool and dyes, 55 × 85½ in.
Gift of Gayle and Charles Pancerzewski, in honor of the
75th Anniversary of the Seattle Art Museum, 2007.38

She and her husband, Michael, spent more than a decade collecting the wool for it. When the robe was finished in 2007, it was the first fully twined mountain-goat wool garment woven in one hundred years. The blanket pin and carved cedar chest accompany the robe (plates 126, 127). This special artwork truly enacts the museum's mission to connect art to life.

Nine beautiful hard-coiled baskets have recently entered the collection through the generosity of the Bedal family estate and the Sauk-Suiattle tribe (plate 128). Created by Susan Wawatkin Bedal, the last traditional Sauk weaver, who died in 1947, they afford an excellent opportunity to spotlight women artists and their life stories, for Bedal's family history has been extensively documented. She and her husband, James, homesteaded on a hundred acres near

126 **Andy Wilbur-Peterson**
Coast Salish, Skokomish/Squaxin, born 1959
Bent-corner Chest: *The Naming Ceremony,* 2007
cedar and paint, 22 × 32 × 19 in.
Gift of Gayle and Charles Pancerzewski, in honor of the
75th Anniversary of the Seattle Art Museum, 2007.39

127 **Michael Pavel** (CHiXapkaid)
Coast Salish, Skokomish/Squaxin, born 1959
Blanket pin, 2007
deer bone, l. 9½ in.
Gift of Gayle and Charles Pancerzewski, in honor of the
75th Anniversary of the Seattle Art Museum, 2007.40

Darrington, Washington, in a community of whites and Natives in
the 1890s. Bedal wove baskets for use in the community, but she was
also known to take the Speeder train to Everett to sell her baskets,
which were highly desired because of their extraordinary artistry.
She excelled in several weaving techniques, using materials that
she gathered herself, such as cedar root, horsetail root, cedar bark,
and cherry bark. The signature feature of her decorated baskets is
the striking rose-colored dye she used to create designs depicting
butterflies, clouds, and snake tracks—imagery that reflects the intimate connection she had with the beauty and natural elements of
the Sauk homelands. Fortunately, Bedal's work has found its way to
the Seattle Art Museum, only a short distance from where she lived
and died. Keeping these pivotal works close to "home" will allow

128 Susan Wawatkin Bedal
Coast Salish, 1865–1947
Coiled Basket, c. 1900–1930
cedar root, horsetail root, cedar bark, and cherry bark,
11½ × 15 × 13 in.
Gift of Jean Bedal Fish and Edith Bedal, in honor of the
75th Anniversary of the Seattle Art Museum, 2005.99

the next generations to learn from the remarkable life and artistry of Susan Bedal.

A family heirloom from Vi taqšeblu Hilbert—a longtime adviser to the museum—graces the museum's installation of Puget Sound baskets (plate 129). This elegant hard-coiled cedar-root container was created in the late nineteenth century by Hilbert's aunt, who is known only by her Native name, tsisdauš. As is common for artists of an older generation, little was recorded about this basket maker who had perfected the complex coiling techniques. Such sturdy containers were the mainstay of food gathering, preparation, cooking, and storage. In later times, they were joined by trade wares such as copper kettles and enamel bowls. An avid collector of baskets, Vi Hilbert previously gifted several baskets and a traditional cedar-bark dress to the museum.

129 **tsisdauš**
Coast Salish, Upper Skagit, act. late 19th century
Coiled Basket, late 19th century
cedar root, horsetail, bear grass, and red huckleberry,
12 × 13 × 10 in.
Gift of Vi Hilbert, in honor of the 75th Anniversary
of the Seattle Art Museum, 2005.176

Michael Darling

Studio Glass
Tradition and Innovation

One of Seattle's best-known cultural exports in recent decades has been studio glass. With the founding in 1971 of the Pilchuck Glass School, legions of glass artists have learned and honed their craft in the Northwest, often under the tutelage of the world's leading practitioners. As a result, the local glass scene has long been an international affair, with resident artists and visitors collaborating in often exciting ways. Any studio glass collection in the Northwest, therefore, should represent not only artists who live and work here but also those foreign colleagues who have contributed significantly to the area's glass tradition. Prior to 2005, the Seattle Art Museum had a modest collection of glass, with holdings by many of the leading characters in the story of Northwest

130 **Ginny Ruffner**
American, born 1952
The Invention of the Games, 1991
lampworked and painted glass, 25 × 37 × 20 in.
Gift of Jon and Mary Shirley, in honor of the
75th Anniversary of the Seattle Art Museum, 2005.264

131 **Dale Chihuly**
American, born 1941
Venetian, 1991
blown glass, 16¾ × 13½ in.
Gift of Jon and Mary Shirley, in honor of the
75th Anniversary of the Seattle Art Museum,
2005.210

studio glass. But in that year Jon and Mary Shirley made a trans-
formational gift of 117 works, equipping the museum to properly
reckon with this artistic juggernaut in all its diversity.

Dale Chihuly, the cofounder of Pilchuck, was represented within
the museum's collection, but the Shirleys' gift provides a basis
from which to survey many different phases of his career, including his *Venetian* vessels from 1991 (plate 131). Also abundant in this
newly energized area of the museum are works by fellow Pilchuck
artists and teachers William Morris, Joey Kirkpatrick, Flora Mace,
Richard Marquis, and Ginny Ruffner, all of whom witnessed and
facilitated Pilchuck's evolution from rustic studio in the woods to
internationally recognized center of the glass world. Ruffner's *The
Invention of the Games* (1991, plate 130) illustrates the joyful exuberance and formal daring of the best examples from this group, while
Morris's *Petroglyph Vessel* (1989, not illustrated) reflects the primordial associations of the medium.

132 Harvey Littleton
American, born 1922
Form 12.89.6, 1990
drawn glass, 15¾ × 15¾ × 6 in. overall
Gift of Jon and Mary Shirley, in honor of the
75th Anniversary of the Seattle Art Museum,
2005.229

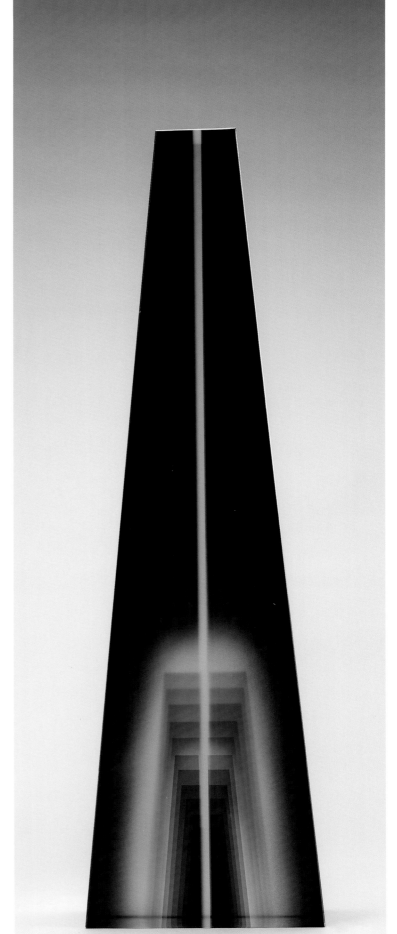

133 **Zoltan Bohus**
Hungarian, born 1941
Bronze Pylon, 1992
laminated glass, 30 × 8½ × 4 in.
Gift of Jon and Mary Shirley, in honor of the
75th Anniversary of the Seattle Art Museum,
2005.203

Among the important visitors whose work can now be tracked are Harvey Littleton (plate 132) and Marvin Lipofsky—who laid the initial foundations for the growth of the studio glass movement in the United States—and subsequent inheritors of their exacting techniques and innovations such as Thomas Patti, Mark Peiser, and Toots Zynsky. International influences and advances are also richly documented, including Italian, Czech, Japanese, German, Hungarian, and Australian glass artists from Lino Tagliapietra, Stanislav Libenský, and Jaroslava Brychtová to Zoltan Bohus (plate 133) and Klaus Moje, to name just a few. Tagliapietra has been particularly noteworthy in the writing of the Pilchuck story, for his legendary 1979 visit there forever transformed American glassmaking when he introduced centuries-old, long-secret Venetian techniques, and he continues to visit the Northwest to share his expertise with new generations of artists. Several fantastic Tagliapietra works now grace the collection, such as his *Spirale* (1991, plate 134), as do works by the quasiminimalist Czech masters Libenský and Brychtová, which together trace a wide spectrum of the possibilities of glass.

134 **Lino Tagliapietra**
Italian, born 1934
Spirale, 1991
blown glass, 32⅜ × 5¾ in. overall
Gift of Jon and Mary Shirley, in honor of the 75th Anniversary
of the Seattle Art Museum, 2005.275

Beyond technical and formal innovations, the cultural and asso-
ciative qualities of glass have been slyly investigated by a younger
group of artists including Josiah McElheny and the brothers Oscar
Tuazon and Eli Hansen. McElheny, whose representation within the
collection grew with the Shirley gift, has been one of the leading
forces of a more conceptual approach to glass which recognizes the
tradition and craft inherent in the genre but also exploits the conventions and clichés that have grown up around it. This is especially
apparent in the collaborative work by Tuazon and Hansen, who witnessed the infancy of the studio glass movement in the Northwest
as children traipsing through the forest to backwoods foundries

and hot shops, and yearn for the direct, raw, and do-it-yourself spirit of the early days. That attitude is recaptured in their recent projects, albeit with contemporary inflections of what off-the-grid lifestyles can entail. *Crystal Math* (2007, plate 135), for instance, combines the high bourgeois craft of faceted crystal with the geodesic structures of Buckminster Fuller (high priest of D-I-Y) and the dark reality of drug culture in a single, beguiling sculpture. Both recognizing the roots of studio glass and turning away from its more flamboyant contemporary iterations, Tuazon and Hansen prove that there is much potential in this now historic and distinctly Northwest tradition.

135 **Oscar Tuazon**
American, born 1975
Eli Hansen
American, born 1979
Crystal Math, 2007
blown, cut, and assembled glass and plywood, 36 × 30 in.
Gift of Merrill Wright, in honor of the 75th Anniversary of the Seattle Art Museum, 2007.69

Josh Yiu

The Chinese Connection and the Chinese Collection at the Seattle Art Museum

The Seattle Art Museum recently acquired fifteen Chinese artworks in celebration of its seventy-fifth anniversary. This number might seem modest when compared to the thousand or more items that entered the museum in 1933, when it was founded. At that time, Western collectors could amass objects, especially ceramics and sculpture, at favorable prices due to the political turmoil that had afflicted China for much of the preceding century. Accordingly, Richard E. Fuller, the founding director of the museum, readily purchased a large quantity of works, even though English-language writings on Chinese art were very few at the time. The combination of low cost and steady supply created an encouraging environment for collecting Chinese art. Acquisition policies were also much less rigid then, which facilitated efforts by collectors and museums to refine their holdings though acquisition and deaccession. There was much less at stake in buying an artwork, and it was common to acquire things based on aesthetic merit even before their historical significance had been firmly established. Although problematic works may have crept in, lesser-known objects were given the benefit of the doubt and preserved for future study.

This expansive approach provided a foundation for building rich collections and generating scholarship. For example, Fuller, a gemologist by training, had a predilection for jades, and he built a large collection during his tenure from 1933 to 1973. By the time the jade collection was published in 1989, the museum could boast a comprehensive collection from the Neolithic to Qing periods.[1] The museum similarly acquired many important ceramics, bronzes, and snuff bottles at an early date. When the museum's collecting practices diversified during the second half of the twentieth century, the acquisition of Chinese art became increasingly selective and varied.

THE EFFECT OF THE ART MARKET ON COLLECTING

Multiple factors contributed to the shift in the museum's collecting habits. In its early years the museum emphasized Asian art, primarily Chinese and Japanese, but later, as it moved to develop a more general collection, the museum expanded its holdings into art from Europe, the Americas, Africa, and Oceania. Furthermore, stricter government control on exporting cultural properties from China and mounting demand within China for its arts created a less favorable collecting atmosphere in the United States.

Under the Chinese Antiquity Protection Law (2002), cultural relics produced before 1949 and works by famous late calligraphers and painters made after 1949 can be exported only with a license from the State Bureau of Cultural Relics. Cultural artifacts produced before 1795 are simply forbidden from export.[2] This is but one effort to keep Chinese antiquities on Chinese soil. The Chinese government has also tried to gain support from other countries to protect its antiquities. Believing that American demand for Chinese art objects was fueling a sharp increase in the looting of archaeological sites and even thefts from museums, in May 2004 Chinese officials asked the U.S. State Department to impose restrictions on the importation of a wide range of artifacts from the prehistoric period through the early twentieth century. It has been estimated that as many as 400,000 tombs have been pilfered in the last twenty-five years.[3]

The main buyers of Chinese antiquities at international auctions are Asian. Since the 1970s, collectors in Asia, especially Hong Kong, have grown knowledgeable about Chinese art and have competed for the best pieces. The Chinese art market has been increasing steadily over the past three decades, and in recent years, collecting by mainland Chinese has taken off. In 2005 there were 320,000 millionaires in China, and the number of committed collectors is estimated at two hundred times that figure, at 68 million.[4] The government legalized the private art market in 1992, and there are now more than four thousand auction houses, which sold art valued at $1.25 billion in 2005, up from $100 million in 2000.[5] Many top-quality Chinese artworks brought to the West decades ago are now being repurchased by the Chinese, despite higher prices. The Beijing Municipal Administration of Cultural Heritage has estimated that ten thousand Chinese ancient works of art have been returned to mainland China in 2006.[6] Despite a diminishing number of proactive acquisitions, the Seattle Art Museum is fortunate to have garnered support from dedicated collectors who are willing to share their passion with the public. The new acquisitions in honor of the museum's seventy-fifth anniversary are the result of their generous donations.

COLLABORATIVE COLLECTING AND SPECIAL GIFTS

Because private collectors buy, first and foremost, to satisfy themselves, they tend to be more adventurous than institutions. Oftentimes the remarkable objects they obtain broaden the horizons of the museums that eventually receive them. The wide-ranging objects donated to celebrate the museum's seventy-fifth anniversary highlight Chinese practices related to imperial funerals, traditional weddings, time management, and architecture.

A large golden box of lacquered wood from the Qing period (1644–1912) once held jade tablets that eulogized a deceased emperor's deeds (plate 136). Such objects have not been widely collected, but extant examples can be found in the National Palace Museum, Taiwan, and among the Qing imperial objects housed at the Shenyang Palace Museum (Liaoning province). The boxes in

136 *Imperial Document Box*
Chinese, Qing period, 1735–96
lacquered wood, lined with cotton, 17 × 18¾ × 12⅞ in.
Gift of Henry and Mary Ann James, in honor of the
75th Anniversary of the Seattle Art Museum, 2007.19

these collections are very similar, although they were made in different times for different emperors. For instance, one example in the National Palace Museum, made for the Shunzhi emperor (reign 1638–61),[7] is identical to a box from Shenyang that commemorated the Qianlong emperor (reign 1736–95). The jade tablets in the National Palace Museum are framed and connected by a sashlike fabric. Although it is unclear when the practice of storing eulogy texts in elaborate lacquer boxes began, prototypes of boxes with canted lids can be found in earlier times and were used in Buddhist contexts, as shown by ninth-century caskets excavated from the Famensi monastery in Shaanxi province, and thirteenth- and fourteenth-century sutras boxes from Korea.[8] A similarly shaped wooden box with golden dragons has been attributed to the Wanli period (1573–1620), but its function has not yet been established.[9]

A box associated with a more joyous occasion is a dowry chest (*taihe* 抬盒) from the late Qing period (plate 137). Both ends are inscribed "Jiangxia qian shi" 江夏遣適 (to send in marriage from Jiangxia). The chest was used to transport a bride's ceremonial and personal items from her parents' home to that of her husband. Its sumptuousness is a reflection of the stature of the bride and, by extension, of the groom and his family. The reticulated design, probably derived from scenes from Chinese opera, allows ventilation, although two built-in panels behind the door could be raised to block dust when the chest was paraded through the streets. To facilitate lifting and carrying, a hefty pole was slid through the openings on top and shouldered by a man at each end. The container fulfilled a dual purpose of transport and display as part of the wedding procession that moved through public spaces, past neighbors and relatives, ending at the bride's new home.

The items in the bride's dowry could have included an "alarm clock" in the form of a lively dragon boat painted in gold (plate 138). Although mechanical clocks were introduced to China by the late Ming period (1368–1644), ancient Chinese often measured time in units that corresponded to daily or conventional activities, such as the-time-needed-to-cook-a-pot-of-rice and the-time-needed-to-burn-an-incense-stick, which transpired at a consistent rate. Activating the alarm involved the burning of incense. The user placed an incense stick horizontally on the boat and then draped a thread with a bell at each end across the incense at the interval he or she wished to be alerted. When the incense burned down to the thread, it broke, thus dropping the bells, whose noise presumably roused the user. Most extant dragon boat alarms from the eighteenth and nineteenth centuries are made of wood, with some of metal.

The dragon is arguably the most prevalent symbol in Chinese art, appearing in numerous objects, including roof tiles, a pair of which has recently been acquired to complement the museum's existing collection of Chinese tiles. Roof tiles were highly popular collectibles in the West during the late nineteenth and early twentieth centuries. Chinese buildings were largely constructed of perishable wood, but their durable tile roofs have stood the test of time, becoming a representative feature of Chinese architectural art. Ceramic roof tiles provided greater protection than thatch against fire and weather, and their history goes back to the Western Zhou period (c. 1050–771 BC). Many contain auspicious motifs that were

137 *Dowry Chest*
Chinese, south China, Qing period, 1873
gilded and lacquered wood with metal fittings,
44 × 36½ × 23 in.
Gift of Henry and Mary Ann James, in honor of the
75th Anniversary of the Seattle Art Museum, 2007.20

138 *Dragon Boat Alarm*
Chinese, Qing period, 19th century
lacquered wood with pigment and metal, 7¼ × 27⅝ in.
Gift of Ruth, Nancy, and Kal Kallison in memory of James M. Kallison,
in honor of the 75th Anniversary of the Seattle Art Museum, 2007.68

139 *Roof Tiles in the form of a Figure Mounted on a Dragon*
Chinese, Shanxi province, Ming period (1368–1644)
ceramic tiles with low-fired lead glazes, approx. 30 × 31 × 8½ in. each
Gift of Henry and Mary Ann James, in honor of the 75th Anniversary
of the Seattle Art Museum, 2007.23–.24

140 *Jar*
Chinese, Western Han Dynasty, 206 BC–220 AD
pottery with green glaze, 17½ × 13 in.
Gift of Henry and Mary Ann James, in honor of the 75th Anniversary
of the Seattle Art Museum, 2007.25

believed to convey good luck to the dwelling's inhabitants. These motifs range from carved designs to full-fledged sculptural forms. Zoomorphic ornaments known as *wenshou* 吻獸 were generally placed at the front of a roof's main ridge. This figure mounted on a dragon (*gui longzi* 鬼龍子) would have been part of a series of tiles covering the entire length of the ridge (plate 139).

These fine ceramic roof tiles have a *liuli* 琉璃 glaze, a low-fire glaze that generally employed lead as the fluxing agent, although certain colors required an alkaline flux. *Liuli* glaze colors include yellow, green, blue, and purple, and were used in both monochrome and polychrome. This glaze is most closely associated with Shanxi province, whose *liuli* products were distributed around the empire and whose skilled craftsmen, particularly since the Ming dynasty, responded to state summons to work on major projects. The use of *liuli* glazing for architectural features is known as early as the Yuan dynasty (1279–1368) and continued in greater prevalence into the Qing. *Liuli* objects from different periods are not easily

distinguishable, and many of them, including this pair of roof tiles, are conventionally dated to the Ming period.

Another object that demonstrates the beauty of low-fire lead glazes is a green jar made in the Han period (206 BC–220 AD), when Chinese potters mastered the glazing technique. This jar is an excavated piece, and the weathering effect of burial is shown in its lustrous surface (plate 140). In the centuries between burial and unearthing, the lead-based glaze interacted with the oxidized copper in the mix, giving a silvery sheen to the glaze. As an indication of burial and age, the iridescence becomes an admirable feature in its own right. A myth shared among antique dealers claims that exposure to light causes the iridescence to fade, but it is the permanent result of a chemical reaction, one that weakens the bond of the glaze to the clay body. The "fading" is likely the result of glaze flaking off the vessel.

Even when they are at odds with more credible evidence, stories circulated in the antique circle provide clues about what people

141 *Cat Carrier*
Tibetan, 18th–19th century
wood with mineral pigments, 12 × 11 × 21½ in.
Promised gift of Ruth Sutherlin Hayward and Robert W.
Hayward, in honor of the 75th Anniversary of the Seattle
Art Museum, T2007.5

believed and how they behaved. For objects that are not well doc-umented in books, these tales often become the only source of information we have about them. A rare Tibetan cat-carrier from the eighteenth or nineteenth century is one such object (plate 141). At first glance, it appears to be extraordinarily small for keeping cats. But it is said to have accommodated a small breed found in Tibet and would have protected the cat while preventing it from killing mice, as Buddhism prohibited killing. In any event, the cage may have been better suited for carrying a cat from place to place than keeping it. The openwork with a carved flower on two sides allows air and light into the carrier, and two removable dowels on one end let the cat enter and exit.

The keeping of creatures is documented in the earliest records in China, all the way from the grand scale of the game parks of the emperor to the private housing of birds and crickets.[10] Chinese bird-cages represent the culmination of refinement of this pet-keeping tradition. The appreciation and culture surrounding this pas-time applied not just to birds but also to their cages. The clearest articulation of this aesthetic comes in the Qing dynasty, whose Qianlong emperor is known to have admired caged birds. In this period, simplicity and function dominated cage design to showcase the songbirds within. Connoisseurs often pay attention to the metal hooks on cages, fine examples of which were kept and saved for future use when they outlasted the cage. Some cages were intended for show, as in the case of a delicate bamboo example (plate 142). Constructing this cage without breaking the fragile bamboo sticks must have posed a challenge to its maker. Another example clearly meant for use is a large, sturdy, expandable cage that stretches to more than four feet to allow more space for the birds (plate 143). Although birding and aviculture hold a diminishing place in Chinese society, birdcages continued to be admired for their structural integ-rity and their fine accessories such as porcelain watering dishes and jade decorations.

Of all the gifts that have enriched the Chinese collection in the seventy-fifth anniversary campaign, an exquisite album of paintings by Chen Hongshou 陳鴻壽 (1768–1822) is of particular

142 *Birdcage*
Chinese, 1850–1920
bamboo and metal, 22 × 9 × 9 in.
Gift of Henry and Mary Ann James, in honor of the
75th Anniversary of the Seattle Art Museum, 2007.9

143 *Birdcage*
Chinese, 1850–1920
bamboo and metal, 37 × 19 in., expandable
Gift of Henry and Mary Ann James, in honor of the
75th Anniversary of the Seattle Art Museum, 2007.8

note. While other objects broaden our view of Chinese art and culture, the album directly addresses a weakness in the collection. Chinese painting is one of the most revered art forms in China, but Western appreciation of it has lagged behind that for ceramics, jades, and Buddhist sculptures. Despite the fact that the museum's overall collection of Chinese art is among the best in America, its holdings in Chinese painting are relatively modest. This recent gift fills a gap in flower painting of the late Qing period. The album features twelve vibrant depictions of celebrated flowers and plants, including peony, orchid, loquat, lotus, pomegranate, willow, chrysanthemum, pine branch, bamboo, plum, and narcissus (plate 144). Rapid brushstrokes underscore the confidence and competence of Chen Hongshou, a multitalented artist skilled in calligraphy, painting, seal carving, and the design of teapots. In inscriptions written in cursive script, Chen acknowledged his debt to ancient masters who inspired him, but his style has its own distinctive features. Almost every image shows a fragment of the depicted plant, thereby giving the impression of a close-up view. Using muted

colors, Chen rendered the flowers clearly without outline in the so-called boneless style, which conveys a gentle sentiment that is consistent with the mood of the subject. The album ends with an appreciative colophon, dated 1821, by the scholar-painter Wang Xuehao 王學浩 (1775–1832).

This group of objects, despite being small in quantity, adds immeasurably to the depth of the Chinese collection at the Seattle Art Museum. There may not be a time again in which Chinese art can be amassed in bulk, yet improvement of the collection need not be defined by number. With increasing communication among scholars, advanced technology, and improved access to archival sources, we are better able to understand and research the purpose and function of Chinese art in the museum and of that we might acquire in the future. Through active collaboration with the scholarly and collecting communities, the Seattle Art Museum will further develop a collection that is in line with Chinese connoisseurship and embraces art that illuminates China's multifaceted artistic heritage.

144 a–m **Chen Hongshou**
Chinese, 1768–1822
Flowers and Plants, Qing period,
early 19th century
album, ink and color on paper, 10⅝ × 17½ in. (image)
Gift of Patricia and Thomas Ebrey, in honor of the
75th Anniversary of the Seattle Art Museum, T2008.1

a

b

c

滴露和煙漾碧叢
趑趺臭味与谁同宣
知空谷幽人无只在春
風落蕩中
錢唐陳鴻壽 [印]

d

枇杷不愿者琵琶只為當年識字差
使琵琶能結果滿城簫管畫開花
白石翁有此本并錄其句 鴻壽 [印]

e

繡暈長連技 野風吹不
落金刀劈玉漿夜深清
酒渴
陳鴻壽 [印]

f

167

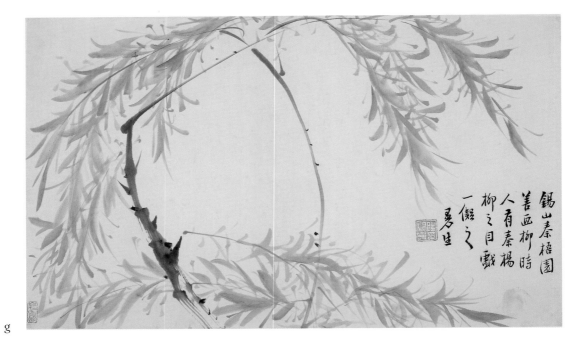

g

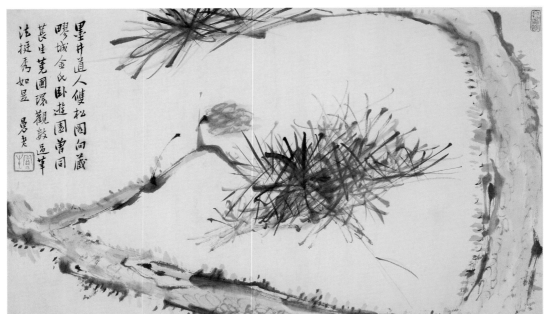

h

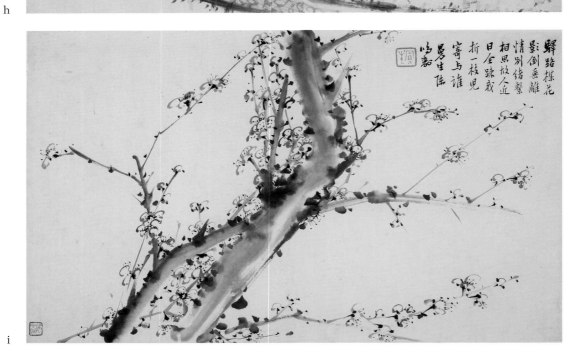

i

j

k

l

m

NOTES

1. The collection catalogue, by eminent jade scholar James Watt, has become a standard reference for jade enthusiasts: James Watt, *Chinese Jades from the Collection of the Seattle Art Museum* (Seattle: Seattle Art Museum, 1989).

2. Shao Xiaoyi, "Foreigners Caught Smuggling Relics," *China Daily* (North American ed.), May 31, 2005.

3. Some argue that Chinese officials have not done enough to protect the nation's cultural patrimony, and therefore the United States should not take the blame, especially when Americans make up only 4 percent of the buyers of Chinese antiquities at auction. The United States relies on its own 1983 art importation law, which protects objects if countries demonstrate adherence to a 1970 United Nations agreement to preserve their cultural heritage. This law applies only to objects at least 250 years old, and therefore the Chinese government's recent request to restrict the import of cultural properties made during the nineteenth and twentieth centuries has been problematic. See Howard French, "The Slow Fight to Save Chinese Artifacts," *New York Times*, April 1, 2006.

4. Will Bennett, "China's New Millionaires See Capital Gain in Art," *Financial Times* (London), Sept. 30, 2006; "China Sets Up Expert Commission to Combat Fake Art," Xinhua News Agency-CEIS, May 13, 2006; Allen T. Cheng, "Art Rush Gains Steam in China," *International Herald Tribune*, July 19, 2006.

5. Cheng, "Art Rush." The sales figure is expected to double by 2010; see Li Jing, "There's No Place Like Home for Chinese Antiques," *China Daily* (North American ed.), Sept. 22, 2006.

6. Even so, approximately one million Chinese objects are currently held outside the country, according to the State Cultural Relics Bureau.

7. See Zhuang Jifa, "Yidai huanghou—Bumu butai," *Gugong wenwu yuekan* 113 (August 1992): 86.

8. For more information about the caskets, see Shaanxi Sheng Kaogu Yanjiuyuan, *Famensi kaogu fajue baogao* (Beijing: Wenwu Chubanshe, 2007), ch. 4.1. For an example of a fourteenth-century lacquered box with an elaborate motif of flying peacocks, see Sherman Lee and Wai-Kam Ho, *Chinese Art under the Mongols: The Yuan Dynasty (1279–1368)* (Cleveland: Cleveland Museum of Art, 1968), pl. 285. For the Korean Buddhist sutra boxes, see Pratapaditya Pal and Julia Meech-Pekarik, *Buddhist Book Illuminations* (New York: Ravi Kumar Publishers, 1988), 246, pl. 78.

9. Grace Wu Bruce, *Zitan Furniture from the Ming and Qing Dynasties* (London: Grace Wu Bruce, 1999), 28, no. 9.

10. For an example of a birdcage from the Warring States period, see Gloria Lannom, "Chinese Birdcages: A New Study Based on the Donegan Collection," *Arts of Asia* 19, no. 5 (Sept. / Oct. 1989): 159–65, fig. 2.

Yukiko Shirahara

Ukiyo-e
The Aesthetics of Pleasure

145 Suzuki Harunobu
Japanese, 1725–1770
Night Rain at Nihonzutsumi, from the series
Eight Elegant Views of Edo, 1769
woodblock print, ink and color on paper, 10⅝ × 7¼ in.
(*chū-ban* sheet)
Promised gift of Mary and Allan Kollar, in honor of the
75th Anniversary of the Seattle Art Museum, T2006.119.9

The Seattle Art Museum is widely respected for its comprehensive collection of Japanese art, but it has had a significant gap in the area of ukiyo-e, or premodern Japanese woodblock prints, whose subjects include every aspect of the ephemeral (*ukiyo*) world. Portraits of beautiful women, Kabuki actors, and sumo wrestlers; landscapes of famous places; historical scenes and daily amusements were all popular subjects. The prints were sold at affordable prices on the street or in shops. Richard E. Fuller, the founding director of the museum, collected contemporary Japanese prints, but he did not have a keen interest in ukiyo-e. Now, on the occasion of the museum's seventy-fifth anniversary and through the generosity of Mary and Allan Kollar, the museum can claim a first-rate ukiyo-e collection, including examples from Torii, Katsukawa, and Utagawa school artists and by Utamaro, Hokusai, and Sharaku. All are in excellent condition and illustrate the artistic peaks in ukiyo-e's development.

The Japanese tradition of single pictorial prints began in the late seventeenth century. Multicolored printing (*nishiki-e*) was perfected about 1765 through the effort of Suzuki Harunobu 鈴木春信 (1725–1770) and his coworkers. Harunobu's skillful compositions of young women and their lovers, combining delicate ink lines and bright color, made him the most successful artist of his generation and influenced many followers. Harunobu's originality is illustrated in a poetic image from the Kollars' collection, for which the artist used jet-black color for the darkness of night (plate 145). The postures of a courtesan and her petite maid elegantly link the snugness of the room to the night scene outside, where passersby walk along the Nihon embankment leading to the Yoshiwara pleasure quarter in the city of Edo.

Although he was a central figure a few decades later in the same genre as Harunobu, Kitagawa Utamaro 喜多川歌麿 (1753–1806) gives us a totally different impression. The women in his prints not only display a mature and sensual appeal but also convey something of their personal psychology. The narrow eyes and small lips in an oval face characteristic of his beauties are regarded today as the classic signs of the ukiyo-e woman. Utamaro's *ōkubi-e* (close-up portraits of courtesans and actors) and incomparable *shunga* (erotica) made the artist a popular printmaker. His streak of success ended suddenly in 1804, however, when he published prints that were perceived by the shogunate to satirize its authority.

The women in Utamaro's prints are often depicted expressing sadness over parting with a lover, raptly reading his letters, or keenly

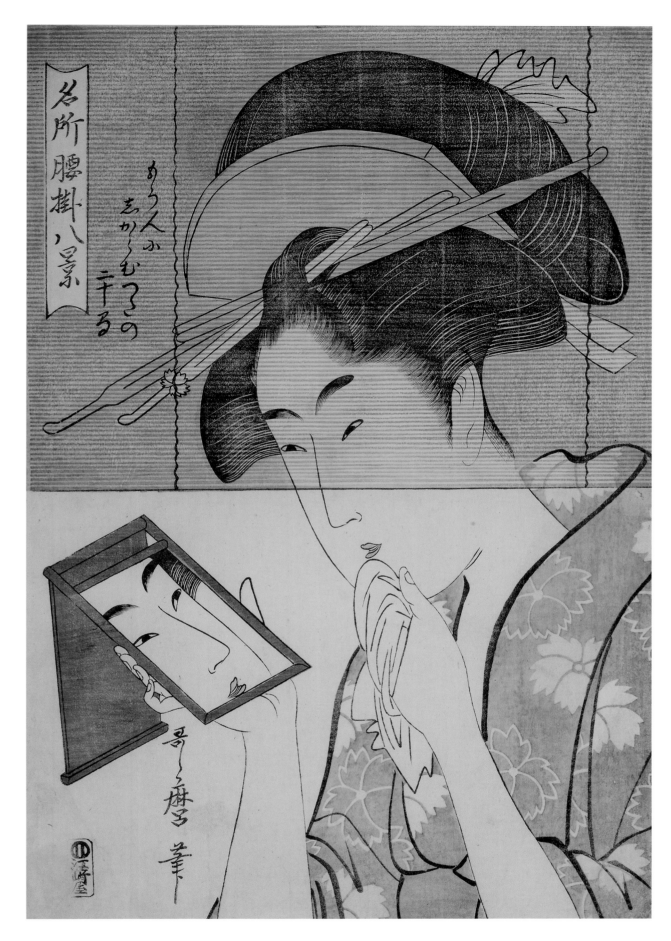

146 **Kitagawa Utamaro**
Japanese, 1753–1806
Woman's Beauty Rituals, from the series *Eight Views of Tea Stalls in Celebrated Places,* Edo period, 1790s
woodblock print, ink and color on paper, 15⅜ × 10¼ in. (ō-ban sheet)
Promised gift of Mary and Allan Kollar, in honor of the 75th
Anniversary of the Seattle Art Museum, T2006.118.5

147 **Katsushika Hokusai**
Japanese, 1760–1849
Under the Wave, off Kanagawa (Great Wave),
from the series *Thirty-Six Views of Mount Fuji,*
Edo period, 1830–33
woodblock print, ink and color on paper, 10¼ × 15 in. (*ō-ban* sheet)
Promised gift of Mary and Allan Kollar, in honor of the
75th Anniversary of the Seattle Art Museum, T2007.144

waiting for his visit. Visually, Utamaro excelled at using reflection and transparency, as seen in this excellent example (plate 146). The artist knew well how intently a woman looks into a mirror in her daily life. For the viewer of the print, the mirror captures not only the woman's gaze but a sense of her true self. Compositionally, the mirror plays an important role, creating the space between it and her body. Moreover, the presence of the mirror made it possible for Utamaro to show different angles of the beauty in one image.

In the early nineteenth century two ukiyo-e masters, Katsushika Hokusai 葛飾北斎 (1760–1849) and Utagawa Hiroshige 歌川広重 (1797–1858), established a genre in Japan that separated landscape from the literary and conceptual contexts with which it was traditionally associated. Accordingly, not only famous but ordinary sights began to be depicted for the enjoyment of their intrinsic features. Depth

of field was created with linear perspective, a technique introduced from the West through China. With great creativity, Japanese artists effectively employed this new method to create simple and impressive imagery.

There is no doubt that *Under the Wave, off Kanagawa* and *Red Fuji* are the most popular prints of the versatile Hokusai, whose work epitomizes Japanese ukiyo-e. Both are promised gifts to the museum's collection. In *Under the Wave, off Kanagawa* (plate 147), a hawklike claw of water (a metaphor used by Vincent can Gogh) rises to its crest, giving a dynamism to the circular composition, at whose center Mount Fuji is viewed in the far distance. More than any other illustration, in this print the menace and beauty of nature are successfully expressed in the brilliantly contrasting white and blue color scheme. The French composer Claude Debussy is famously said to have placed a print of *Under the Wave, off Kanagawa* on his piano when he composed the orchestral piece *La Mer* in 1905. Today, this strong and vivid image is regarded among art lovers as second in fame only to the mysteriously smiling Mona Lisa of Leonardo da Vinci.

Influenced by Hokusai's landscapes, Utagawa Hiroshige looked at nature on a more human scale, as seen in his print series *Fifty-three Stations on the Tōkaidō Highway* and *One Hundred Famous Views of Edo*. In the print selected here, a windy shower suddenly strikes a slope at Shōno (Mie prefecture) on a summer day (plate 148).

This is not a famous place but simply a typical road. Two travelers rush downhill, clutching at their straw hat and umbrella, while palanquin bearers carrying a passenger hurry in the opposite direction. Trees bent by a strong wind are beautifully rendered in gradated *sumi* ink. Hiroshige actually traveled the Tōkaidō highway in 1832 and viewed the topography of each station. He possibly witnessed the effect of a sudden change in weather at a certain moment and then recreated it in this excellent work. The intersecting angles of the slope, the pounding rain, and the bowed trees form multiple triangles in the composition and convey a feeling of anxiety to viewers.

Soon after Japan fully opened its borders to foreigners and trading in 1854, ukiyo-e helped to spark the *japonisme* movement in Western art. In one popular account, the French print artist Félix Bracquemond is said to have stumbled across crumpled ukiyo-e prints used to cushion exported ceramics in 1856. The poster art of Toulouse-Lautrec, the color and decorative flatness of Van Gogh's paintings, and the female portraits of Mary Cassatt are only a few examples of the artistic fruit borne by ukiyo-e. Its impressive design and color illustrate the strength of Japanese art in the premodern period and would became sources for modern art in both Japan and the West.

148 **Utagawa Hiroshige**
Japanese, 1797–1858
Sudden Shower at Shōno, from the series
Fifty-three Stations on the Tōkaidō Highway,
Edo period, 1833–34
woodblock print, ink and color on paper, 9⅝ × 14¾ in. (*ō-ban* sheet)
Promised gift of Mary and Allan Kollar, in honor of the
75th Anniversary of the Seattle Art Museum, T2006.118.3

Yukiko Shirahara

Tsuji Kakō and the Modern Spirit

The political and social changes of the later nineteenth century that catapulted Japan from the feudal to the modern era were felt throughout Japanese culture, including the arts. For example, no longer isolated from the larger world, Japan as a nation participated for the first time in a world art exposition in Vienna in 1873. In this period of transition, the strict master-student relationship that had defined Japanese art practice began to dissolve, and Japanese painters could not avoid becoming aware of their individual identities. It was during this time that painter Tsuji Kakō 都路華香 (1871–1931) was active in Kyoto.

In this atmosphere of flux, artists were seriously exploring personal modes of expression suited to the modern age. Kakō started his painting training under the direction of the brilliant Kōno Bairei, participated successfully in official exhibitions, and was counted as one of the essential figures in the Kyoto painting circle. But Kakō's artistic individuality and habit of exploring various styles at times mystified contemporary artists and critics, and in the years after Kakō's death, interest in his art gradually declined.

Only in the last decade has an evaluation of his achievements and wide-ranging creativity taken hold. A retrospective exhibition held in Japan in 2006–7 was a milestone in the new appreciation for this little-known artist, and among the exhibited works were selections from the collections of Griffith and Patricia Way and of Henry and Mary Anne James. Recent gifts made to the Seattle Art Museum by these collectors allow an unparalleled opportunity to examine this modern artist's creative process through pivotal examples of Kakō's *Wave* paintings.

Sound of Waves (fig. 1), created in 1901, reveals Kakō's inheritance from a past master, Maruyama Ōkyo (1733–1795). In a panoramic view of the seashore that stretches across twelve panels, rough waves wash a rocky shore where an eagle spreads his wings. The water's spray is depicted dynamically with detailed touches of white pigment, while the sea itself is roughly brushed in a thin blue. Naturalistic and magnificent, Kakō's representation shows the influence of Ōkyo's realistic painting style and traditional compositional form.

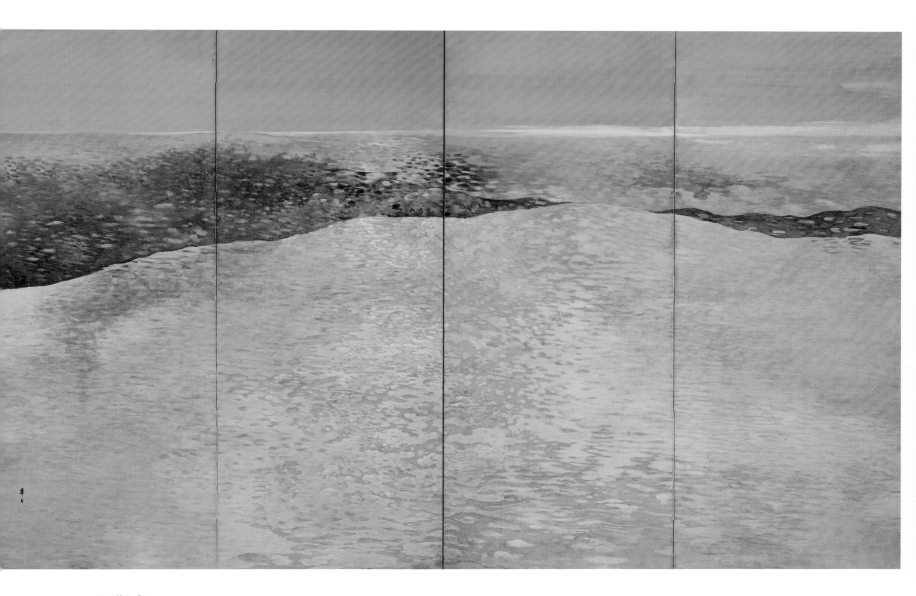

149 **Tsuji Kakō**
Japanese, 1870–1931
Green Waves, Meiji period, c. 1910
Four-panel screen, color and gold on silk, 66⅜ in. × 9 ft.
Promised gift of Griffith and Patricia Way, in honor of the
75th Anniversary of the Seattle Art Museum, T97.198.41

Figure 1. Tsuji Kakō (Japanese, 1870–1931), *Sound of Waves*,
Meiji period, 1901, one of a pair of six-panel screens, ink
and color on gilded paper, 65⅝ in. × 12 ft. Gift of Henry
and Mary Ann James, 98.45

150 **Tsuji Kakō**
Japanese, 1870–1931
Waves and Plovers, Meiji period, c. 1911
Pair of six-panel screens, ink and light color on paper,
48¾ in. × 8 ft. 7 in. each
Promised gift of Griffith and Patricia Way, in honor of the
75th Anniversary of the Seattle Art Museum, T97.198.42.1–.2

Figure 2. Unknown Japanese artist, *Voyage to Tsukushi,
detail from Legend of the Origin of the Kitano Shrine*, Kamakura
period, 13th century. Hanging scroll, ink and color on
paper, 11⅞ × 20½ in. Eugene Fuller Memorial Collection,
48.169

Kakō created the four-panel screen *Green Waves* (plate 149) around 1910, when he was in his early forties. Here he rose to the challenge of handling color under the impact of impressionism. Kakō first painted the silk cloth of the screen in gold, onto which he layered green and blue pigment, gradually building up a finely textured surface. The work beautifully expresses the fleeting appearance of sunlight reflecting on the calm surface of water. Less showy than gold foil, the painted gold displays a mild brightness and perfectly fuses with the green and blue. Although Western influenced in its technique, this is a very Japanese painting in its limited palette of traditional mineral pigments and gold. Evocatively suggesting the changeability of nature, *Green Waves* is regarded among Kakō's masterpieces.

Kakō created another masterwork, *Waves and Plovers* (plate 150), a pair of six-panel screens, at the same time, but he chose a completely different technique. Here the movement of the waves is conjured by ink lines alone. To create a sense of depth, the waves diminish in size and grow fainter and closer together as they reach the tops of the screens. Flying plovers give a feeling of open air above the water and provide another rhythm to the painting. Unlike *Green Waves*, the style of *Waves and Plovers* is a traditional one Kakō would have encountered as a student copying classic paintings such as the famous *Voyage to Tsukushi*, from the thirteenth-century handscroll *Legend of the Origin of the Kitano Shrine* (fig. 2). After studying the undulating fine line of a traditional work such as this and the later Rimpa style of swelling surf, Kakō devised his own elegantly rhythmic flowing waves.

Each of these paintings, created at the beginning of the twentieth century when Kakō seriously pursued the wave motif, is an accomplished work in a different style. The changeability that has made it difficult for some to comprehend this artist's nature is a sign of the searching nature of a modern artist, and one element of the charm of Kakō's art. Released from the restrictions of traditional painting methods, Kakō used experimental techniques to mine the artistic possibilities of his subjects. At a time when many Japanese painters were seeking to be recognized by a single mode of expression, Kakō took on various styles and moods as he sought to satisfy not critics but his own artistic impulses. Such unforced, accomplished paintings could only have been made by an artist of intellectual depth who took great pleasure in his creations.

Chiyo Ishikawa

A Restless Heart

"My heart is restless until it comes to you." Augustine of Hippo (354–430) addressed these words to God when he wrote his *Confessions* at the age of forty-four. This unvarnished record of a personal spiritual journey is often called the first autobiography in the Western world. Neither an active sensual and intellectual life nor his exalted academic position had satisfied Augustine's quest for meaning. Only when he embraced Christianity, in his thirties, did he find the course that gave his life purpose and led to his influential teachings, which are still widely read and appreciated.

In Bartolomé Murillo's painting, Augustine has laid aside the miter and crozier that are part of his bishop's office; he kneels in a heavily embroidered cope bearing images of the apostles (plate 151). Turning from the books that record his struggle and teachings, he experiences a mystical vision of a flaming heart encircled by the words quoted above. Murillo suggests intelligence, self-doubt, and humility in his portraitlike rendering of the saint. The design of the painting embodies Augustine's description of his own earlier religious conversion as a passage from darkness into light.

This image of spiritual dedication and reward was commissioned to inspire monks in the Convent of Saint Augustine in Seville, in southern Spain. One of the richest convents in a city with more than a hundred religious institutions, it sheltered the Holy Crucifix of Saint Augustine, a fourteenth-century sculpture of the crucified Christ which was said to have performed many important miracles. It was also an artistic treasure-house rich in the paintings of Murillo, Seville's leading painter, who in 1678 was commissioned to paint two images for the central altarpiece of the convent's church. Murillo created several other paintings for the convent, including this image. It was installed in the sacristy, a room near the altar where priestly vestments, sacred vessels, and other precious objects were stored. The sumptuously embroidered cope that Saint Augustine wears in the painting was justified by his role as bishop of Hippo, but it must also have been chosen because of its relation to the splendid garments kept in the sacristy.

Located on the Guadalquivir River in the southern province of Andalusia, Seville became the wealthiest and most cosmopolitan city in Spain after being named the exclusive embarkation point for New World trade in the early 1500s. By the second half of the seventeenth century, however, Seville was shaken by the declining fortunes of the Spanish empire and a loss of trade as the Guadalquivir silted up. A series of biblical-scale disasters threatened the city itself: terrible food shortages, floods, and a devastating outbreak of the plague in 1649, which killed nearly half of the city's population. The already great disparity of wealth in the city, documented by Murillo in his paintings of scruffy beggar children, became more extreme with the dramatic economic downturn. Nonetheless, the church retained its power and continued to order works of art for the embellishment of churches, monasteries, and confraternities, and Murillo was kept busy his entire career. His death in 1682 was caused by injuries from a fall from a scaffold in a church where he was working.

In the early nineteenth century Napoleon's occupation of Spain extended to Andalusia, and Seville fell to French troops without a struggle in 1810. The city remained occupied for two years. Napoleon suppressed convents throughout Europe and confiscated their property, and though this order was reversed with the resumption of Spanish rule in 1814, in 1835 a federal decree once again ordered the dismantling of monasteries; many were sold or converted to other purposes. The Convent of Saint Augustine became a prison in 1838, and its church was destroyed. (In 2007 plans were being made to convert the remains of the monastery into a luxury hotel.)

With the suppression and often destruction of the monasteries, more than 1,500 paintings were rounded up. Some were sent to Madrid to become part of the collection of a new national museum, and others were taken to France. Paintings created to aid in religious devotion were now desirable as collectible objects. *Saint Augustine in Ecstasy* was among 180 paintings seized by Marshal Nicolas Jean de Dieu Soult (1769–1851) for his personal art collection during the French occupation of Spain. When Soult returned to Paris in 1812, he donated some of the paintings to the Musée Napoleon and displayed the rest in his home. Spanish painting had been virtually unknown in France, and Soult's collection created a reverence for Spanish painting among French artists such as Eugène Delacroix and Édouard Manet that would strongly influence the development of French painting in the late nineteenth century.

In the mid-1840s Soult sold several works to British collectors, who especially favored the works of Bartolomé Murillo. George Tomline of Orwell Park, whose collecting motto was "few, but good," purchased *Saint Augustine in Ecstasy* in about 1846 from Soult's British agent, William Buchanan. It stayed within the family collection until 1933, when it was sold at Christie's, London. The painting was on the art market for a short period before being purchased by Father Thomas Molloy, bishop of St. James Cathedral in Brooklyn,

New York, for his personal collection. On his death in 1956 Molloy left his collection to the Roman Catholic Diocese of Brooklyn. Sold at Christie's in 2005, the painting was purchased by Seattle collectors Richard and Elizabeth Hedreen, who in recent years have introduced a dialogue between past and present by introducing several stupendous Old Master paintings into their stunning collection of modern and contemporary painting and sculpture.

151 **Bartolomé Esteban Murillo**
Spanish, 1618–1682
Saint Augustine in Ecstasy, 1670s
oil on canvas, 76½ × 55 in.
Promised gift of Richard and Elizabeth Hedreen, in honor of the 75th Anniversary of the Seattle Art Museum, T2006.34

Patricia Junker and Julie Emerson

British Taste in Colonial Boston

By 1770 John Adams had seen his native Boston so transformed by material wealth that he openly disparaged what he considered a growing tendency toward pretension, which he termed the "fribbling Affectation of Politeness."[1] The future president was among the few of the newly moneyed Bostonians who resisted the temptation to surround themselves with lavish displays of the luxuries that came with increasing economic prosperity in the colonies.

Bostonians were never more enamored of British aristocratic taste than they were on the eve of the Revolution. Boston's early position as the leading commercial center of the colonies created in that city both a merchant class, whose fortunes were tied to material goods, and a proud artisan class that enjoyed unparalleled access to British imports and an unprecedented level of patronage among those who relished fine things. By the early eighteenth century, Boston was already home to silversmiths and furniture makers whose work was comparable to that of their London counterparts. This flourishing environment of aspiration and display was ideal for the portraitist John Singleton Copley (1738–1815), indisputably the finest painter in the colonies and an artist of uncommon talent who would ultimately win recognition on both sides of the Atlantic. Copley's exquisite paintings are the ultimate expression of the social and cultural conditions of colonial Boston.

A SILVER TANKARD BY JEREMIAH DUMMER

Paintings were rarely found in the low, dimly lit rooms of the early colonial era. Silver was the revered object of pride, and the silversmiths of Boston, New York, and Philadelphia are regarded as the first great colonial artists. Always an indication of wealth and social status, silver took many shapes for drinking and dining and as ecclesiastical and presentation pieces.

This three-quart tankard ranks among the rarest objects in American silverwork because of its impressive size and unusual decoration (plate 152). An early example of America's fascination with exotic ornamentation from the East, the popular flowering-tree and bird motif was taken from Chinese silks and Indian cotton chintzes. The tankard's maker, Jeremiah Dummer (1645–1718), apprenticed in the shop of John Hull and Robert Sanderson, the first established silversmiths in the North American colonies. The tankard was probably made for the wedding in 1685 of Simeon Stoddard (1650–1730), who, through inheritance and the shipping trade, primarily in textiles, would become one of the wealthiest men in Boston. Stoddard and Dummer were part-owners of the ship *The Expedition* and would have shared a friendship as well as access to the latest decorative designs coming from Asia. This tankard's history can be traced through eight generations of the Stoddard and Greenough families.

152 Jeremiah Dummer
American, 1645–1718
Tankard, Boston, c. 1685
silver, h. 8¾ in.
Promised gift of Ruth J. Nutt, in honor of the
75th Anniversary of the Seattle Art Museum,
T93.50.1

153 John Singleton Copley
American, 1737–1815
Dr. Silvester Gardiner (1707–1786), probably 1772
oil on canvas, 50 × 40 in.
Gift of Ann and Tom Barwick, Barney A. Ebsworth, Maggie and
Douglas Walker, Virginia and Bagley Wright, and Ann P. Wyckoff;
and gift, by exchange, of Mr. and Mrs. Sidney Gerber; Mr. and
Mrs. Louis Brechemin; Mrs. Reginald H. Parsons Memorial;
Anne Parsons Frame, in memory of Lieutenant Colonel Jasper
Ewing Brady, Jr., and Maud B. Parsons; Estate of Louise
Raymond Owens; anonymous donors; and Eugene Fuller
Memorial Collection; with additional funds from the American
Art Support Fund and the American Art Acquisition Fund,
in honor of the 75th Anniversary of the Seattle Art Museum,
2006.125

DR. SILVESTER GARDINER
BY JOHN SINGLETON COPLEY

Just how Silvester Gardiner (1707–1786) came to be painted by Copley is not known (plate 153). The men were acquaintances, and some have speculated that Copley may have offered the portrait to Gardiner as partial payment on a Boston land purchase. It is also possible that it was painted when Gardiner commissioned a portrait of his second wife, the widow Abigail Pickman Eppes, whom Gardiner married in 1772.[2] The commissioning of such costly painted likenesses tells us something about the cultural aspirations of Gardiner, an admired Boston physician who lived the life of a New England nobleman. In his Boston mansion Gardiner "entertained lavishly the grandees of the day,"[3] and he was devoted to the king of England, having prospered under royal patronage. Gardiner established a hospital for the British navy and by royal charter acquired extensive landholdings in rural Maine.

Copley could have shown Gardiner as a man of fine possessions and professional distinction, which he was. But instead of focusing on rich qualities of the sitter's costume or furnishings, Copley painted the doctor without any props to easily reference his social class, economic status, or professional accomplishment. Copley knew Gardiner well, and in this portrait he let the irrepressible spark of curiosity and bemusement in his friend's eyes speak for the man's experience and character.

By the time Copley painted *Dr. Silvester Gardiner,* he was turning to the most advanced carver in Boston to obtain frames of unmatched beauty and quality. John Welch (1711–1789), a London-trained frame designer, had helped to introduce into the staid decorative arts in Boston the new flowing, floriated style of the rococo. The highly sculptural frame chosen for Gardiner's portrait is among the most stylish of Welch's designs. The use of easily carved white pine enabled Welch to create bold curls and cutouts enhanced by leaf, vine, and floral details in, at times, high relief.

At the outbreak of the Revolution, the loyalist Gardiner and his wife left Boston for England, and his hospital, apothecaries, and personal property—including the Copley portrait—were confiscated when General George Washington's Continental Army marched into Boston. Gardiner remained abroad until 1785, when he returned to America, settling in Newport, Rhode Island. There he practiced medicine to the end of his life. So beloved was the charming, hardworking, and pious Gardiner that, when he died, his obituary in the *Newport Mercury* extolled his character: "He was possessed of an uncommon vigor and activity of mind. . . . His Christian piety and fortitude were exemplary as his honesty was inflexible and his friendship sincere." On the day of his funeral at Newport's Trinity Church, on August 14, 1786, the flags on all the ships in Newport harbor were lowered to half-mast, "and every other mark of respect [was] shown by the citizens on this mournful occasion."[4]

Gardiner's landholdings in Maine were restored to the doctor's heirs, and the Copley portrait was also returned to them after the war. Until it was acquired by the Seattle Art Museum in 2006, the portrait had remained for more than 250 years in the sitter's family, in their home in Gardiner, Maine, the town that honors Silvester Gardiner.

NOTES

1. John Adams, writing in 1770, in *Diary and Autobiography of John Adams,* vol. 1, ed. Lyman H. Butterfield (Cambridge, Mass., 1961), 293; quoted in Theodore E. Stebbins, Jr., "An American Despite Himself," in Carrie Rebora et al., *John Singleton Copley in America* (New York: The Metropolitan Museum of Art, 1995), 94.

2. For a discussion of the possible circumstances surrounding the Gardiner portrait commission, see Rebora, *John Singleton Copley in America,* 309–12. Copley's portrait of Abigail Pickman Eppes Gardiner is in the collection of the Brooklyn Museum, New York.

3. James A. Spading, "Silvester Gardiner," in *Dictionary of American Medical Biography,* ed. Howard A. Kelly and Walter L. Burrage (London and New York: D. Appleton, 1928), 451.

4. *Newport Mercury,* August 14, 1786; quoted in Wilkins Updike, *History of the Episcopal Church, in Narragansett, Rhode-Island* (New York: Henry M. Onderdonk, 1847), 127–28.

Patricia Junker

America in the Artful Age

A large Boston audience gathered in 1867 to hear Charles Eliot Norton, a charismatic Harvard lecturer, address the spiritual and cultural importance of the arts to America. That there should be wide interest in Norton's topic is not surprising. With the Civil War behind them, Americans had begun a process of self-examination and rebuilding of their land, society, and culture. Norton presented a sweeping overview of world history intended to show that the most virtuous civilizations produced the finest art.[1] To the extent that America was an enlightened society, Norton believed, its arts, too, would rise to enviable levels:

> In their highest achievements the arts are not so much the instruments and expression of the solitary individual artist as the means which the nation adopts, creates, inspires for the expression of its faith, its loftiness of spirit. They are the embodiment of its ideals; the permanent form of its poetic moods. When the nation is great enough to require great art, there will be artists ready for its need.[2]

The cultural reawakening that swept through American society following the bleak years of the Civil War corresponded with the growth of American interests and influence around the world. In this new era of internationalism, which extended until the outbreak of war in Europe in 1914, America's artists and arbiters of taste came to appreciate their country's cultural possibilities while becoming more knowledgeable about the arts in other parts of the globe. World's fairs brought together art objects from many nations and historic periods in grand displays. Illustrated books documented archaeological discoveries, catalogued collections of exotic-seeming objects from around the world, and offered the armchair traveler a glimpse of foreign locales. Collections of ancient, Old Master, Asian, and modern American art, both privately held and in recently founded museums, were opened to the public, and thus the obsessive desire for objects of taste and beauty spread from the newly wealthy and the cultural elite to an ever-widening circle of Americans.

Equally important, by the time of the country's much heralded Centennial in 1876, the production of American art, craft, and technology had advanced in quality to equal that of any country in the world. At home and abroad, America's artists enjoyed expanded exhibition opportunities through art clubs, regional industrial fairs, and international expositions. And with a burgeoning field of art periodicals and illustrated magazines to promote their work, American artists reached a broader national and international audience.

THE CULT OF THE EXOTIC EAST

The opening of trade between Japan and the Western world in 1854 provided a vital source of artistic ideas. By the 1880s an enthusiasm for things Japanese was pervasive among Americans, who also collected Chinese ceramics, bronzes, and jades; Persian carpets; and all manner of Turkish, Moorish, and Indian objects. Designers were enchanted by exotic artifacts and adapted them to new uses, turning Chinese porcelain decorations or Persian rug motifs, for example, into patterns for wallpapers or textiles. The well-appointed home might mix Japanese, Chinese, or Moorish themes in interiors designed specifically to encourage flights of fancy.

In this spirit of playful reinterpretation, Tiffany and Company created an impressive, fanciful tankard (plate 154) as a showpiece for the World's Columbian Exposition (fig. 1), Chicago's great 1893 world's fair celebrating the New World. The tankard at first glance recalls a Renaissance form, but its decoration in high relief features vegetation from America's southern climes: oranges, cacti, palm fronds, banana leaves, and magnolia flowers. Catering to the vogue for things exotic, Tiffany marketed the tankard with the title "Son Chow," a Chinese-sounding though wholly capricious name meant to convey something of the strangeness of the flora with which it is encrusted.

Japanese woodblock prints, especially the genre scenes known as ukiyo-e, exerted enormous influence on American art and culture

154 Tiffany and Company
Tankard, New York, 1893
silver, h. 10¼ in.
Promised gift of Ruth J. Nutt, in honor of the
75th Anniversary of the Seattle Art Museum,
T98.5.4

Figure 1. Tiffany and Company tankard (Son Chow),
exhibited at the World's Columbian Exposition, 1893,
published in *The Illustrated American*, May 20, 1893.
Tiffany and Company Archives

155 Mary Cassatt
American, 1844–1926
The Banjo Lesson, c. 1893
drypoint and aquatint with additions in monotype
on paper, 15¼ × 10 in. (sheet)
Partial and promised gift from a private collection,
2003.125

156 Mary Cassatt
American, 1844–1926
The Banjo Lesson, c. 1893
drypoint on paper, 14⅛ × 12¼ in. (sheet)
Partial and promised gift from a private collection,
2003.124

157 Mary Cassatt
American, 1844–1926
The Banjo Lesson, c. 1893
drypoint and aquatint with additions in monotype
on paper, 15⅞ × 10¼ in. (sheet)
Partial and promised gift from a private collection,
2003.126

158 Suzuki Harunobu
Japanese, 1725–1770
Two Lovers Playing Shamisen, Edo period, c. 1769
woodblock print, ink and color on paper, 11⅛ × 8¼ in.
(*chū-ban* sheet)
Promised gift of Mary and Allan Kollar, in honor of the
75th Anniversary of the Seattle Art Museum, T2006.118.11

through the second half of the nineteenth century. In Paris, American Mary Cassatt (1844–1926) began to imagine how the introduction of subtle color could enhance her work in etching, a print technique advanced by Rembrandt in the seventeenth century and revived in the nineteenth. Cassatt surely admired the charming intimacy of the scenes of daily life often depicted in ukiyo-e prints, and it is easy to imagine that her renditions of *The Banjo Lesson* (plates 155–157) were directly inspired by the example of Suzuki Harunobu (1725–1770, see plate 158), one of the great Japanese masters of color printmaking.

Cassatt loved the subtle qualities of etching, especially the delicate drypoint lines made directly into the copper plate, and the variable tonal qualities of aquatint, suggestive of watercolor. She was not interested in printmaking for its process of replication and carefully controlled sameness. Instead Cassatt enjoyed variation from printing to printing, using different papers or adding color through monotype to create unique effects among impressions of the same image. We can begin to comprehend Cassatt's experimentation and versatility only by studying multiple impressions pulled from the same plate but printed in different ways, as in the three variant images of *The Banjo Lesson*.

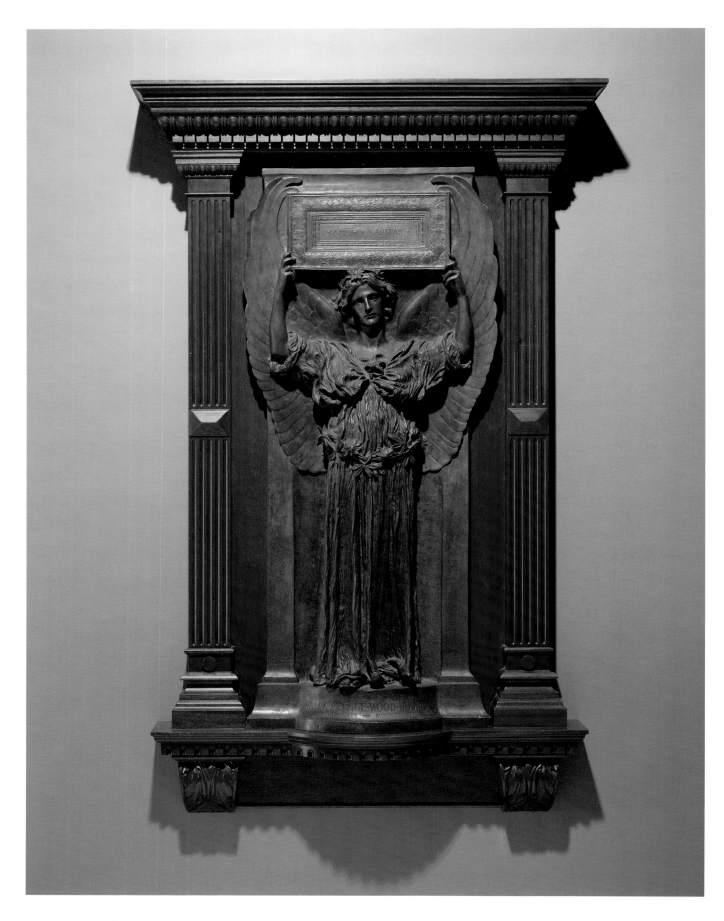

159 Augustus Saint-Gaudens
American (born Ireland), 1848–1907
Amor Caritas, modeled 1898; this cast probably 1898
bronze, 39⅞ × 17 × 4½ in.
Gift of Ann and Tom Barwick, the General Acquisitions Endowment,
the Gates Foundation Endowment, the Utley Endowment, the
American Art Endowment, and the 19th Century Paintings Fund,
in honor of the 75th Anniversary of the Seattle Art Museum, 2006.4

AN AMERICAN RENAISSANCE—A TASTE FOR CLASSICISM

In the decades following the Civil War, American artists often consciously allied their creations with the great art traditions of ancient Greece and Rome and of the Italian Renaissance, thus advancing a proud national sense of the high aspirations of American culture. In every area of society and thought, this was the American Renaissance. By 1876 the United States was, in the minds of many, on the verge of becoming a new Athens or a modern Florence, such was the perceived economic, intellectual, and artistic potential of the republic.

One of the greatest exemplars of the Renaissance spirit in America was the sculptor Augustus Saint-Gaudens (1848–1907). He lent his talents to extraordinary civic projects and collaborated with fellow artists, designers, craftsmen, and architects in the spirit of artistic brotherhood. For his sculptures he selected subjects that might uplift and ennoble his audience. In the bronze relief *Amor Caritas* (plate 159), an angel—the classical form of feminine beauty—symbolizes what Saint-Gaudens considered the greatest measure of humankind, our exalted capacity for love (*amor*) and charity (*caritas*). Saint-Gaudens equated the highest moral ideals with exquisite physical beauty, and in the small angel he found a recognizable symbol of physical perfection and moral purity. The form of the relief tablet itself recalls an ancient Greek grave marker, or stele, and its iconography is reminiscent of a Christian tombstone. This cast was commissioned by the children of Nancy Legge Wood Hooper (1819–1898) to honor their late mother. The angel form, coupled with the sculpture's express sentiment of selfless love and giving, made the bronze an appropriate memorial to a woman and a mother.

160 **Herter Brothers (Christian Herter)**
American, active 1864–1906
Cabinet, New York City, c. 1881–82
ebonized oak, brass, gilded bronze, and agate,
60½ × 75¾ × 13¼ in.
The Guendolen Carkeek Plestcheeff Endowment for the
Decorative Arts, The Decorative Arts and Paintings Council,
and the Decorative Arts Acquisition Fund, in honor of the
75th Anniversary of the Seattle Art Museum, 2006.5

To nineteenth-century Americans, classicism denoted both refinement in form and a time-honored tradition of informed taste. Architects, designers, and furniture makers were eager to adapt Greek shapes and Roman ornamentation to their productions in silver, ceramics, glass, wallpaper, textiles, and furniture, while painters and sculptors collaborated on elaborate enterprises on the scale of the Italian Renaissance, whether working in the great houses of America's elite or designing grand civic projects such as public squares or military monuments. In the Manhattan mansion of William Henry Vanderbilt, designed in the early 1880s, the ornate classicism of the Italian Renaissance could be found among rooms keyed to every possible taste or mood, from exotic and playful Persian or Japanese rooms to evocations of fifteenth-century Florence. A product of the eminent design firm of the German-born Herter Brothers, the interior of Vanderbilt's residence drew heavily on Renaissance sources as especially appropriate for the home of an American Medici. From the moment one entered the mansion through amazing full-scale bronze reproductions of Lorenzo Ghiberti's great fifteenth-century *Gates of Paradise*, created for the Baptistry in Florence, one was reminded, and never subtly, that Vanderbilt's wealth and glory were no less than that of the early Italian merchant princes. The ebonized oak cabinet (plate 160) is in the style of the mansion's dining room (fig. 2), which was richly decorated with heavily carved oak panels dominated by garlands and swags in the high relief that also characterizes the carved decoration on the chest. The cabinet features putti and swags of flowers and fruit representing the four seasons. The gilded brasses, studded with cabochon-mounted agates, were inspired by classical roundels used as ornamentation on ancient furniture and dress. Seen in full flower in the William Vanderbilt house, the Renaissance Revival in America was more than a mannered adaptation of style. It was at its core a manifestation of the nation's need to instill purpose, a high artistic standard, and a noble spirit in its art and architecture.

Figure 2. William Vanderbilt dining room, from Edward Strahan (pseud. Earl Shinn), *Vanderbilt's House and Collection,* vol. 2 (New York, 1883–84).

161 Lilian Westcott Hale
American, 1881–1963
Daydreams, 1908
charcoal on paper, 28½ × 20 in.
Private collection, T2006.121.4

162 Lilian Westcott Hale
American, 1881–1963
The Old Mirror, c. 1905
charcoal and graphite on paper, 15¾ × 14¼ in.
Private collection, T2006.121.3

"WHAT SHALL WE DO WITH OUR WALLS?"

In 1880 the American critic Clarence Cook published a promotional pamphlet on wallpapers whose title—"*What Shall We Do with Our Walls?*"—suggests another obsessive tendency of the period, the collecting of pictures for the artful interior.[3] The decorative impulse and the making and collecting of paintings understandably went hand in hand. Painters enjoyed patronage on a level never before seen in the United States as their productions assumed ever greater importance as domestic objects.

Hungry for new pictorial effects and willing to accord equal stature to all the pictorial arts, progressive painters of the late nineteenth century expanded beyond oils to experiment with etching, watercolor, and drawing techniques (plates 161, 162). Watercolor painting and printmaking had long been associated with the prosaic art of illustration, while drawing traditionally had been valued merely as a building block to painting. In reviving outmoded or unappreciated artistic practices, painters elevated them to highly respected creative forms. As American artists explored new areas of interest, they founded professional organizations to promote them, including the American Watercolor Society (1866), the New York Etching Club (1877), and the Society of Painters in Pastel (1882).

163 **John La Farge**
American, 1835–1910
Roses, 1880
watercolor on paper, 9 × 10⅞ in.
Partial and promised gift from a private collection, 2005.159

John La Farge excelled equally in painting, decorative work, and the so-called minor arts, and he, more than any other American of his generation, embodies the period's artistic openness. La Farge became convinced of his artistic calling by early experiences in Europe, and he readily explored new ideas from abroad, such as painting in the open air like the French impressionists and distilling unconventional design concepts from ukiyo-e prints. When the opportunity presented itself, he turned to the decorating of interiors in the Italian Renaissance manner on an unprecedented scale, creating sumptuous decorations for the wealthiest private patrons of the Gilded Age, including William Vanderbilt, from whose home the museum's Herter Brothers cabinet (see plate 169) probably comes.

La Farge felt a compulsion, as he put it, to create "light by colors," which he did in both transparent watercolor and pictorial glass (most notably for Boston's Trinity Church).[4] For a tiny still life of roses in a porcelain bowl (plate 163), he exploited the translucency of watercolor with an exceptional economy of means. He sparingly applied the delicate, sheer tints of the light-bathed pink and yellow rose petals; elsewhere he layered hues carefully and richly, the overlapping colors creating luminous dark passages. The spare composition itself is almost wholly unremarkable, and yet *Roses* is a spellbinding work of art. The iridescent glazed porcelain bowl, gently illuminated in an otherwise dark room, creates a dazzling reflection on the highly polished tabletop. Everything about the painting seems designed to invite our close inspection and quiet contemplation—its small dimensions and tight cropping, the measured layering of transparent colors, the almost magical effects of light upon so many different elements, the mournful character of limp, withering blooms. These mesmerizing qualities remind us, too, of the careful observation and deliberate practiced execution required by this deceptively simple painting.

164 John Singer Sargent
American (born Italy), 1856–1925
Yachts at Anchor, Palma de Majorca, 1912
watercolor on paper, 12 × 16 in.
Partial and promised gift from a private collection, 2005.164

John Singer Sargent came to watercolor painting later than his contemporaries, who had embraced the medium by the early 1880s. But when he did come to watercolor, he made it a specialty. Portraiture had defined the first half of Sargent's career, from the 1870s to around 1900, but watercolor defined the second half, a time when he traveled widely. Sargent's increasing regard for watercolor points to another fundamental characteristic of the artful age. Peripatetic artists of the late nineteenth century quickly and enthusiastically seized upon watercolor for its usefulness as a traveler's medium. Sargent painted loosely and vigorously in watercolor, undaunted by its inherent challenges to control, and this ease speaks to his love for it as a leisure pursuit. No matter what their nominal subject, Sargent's watercolors have in common a primary focus on effects of light. He worked always with transparent washes, keying every stroke of color to the bright white of the paper, which in his paintings is light itself. Small wonder that he was captivated by the kind of evanescent scene he sketched in watercolor in the port of Palma, on the Spanish island of Majorca (plate 164), in 1912. Sargent's inscription identifies the otherwise anonymous harbor scene, though the painting does exude a Mediterranean light and heat. Light flashes off the water and the shiny white hulls of the ships and the long, broad expanses of their headsails. The architecture of so many ships at anchor, all compressed into a close space,

165 **Theodore Robinson**
American, 1852–1896
Claude Monet, 1890
charcoal on paper, 27 × 13 in.
Partial and promised gift from a private collection,
2005.163

166 **Theodore Robinson**
American, 1852–1896
On the Canal, 1893
oil on canvas, 19 × 23 in.
Partial and promised gift from a private collection,
in memory of Anne S. Thaanum, 2005.161

is exceedingly complicated, and yet, even among the dizzying glints of light and intricate shadow patterns, Sargent presented the various forms convincingly in a rhythmic arrangement of hulls, masts, booms, and rigging. From his vantage at sea, Sargent made a study of the blues of sky, water, and reflections playing on and around the ships rafted together in the harbor.

Theodore Robinson (1852–1896), an irrepressible experimenter, created finished work in drawing, watercolor, and oils; used photographs as an aid to painting; and experienced French impressionism firsthand through his friendship with Claude Monet. He came to know Monet during an extended stay in the French painter's hometown of Giverny in the late 1880s. Robinson's informal drawing of Monet (plate 165), an illustration for a popular magazine, is a touching record of their friendship. For all his closeness to Monet, Robinson remained an independent, holding up his friend's inventiveness and color sensibility as standards but never slavishly imitating Monet's work.

When Robinson returned to New York in 1892, after nearly a decade of living abroad, he faced his native land with a fervent desire to rediscover and celebrate it. He spent his remaining years applying French-inspired impressionism to distinctly American subjects, especially rural scenery that he found to be as poetic as that of Giverny, such as the countryside seen in *On the Canal*

(plate 166), a view on the Delaware and Hudson Canal, at Port Ben, near Naponach, New York.

Although the painting refers to a specific landmark, Robinson might have thought of it as a cloud study, for he often commented upon the role that clouds played in inspiring him and in cementing a lasting impression of a place in his mind's eye. In the Port Ben work, capturing the harmonious allover light and color effects through the changing atmosphere of early autumn days had been hard won. He noted in his diary: "Worked on a grey day, but trying to keep my first impression—a very luminous sky and water—difficult as there are many kinds of greyness" (September 15, 1893). He painted three versions of the scene, working sometimes on multiple canvases simultaneously, so intent was he on portraying the light variations in all their subtlety.[5]

For Cincinnati-born and European-trained John Twachtman (1853–1902), the intense study of landscape and atmosphere in its ever-changing complexity led at times to intuitive experiments in color and form, especially when his meditative scrutiny focused on one favorite corner of his world, the hemlock pool at his Connecticut farm property. Twachtman painted the quiet wooded glade time and time again, but never in such a cursory and wholly suggestive manner as in the small, intimate canvas that has come to the Seattle Art Museum (plate 167). Its somber autumnal palette suggests that

167 **John Twachtman**
American, 1853–1902
Hemlock Pool, Autumn,
possibly 1894
oil on canvas, 15½ × 19½ in.
Partial and promised gift from
a private collection, 2005.166

(opposite)
168 **Willard Metcalf**
American, 1858–1925
The Cornish Hills, 1911
oil on canvas, 35 × 40 in.
Partial and promised gift from
a private collection, 2005.160

it might be the work that Twachtman submitted as *Hemlock Pool (Autumn)* to the 1894 winter exhibition at the Pennsylvania Academy of the Fine Arts in Philadelphia. Twachtman's 1894 Academy picture, though awarded the gold medal as the best painting in the show by a jury of artists, was widely considered to be highly idiosyncratic and a travesty of landscape art—"a misty agglomeration of blues and reds—a thing of shreds and patches," one outraged critic declared. Another dismissed it as "hardly a picture."[6] Especially at the Pennsylvania Academy, such a picture could easily be seen to mock the discipline that was fundamental to academic practice. In a period when Americans valued tradition over innovation, Twachtman's unconventional picture crossed a line for some.

Willard Metcalf (1858–1925) came to impressionism as Robinson had, through the example of Monet, whom Metcalf met in Giverny. After he returned to New York from France in 1888, Metcalf enjoyed a successful career as a teacher, illustrator, and painter of colorful, loosely brushed spring and fall studies of picturesque Gloucester, Massachusetts, and Old Lyme, Connecticut. Then rather suddenly,

as a mature painter at the age of fifty, Metcalf found a subject that would engage him as never before. In the winter of 1909 Metcalf traveled to the artists' enclave of Cornish, New Hampshire, to visit friends. In the snow-covered hills there he discovered the beauty of the winter landscape, a landscape reduced to a few solid forms, so different in structure from the soft tapestries of spring and autumn. The stillness of winter engaged Metcalf's spiritual side, bringing a deeply meditative presence to his work. With his first Cornish canvases, Metcalf garnered immediate critical attention.

Metcalf made a second visit to Cornish in the winter of 1911, and in an exceptional season of work he surpassed even the highly acclaimed paintings of 1909. Among many outstanding canvases, Metcalf produced one that arguably now stands as the centerpiece of his entire career, the monumental *Cornish Hills* (plate 168). The exhilaration that Metcalf must have felt in these weeks in Cornish, typically painting outdoors, undeterred by the New England winter, is especially apparent in the brilliant blue sky and shining white, crystalline snow of this picture.

"To define beauty, not in the most abstract, but in the most concrete terms possible. To find not a universal formula for it, but the formula which expresses most adequately this or that special manifestation of it, is the aim of the true student of Aesthetics."[7] So declared the widely influential English critic Walter Pater in 1873, aptly describing the pattern that emerged in American culture in the last decades of the nineteenth century, when artistry was found to exist in many forms and no one school of taste could encompass the notion of beauty. It is in the individuality—the sheer variety and eclecticism—of these creations that we can identify the essence of this age. The virtuosity on display in the art of the period speaks to a passionate pursuit of excellence as a universal aesthetic ideal. The inventiveness surrounding these productions conveys above all a strong new undercurrent of artistic freedom, one that nurtured, as never before, the creativity of America's artists, all very different yet each so self-assured.

NOTES

1. For a detailed overview of Norton's life and ideals, see Theodore E. Stebbins, Jr., with Susan Ricci, "Charles Eliot Norton: Ruskin's Friend, Harvard's Sage," in Theodore E. Stebbins, Jr., et al., *The Last Ruskinians: Charles Eliot Norton, Charles Herbert Moore, and Their Circle* (Cambridge: Harvard University Press, 2007), 13–29.

2. Charles Eliot Norton, "American Culture," 1867, quoted in Kermit Vanderbilt, *Charles Eliot Norton: Apostle of Culture in a Democracy* (Cambridge: The Belknap Press of Harvard University Press, 1959), 205.

3. Clarence Cook, "What Shall We Do with Our Walls?" (New York: Warren Fuller, 1880).

4. John La Farge, in *The Higher Life in Art*, 1908; quoted in Kathleen A. Foster, "John La Farge and the American Watercolor Movement: Art for the 'Decorative Age,'" in Henry Adams et al., *John La Farge* (New York: Abbeville Press, 1987), 150.

5. For Robinson's entries for the early fall of 1893 referring to his work at Port Ben, see his "Diary 1892–1896," Frick Art Reference Library, New York; quoted in Sona Johnston, *Theodore Robinson, 1852–1896* (Baltimore: Baltimore Museum of Art, 1973), 50–51. Other canvases in this series include a larger version (30½ × 34¾ in.) in the collection of the Pennsylvania Academy of the Fine Arts, Philadelphia, and another of this small size (18¼ × 22¼ in.) in the collection of the Nebraska Art Association, Sheldon Memorial Art Gallery, Lincoln. All three variants are signed and dated 1893.

6. December 1894 reviews quoted in Lisa N. Peters, *John Twachtman (1853–1902): A Painter's Painter* (New York: Spanierman Gallery, 2006), 67.

7. Walter Pater, from *Studies in the History of the Renaissance*, 1873; quoted in Lionel Lambourne, *The Aesthetic Movement* (London: Phaidon Press, 1996), 9.

Patricia Junker

New York Stories

The parades, processions, bugles playing, flags flying,
drums beating;

A million people—manners free and superb—open voices—
hospitality—the most courageous and friendly young men;

The free city! no slaves! no owners of slaves!

The beautiful city, the city of hurried and sparkling waters!
the city of spires and masts!

The city nested in bays! my city!

—Walt Whitman, "Mannahatta," 1871

The city of New York has always seemed fundamentally American in its diversity and openness, its energy, its embrace of the new. When artists and writers have dug deep for definitions of Americanness, many have found it in New York, especially in the cacophony of voices and patchwork of faces that fill the city's streets. It is a place defined by its people as much as its skyscrapers and its geographical position as the gateway to the United States. The human dimension of this ever-modern city has been an essential element of America's art.

The Seattle Art Museum's collection of early twentieth-century art once focused largely on the Pacific Northwest, but recent and promised gifts of early modern American art have added a New York dimension. By the turn of the twentieth century, New York had become the center of the artistic universe for many of the country's vanguard painters and sculptors. Each of the works of art introduced here in its own way represents an effort on the part of an American artist to establish his or her identity by association with New York. Sometimes the artist chose New York as a subject that was both modern and peculiarly American. Others made a calculated effort to attract a national audience through exhibitions in New York and coverage in its influential art press. Each of the following vignettes shows a modern American artist at work in the most modern American city, and in them we can see how this one place—New York—reveals common cultural experiences that speak to the nation's broad and fundamental diversity.

OFF MADISON SQUARE, NOVEMBER 3, 1903

It was quite a scene: New York on election night, November 3, 1903, the night when the legendary Tammany Hall political machine managed to oust the reformist mayor Seth Low and elect, by an overwhelming majority, the young Colonel George B. McClellan Jr., son of the famous Civil War general. Mayor Low had run afoul of the city's power brokers by, among other things, working to control gambling and to restrict liquor sales. He had been a fresh change from the entrenched corruption of Tammany Hall, and his political and social reforms had represented the very idea of decency. McClellan raised fears that he would be little more than a puppet for the corrupt elite. The contest between Low and McClellan, at its most fundamental level, seemed a battle between the forces of good and evil.

With the ballot count under way that evening, and with so much at stake, New Yorkers poured into Manhattan's streets to read election results as they were posted on the bulletin boards of the city's newspapers. The largest gathering was just off Madison Square, where the *New York Times* had stretched a large banner across Twenty-third Street and Broadway to carry updated announcements. "When it was seen that *The New York Times* had conceded the election of Col. McClellan there were wild scenes of jubilation on the part of the Tammany crowd," the *Times* later reported.[1] A Fourth of July atmosphere quickly engulfed the city on this cold, wet night. At Madison Square, celebrants organized a spontaneous parade. Young boys appropriated the city's red safety lanterns and carried them aloft on broomsticks. Bonfires burned before many of the saloons and at points along the route of the boisterous, ragtag procession.

Everett Shinn (1876–1953) was on the spot that evening at Madison Square. His pastel drawing *Election Banner, Broadway and Twenty-third Street* (plate 169) is a dizzying record of the electrifying spectacle of firecrackers, lanterns, and bonfires. In the rich hues of pastels in soft, blended strokes, Shinn re-created the magical effect of brilliant flashes of colored light filling the thick atmosphere of a snowy night. The enormous *New York Times* election banner, which had announced McClellan's victory, is in this view a rather ghostly specter, just a faint reminder of the campaign over which the city's emotions had run so high.

The people, the noise, the garishness of Manhattan at night— these things particularly fascinated Shinn. He regularly supplied *Harper's Weekly* with lively illustrations of the city's colorful street life, and in doing so, he had rediscovered pastels, a medium he had used as a student. Reportage required that he work in shorthand, and the atmosphere of New York at night demanded interpretation in intense, saturated color, and for this, pastel served Shinn's needs best.

By 1904 New Yorkers had become accustomed to seeing Shinn's latest pastels exhibited nearly every year at one of the prominent Fifth Avenue galleries. *Election Banner, Broadway and Twenty-third Street* was a highlight of Shinn's show in March 1904 at the Durand-Ruel Gallery, which had become a showcase for the work of French and American impressionists. *Election Banner* was one of only a few New York scenes included among a large group of pastels inspired by Shinn's lingering recollections of Paris. For the *New York Times* critic, Shinn's pastels of Parisian ballerinas were mannered: "He follows Degas too closely."[2] The writer found Shinn's New York subjects more engaging. These were the works, after all, born of this artist-journalist's close familiarity with the people, landmarks, and events that shaped a New Yorker's world.

169 **Everett Shinn**
American, 1876–1953
Election Banner, Broadway and Twenty-third
Street, 1903
pastel on paper, 23 × 15½ in.
Partial and promised gift from a private collection,
2005.165

291 FIFTH AVENUE, MAY 14, 1916

On May 14, 1916, New York's Fifth Avenue between City Hall and Fifty-seventh Street was the scene of one of the largest public displays of American patriotism that the country has ever known: the Preparedness Day parade. As war with Germany loomed, President Woodrow Wilson moved to fire up reluctant citizen-soldiers with this rally for national preparedness. Americans were torn over the issue of war with Germany, though many had become increasingly bellicose after a German submarine torpedoed the British luxury liner *Lusitania* on May 7, 1915. More than half of the 2,500 passengers on board drowned, and 127 of the victims were Americans. In the aftershock, some Americans immediately pushed to enter the war against Germany, but many others wanted nothing to do with further violence. Between these two extremes lay the majority of Americans who, as one contemporary historian described them, "felt shock and anger which they wished to express as loudly as possible so long as it did not lead to war."[3]

Even in a city famous for parades, New York's Preparedness Day event surely must stand as one of the largest and most emotionally charged parades ever mounted. More than 137,000 people—laborers, businessmen, doctors, teachers, mothers, engineers, clergymen, artists—marched over almost thirteen hours. For all the diversity of interests represented among the marchers, there were no signs of individual or group identity; official regulations stipulated that there would be "no display of banners and no advertisements of any sort carried—only the American flag."[4]

The photographer and art impresario Alfred Stieglitz (1864–1946) probably watched the parade from his Little Galleries of the Photo-Secession. He was located right above parade central, on the top floor of an unremarkable commercial building at 291 Fifth Avenue. In those especially tense weeks of April–May 1916, Stieglitz had on view at 291 (as his gallery was most often called) an exhibition of new paintings by his friend Marsden Hartley (1877–1943), who was just back in New York after a two-year sojourn in Berlin. The timing of the show could not have been worse. Hartley's paintings—paeans to the German imperial military and memorials to the German war dead—were on view at the same moment when officials had restricted public expressions of political sentiment to the flying of the American flag alone, fearful that any other flag or placard might incite a riot.

What were Hartley and Stieglitz thinking in mounting this exhibition in New York at this time? There can be no question that Stieglitz fully understood what the pictures were about—Hartley had confided much to Stieglitz in his frequent letters from Berlin. And one American critic, who had seen a large show of Hartley's German work in Berlin in the spring of 1915, had already questioned if the paintings might represent pro-German sentiment.

But Stieglitz was eager to show Hartley's new work. He had recognized Hartley's immense talent in 1909 when this slight man first walked through the door of 291 with his brilliantly colored paintings of his beloved Maine hills. With Stieglitz's financial assistance, Hartley had gone to Europe to expand his artistic horizons even while struggling to set himself apart from the European modern artists then shaping aesthetic debate in Paris and Munich.

Stieglitz's enthusiasm for the originality of Hartley's German abstractions might have simply blinded him to the political folly of showing work that might be viewed as pro-German. Then again, Stieglitz, the American-born and Berlin-educated son of German immigrants, openly expressed an admiration for Germany and a belief that war was a natural, inevitable consequence of living in the world—a stance that appalled some of his American friends. Stieglitz saw the rarefied art milieu of 291 as quite apart from the mundane concerns of commerce, politics, or fashion, and he would have staunchly asserted that Hartley's paintings should be taken on their own terms, and that no artist should hew to the concerns of any audience.

Hartley never actually explained this series of war motif pictures. Our understanding of them today is based on statements he made privately in letters and notes. The paintings would have been obscure to all but a few of Hartley's closest friends from Berlin, and Stieglitz was almost alone in knowing the depth of Hartley's associations with Germany.

"I have every sense of being at home among Germans and I like the life color of Berlin," Hartley wrote to Stieglitz in 1913. "It has movement and energy and leans always a little over the edge of the future instead of leaning so heavily on the past. . . . The military life adds so much in the way of a sense of perpetual gaiety here in Berlin."[5] Hartley's first Berlin canvases re-created the visual sensations of Kaiser Wilhelm's military parades; these dynamic compositions of simple, bold stripes and checkerboard patterns recall uniforms, pennants, and medals. Once Germany declared war on France and England in August 1914, however, the character of Hartley's German designs changed, and the proud symbols of the German military took on a somber meaning: "It is all very hard as a friendly spectator to have seen and still see the countless fine specimens of manhood go out and never come back," Hartley said in a mournful letter to Stieglitz.[6]

And then the war became suddenly personal for Hartley. On October 7, 1914, his friend the imperial cavalryman Lieutenant Karl von Freyburg was killed in France. Hartley wrote to Stieglitz that he had loved Freyburg. They perhaps had had a physical relationship, and Hartley certainly loved the ideal of youth and beauty that Freyburg embodied. "If there was ever a true representative of all that is lovely and splendid in the German soul and character it was this fellow," Hartley told Stieglitz, "at the age of 24, perfectly equipped for a life of joy and strength and beauty."[7] Over the next months, Hartley considered the horrors of war through the

(opposite)
170 **Marsden Hartley**
American, 1877–1943
Painting No. 49, Berlin, 1914–1915
oil on canvas, 47 × 39½ in.
Partial and promised gift of the Barney A. Ebsworth
Collection, in honor of the 75th Anniversary of the
Seattle Art Museum, 2001.1067

Figure 1. George Cope (American, 1855–1929),
The Civil War Regalia of Major Levi Gheen McCauley,
1887, oil on canvas, 50 × 36½ in. The Art Institute
of Chicago, Mr. and Mrs. Robert O. Delaney
and Chauncey and Marion McCormick funds;
Wesley M. Dixon Endowment, 2000.134

wasteful death of this one beautiful young German man. His intense grief fed an equally strong surge of creativity as he obsessively worked the elements of the cavalryman's uniform into a series of pictorial laments.

Painting Number 49, Berlin (plate 170), also known as *Portrait of a German Officer,* is a complex arrangement of symbols that can refer generally to all German cavalrymen. We see the Iron Cross, details of a cavalryman's uniform, and a helmet. One element seems to identify Freyburg specifically: the number "24," Freyburg's age at his death, appears at the left.

This emblematic portrait is emphatically cruciform. "If you knew Freyburg, you would understand what true pathos is," Hartley told Stieglitz, suggesting the intensity of his vision of Freyburg as an innocent, an almost Christ-like figure sacrificed for political ends.[8] The carefully organized arrangement also conforms to the oldest battlefield tribute: the trophy, the ancient Greek *tropaion,* a memorial set up by soldiers on the field of battle at the spot where an enemy had been routed. Traditionally trophy tributes consisted of arms and standards hung upon a tree or stake in the semblance of a man. Trophy designs were popularized in Renaissance emblem books and, much later, in Victorian-era guides to ornament. They appeared as well in European and American still-life painting at the end of the nineteenth century. Hartley might have been recalling similar war tributes in American art, such as George Cope's *The Civil War Regalia of Major Levi Gheen McCauley* (1887; fig. 1).

Hartley offered this explanation of his paintings in the catalogue introduction for his 1916 show:

The Germanic group is but a part of a series which I had contemplated of movements in various areas of war activity from which I was prevented, owing to the difficulties of travel. The forms are only those which I have observed casually from day to day. There is no hidden symbolism whatsoever in them; there is no slight intention of that anywhere. Things under observation, just pictures of any day, any hour. I have expressed only what I have seen. They are merely consultations of the eye . . . my notion of the purely pictorial.[9]

Accept them as graphic designs only, Hartley asked, and know that he would have painted impressions from other cities on the war front if he had been able. Forced by circumstances to hide the joy of life and the love that had inspired these German subjects, Hartley did the politically expedient thing and denied the paintings their content.

The reality of the blood already spilled in 1916 by soldiers and innocents alike minimized the impact of Hartley's intellectualized abstractions on a New York audience facing war. Historical events thus eclipsed Hartley's much-anticipated artistic emergence in America. And because the war changed forever Hartley's relationship to both Berlin and America, he changed artistic direction completely. From this point forward he began the process of rediscovering himself in his native land, a process that would eventually lead to his reputation as one of the great painters of rural New England and of his native Maine. As for Stieglitz, he closed 291 in June 1917, two months after the United States declared war on Germany.

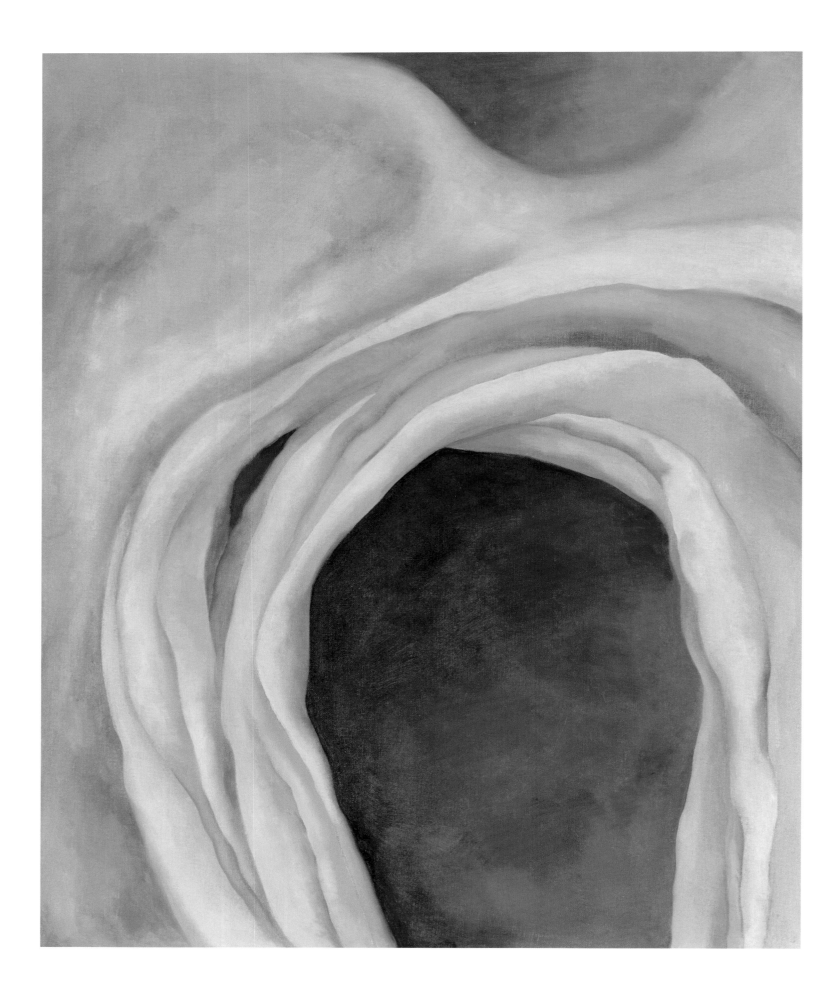

ANDERSON GALLERIES, PARK AVENUE AND FIFTY-NINTH STREET, JANUARY 29, 1923

In the fall of 1922, Georgia O'Keeffe (1887–1986) received a scrapbook from Mitchell Kennerley, director of the Anderson Galleries in midtown Manhattan. In it he had pasted two recent newspaper articles about O'Keeffe. The remaining empty pages, Kennerley believed, would soon hold more clippings about this young artist. Interest in O'Keeffe was building, and she was soon to have a solo exhibition at his galleries.

The upcoming exhibition had not been O'Keeffe's idea. It was arranged by Alfred Stieglitz, her advocate and, now, her lover—O'Keeffe and Stieglitz had lived together since her move to New York from Texas in 1918. Holding her work up to criticism was difficult enough for the self-conscious O'Keeffe, but she was already feeling completely misunderstood even by those to whom she was closest. "The little book looks so clean and fine," she wrote to Kennerley in thanking him for the scrapbook. "I'll paste things in it but I'm sure—every time I do it—I will shiver and have a queer feeling of being invaded the way I do when I read things about myself."[10]

Alfred Stieglitz Presents One-Hundred Pictures, Oils, Water-colors, Pastels, Drawings, by Georgia O'Keeffe, American opened at Kennerley's Anderson Galleries, on January 29, 1923. After the demise of his famous 291 gallery in 1917, Stieglitz kept his circle of modern American artists before the public in a series of mutually beneficial shows in the heavily visited rooms of Kennerley's book and fine arts auction house.

O'Keeffe's work had not been seen publicly since 1917, but Stieglitz had managed to arouse continuing interest in the artist in quite

another way. In 1921 he exhibited a large group of his photographs of her, an extensive serial study of a seductive young woman who had become Stieglitz's obsession. Held at the Anderson Galleries, the show was as much a defining moment for O'Keeffe as for Stieglitz: it was a landmark public unveiling of the new, young woman artist at the center of Stieglitz's life and at the head of the country's artistic vanguard. Of the 145 photographs Stieglitz showed, nearly one third were recent images of O'Keeffe. Some were portraits, a few referenced her art or her art making, but many were nudes and several were shockingly intimate. Stieglitz's provocative photographs of O'Keeffe had attracted much attention, and because of their exhibition, O'Keeffe became, as critic Henry McBride later noted, "a newspaper personality" even before her artistic work was widely known.[11]

The O'Keeffe that the country had come to know by 1923 was very much Stieglitz's creation. He presented her in his photographs as an uninhibited sensualist. In fact, the public was viewing O'Keeffe through the lens of Stieglitz's own erotic obsession. He similarly shaped the way others regarded O'Keeffe as an artist. The men of the Stieglitz circle, when confronted with this woman's esoteric art, could imagine only that it emanated from that which they could not fathom, female sexuality. Even as they celebrated her—and Stieglitz's friends Paul Rosenfeld and Marsden Hartley wrote important early pieces praising O'Keeffe's uncommon vision—their ecstatic prose was sexually explicit. Hartley, in a 1921 essay, "Some Women Artists in Modern Painting," wrote that O'Keeffe's paintings represented "the world of a woman turned inside out" and were "probably as living and shameless private documents as

(opposite)
171 **Georgia O'Keeffe**
American, 1887–1986
Music—Pink and Blue No. 1, 1918
oil on canvas, 35 × 29 in.
Partial and promised gift of the Barney A. Ebsworth
Collection, in honor of the 75th Anniversary of the Seattle
Art Museum, 2000.161

Figure 2. Alfred Stieglitz (American, 1864–1946), *Georgia O'Keeffe: A Portrait—Painting and Sculpture*, 1919, palladium print, 9¼ × 7½ in. National Gallery of Art, Washington, D.C., Alfred Stieglitz Collection, 1980.70.127

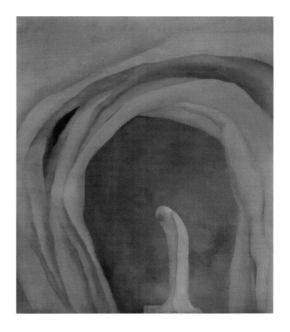

exist, in painting, certainly, and probably in any other art."[12] Rosenfeld's articles, appearing in *The Dial,* the little magazine of art and literature, in 1921 and in *Vanity Fair* in 1922 were especially lurid; one reads in Rosenfeld's critiques that O'Keeffe's paintings are as "great painful and ecstatic climaxes" and so much more.[13]

Stieglitz was happy to supply the public with what the extremely reticent O'Keeffe could not give them, an explanation of her work. O'Keeffe said little publicly that was emphatic enough to directly counter the impressions of her created by Stieglitz, Rosenfeld, and Hartley. Although Stieglitz printed a brief biographical statement by O'Keeffe in a brochure that accompanied her exhibition at the Anderson Galleries, he also reprinted there the Freudian reading that Hartley had published about her art in 1921. Some fifty years after the fact, O'Keeffe could still recall the painful embarrassment Hartley's essay had caused: "I remember how upset I was once by a certain reference Marsden Hartley made to my work in a book. I almost wept. I thought I could never face the world again."[14]

One painting that seems to have particularly supported the case that Stieglitz and Hartley made for a sexual interpretation of O'Keeffe's imagery was the soft, lyrical abstraction she called *Music—Pink and Blue No. 1* (plate 171). Painted in 1918, the canvas was one of a group of expansive oils on musical themes that had evolved from a series of abstractions she had begun in charcoal in 1916. These patterns of rhythmic lines, organic shapes, and tonal variations represented internal visions recorded, she said, almost automatically, and sometimes in direct response to music, as a means to liberate her eye, mind, and hand from the constraints of following pictorial conventions. O'Keeffe had first come to such visualizations in 1915, when she was studying at Columbia University Teacher's College, New York. One day she heard music playing in a classroom:

> Being curious, I opened the door and went in. The instructor was playing a low-toned record, asking the class to make a charcoal drawing from it. So I sat down and made a drawing too. He then played a very different kind of record—a sort of high soprano sounding piece for another quick drawing. This gave me an idea that I was interested to follow later—the idea that music could be translated into something for the eye.[15]

If we read *Music—Pink and Blue No. 1* by its title, it is a visualization of sound. We perhaps see soft notes in the pastel hues and veils that rise and unfold, moving up, over, and around a vaporous blue void—silence, perhaps, or a deeply sonorous infinity. Stieglitz saw this canvas differently. He made an emblematic portrait of O'Keeffe that played on this painting in which the canvas is coupled unsubtly with the phallic form of a sculpture O'Keeffe had created in 1916 (fig. 2). The small plaster is in fact a prayerful votive figure, a work

inspired by the death of O'Keeffe's mother. But Stieglitz employed it as something else entirely. His photograph is a misrepresentation of both the painting and the figurine.

New York's art critics were unprepared for what they saw in O'Keeffe's art in 1923, and when Stieglitz appeared in the galleries to offer his commentary on her work—as he did daily during the course of the exhibition—they came to listen. "The opinions of Stieglitz are not to be taken lightly," wrote Helen Appleton Read in the *Brooklyn Daily Eagle.* Both men and women wrote about the show, and to a person they discussed O'Keeffe's art in the Freudian terms that had been put forth by Stieglitz and Hartley. Read questioned whether "the average intelligentsia would 'get'" O'Keeffe's abstractions without the benefit of Stieglitz's interpretive rhetoric or Hartley's essay in the exhibition brochure. "The shameless naked statements are too veiled," Read said, to be easily understood.[16]

Read and others might have easily looked back to the musical correlation offered up a few years earlier by critic William Murrell Fisher. His sensitive commentary about O'Keeffe's first abstract drawings (previously exhibited at 291 in 1917) had been preserved in the pages of Stieglitz's journal, *Camera Work.* "Of all things earthly it is only in music," Fisher had said, "that one finds any analogy to the emotional content of these drawings, to the gigantic swirling rhythms and the exquisite tenderness so powerfully and sensitively rendered."[17] Yet, Read—and all the other critics—turned instead to Stieglitz and Hartley, believing these two men understood something more deeply psychological about the enigmatic woman artist.

O'Keeffe retreated emotionally and artistically from what Stieglitz had wrought. After the 1923 show, her paintings became thoroughly grounded in things, as if she intended that there would be no question as to the source of her art in nature and the external world. O'Keeffe scholar Barbara Buhler Lynes has shown that of the fifty-seven abstractions included in the 1923 show, most were secreted away by O'Keeffe afterward and not shown again for decades.[18] *Music—Pink and Blue No. 1,* the canvas that had come to define O'Keeffe in Stieglitz's view, was not shown again until 1970, at the first major retrospective of her work at the Whitney Museum of American Art, New York. In 1974 O'Keeffe sold *Music—Pink and Blue No. 1* to the collector Barney Ebsworth. She might have kept the painting close at hand in those intervening years because she recognized its singular importance in her body of work. But to counter Stieglitz's promotion of her art as intensely self-referential, she also may have deliberately suppressed it in order to redefine herself as a painter, not of feelings, but of things.

A NEW YORK CHOP SUEY RESTAURANT, 1929

In artist Edward Hopper's time, few things said New York like chop suey. The dish became thoroughly connected with the city in the first decades of the twentieth century and symbolized then, much more than it does now, the cultural confluences that came to define modern Manhattan.

Chop suey has its source in a bit of New York folklore. It reportedly was a visit to New York in 1896 by General Li Hongzhang that led to the invention of the dish. The general was on an important ambassadorial mission to raise America's consciousness about the Chinese people. Although a guest at the elegant Waldorf Hotel, he refused to eat American food and asked that his own staff prepare his meals. The cooks, unable to obtain genuine Chinese ingredients anywhere in Manhattan, improvised a dish of stir-fried meat and vegetables mixed with steamed rice—*zasui* was the term for it in Mandarin, but "chop suey" is what Americans called it.[19]

In almost no time chop suey was playing an important part in the city's popular culture. By 1903 lively chop suey restaurant–supper clubs had become synonymous with New York nightlife. New Yorkers danced to tunes from a player piano and ate heaping platters of chop suey or, if they were feeling less adventurous, plain old American fare like boiled ham or chicken. Enterprising Chinese cooks established chop suey restaurants to appeal to strictly American taste, and the eateries became wildly popular among working-class New Yorkers as places for a gay time and a cheap meal. A chop suey restaurant was, as one writer pointed out, "an alleviating alternative to the young man who could not afford to act as host to a companion, however fair, at a supper club. The cover charge at a club can . . . easily cover the cost of Chinese comestibles for two, with a sufficient surplus for lunch for a week."[20] Chop suey restaurants were found all across the city, especially in areas that catered to the after-theater crowd. The *New York Times* reported in 1903 that more than one hundred chop suey places had sprung up in just a few months across a large swath of Manhattan.[21]

Chop suey restaurants had a particular look and character. These unpretentious places were located on the upper floors of old commercial brownstones. A large, flashy "chop suey" sign, extending prominently out from a building's facade, identified the restaurant to passersby on the street below. Many were open for lunch, but all catered, at least initially, to a late-night crowd, remaining open as late as 2:00 A.M. Inside, the restaurants might be decorated with bright, patterned wallpaper and festive hanging lanterns and paper parasols, but in the service of food, they were pictures of orderliness.

Because chop suey restaurants appealed to a widely diverse clientele—Irish Catholics, European Jews, and blacks from Harlem—their dining rooms provided a snapshot of modern New York. And as the city changed, the evolution in its social makeup and economic condition was necessarily reflected in the character of its chop suey eateries. By the end of 1925, Bertram Reinitz, a popular social commentator and columnist for the *New York Times*, saw chop suey as a major indicator of cultural transformation. Reflecting on the rapid and dramatic physical and social changes, for better or worse, that his beloved city had seen in the previous months, Reinitz pointed to chop suey as providing the most obvious sign of an all-important if subtle economic shift. "Chop suey," he declared, had suddenly assumed, a "new role." It had been "promoted to a prominent place in the mid-day menu of the metropolis." That might seem a small thing, but it reflected a new and significant economic reality. Chop suey was no longer merely an entertainment but was now "a staple . . . vigorously vying with sandwiches and salad as the noontime nourishment of the young women typists and telephonists of John, Dey and Fulton Streets." Chop suey restaurants, now respectable and omnipresent on the local scene, delivered an essential commodity to working-class New Yorkers, especially the young, single women who had moved into the city's labor force in unprecedented numbers. To them, Reinitz observed, Chinatown was "not an intriguing bit of transplanted Orient. It is simply a good place to eat."[22] The working girls who frequented chop suey restaurants at noontime would have been attracted to the distinctive calm and orderliness of these eateries. They must have seemed peaceful oases to harried shop girls and secretaries, and one can imagine the dining rooms filled with the soft tones of quiet conversations between girlfriends.

Around the time Reinitz published his *Times* piece, Edward Hopper (1882–1967) and his wife, the painter Josephine Nivison Hopper, were frequenting a chop suey restaurant uptown at Columbus Circle, on the west side, not far from his Fifth Avenue dealer, Rehn Gallery, and other art galleries.[23] A close observer of men and women in the quotidian aspects of urban life, Hopper would have been keenly sensitive to the human stories played out within the lunchtime routine of the chop suey restaurant.

The 1929 picture Hopper made is ambiguous enough in its limited action to invite speculation as to its meaning. Yet Hopper specifically titled the work *Chop Suey* (plate 172), firmly grounding the scene in a place known to New Yorkers for the distinctive customs of its hosts and the character of its clientele. The silent individual dramas of two young couples—a pair of smartly dressed girls at center and, at far left, a man dining with a young woman—are made meaningful by being situated in this particular place.

Some painters might favor a Chinese restaurant for its picturesqueness, but Hopper painted an austere place, focusing on the interaction of working girls over a pot of tea. The action that we do not see is as important to the mood of the painting as the view

172 Edward Hopper
American, 1882–1967
Chop Suey, 1929
oil on canvas, 32 × 38 in.
The Barney A. Ebsworth Collection, T97.28

Hopper does give us. Here is a place where no-nonsense Chinese waiters, who rarely spoke and carefully observed the protocol of the dining room, offered diners a standard fare—a strange hybrid Chinese-American concoction that was somehow a staple of New York life. The story of a chop suey restaurant encompassed the intersecting lives of its working-class hosts and guests, both of whom were new, modern urban types who had assumed identities far removed from their traditional roles. *Chop Suey* reminds us that Hopper's modern sensibility lay in his profound sensitivity to America as a culture in flux, the impact of which he measured in individual psychological terms.

YWCA, 144 WEST 138TH STREET, FEBRUARY 14, 1935

On February 14, 1935, the sculptor Augusta Savage (1892–1962) presented an exhibition of some 150 paintings and sculpture created by the scores of adult students she had been nurturing at the Harlem Art Workshop. Affiliated with the State University of New York adult education division, the workshop offered one of the largest free art instruction programs in the city of New York. Savage, who had been dedicated to teaching art in Harlem for years before she became director of the workshop in 1933, was an eloquent spokesperson for the vitality of art making in Harlem. Within a year of the workshop's founding, the classes, held at the Schomberg Center of the 135th Street branch of the New York Public Library, were so popular that Savage was forced to turn away applicants. The exhibition, she hoped, would help her make a case for moving the school to larger quarters, perhaps to the YWCA, which was then accommodating more than three thousand adult students in its trade classes.[24]

The large size of the student show demonstrated the community's enthusiasm for the school's offerings and Savage's pride in what the relatively young program had already accomplished. The character of the student work reflected something more about the workshop, too. These students, among the very first to have been trained in art within Harlem, were the first to gain the benefits of the Harlem Renaissance of the 1920s. Its writers and social theorists had galvanized the community around the issue of its distinct African-American cultural identity, and the art training at the workshop was part of a broader social and educational agenda for asserting the vitality of that culture. The teaching of art at the Harlem Art Workshop was not about artistic currents; rather, students were encouraged to use art to explore their own lives as black people living in the most modern American city, New York.

Savage was admired by her students as much for her stature within the art world as for her teaching. She had trained with the eminent academic sculptor Hermon Atkins MacNeil when he was head of the National Sculpture Society, and she had assisted MacNeil in his studio on major public sculpture projects. Having already earned a reputation as a skillful modeler of portraits in clay, she studied in Paris from 1929 to 1932, thanks to a fellowship awarded by the Julius Rosenwald Fund, established by a Chicago philanthropist for the advancement of African Americans. In 1934 she was the first African American to be elected to membership in the National Association of Women Painters and Sculptors. To young men and women in Harlem, Savage embodied the very idea of individual self-determination and of the viability of a life in art, a milieu then dominated by white men. "By looking at her, I understood that I could be an artist if I wanted to be," recalled Gwendolyn Knight Lawrence, who studied with Savage for some five years in the 1930s.[25]

Savage had established the theme for the student show as Harlem life. There were lively genre scenes included, but portraits figured prominently among the works, an indication of Savage's influence. Some of these were character studies of anonymous men and women, but many were of Harlem luminaries who would have been recognized by both black and white viewers as important figures not just in Harlem but in modern culture: the stage actress and director Rose McLendon; Mrs. Sadie Warren Davis, owner of the important black newspaper the *Amsterdam News*; Leigh Whipper, pictured by many of the student artists in his Broadway roles as Porgy or as the Stevedore; and everyone's favorite, the character actor J. Mardo Brown, the tiny drum major in *Showboat*, who was the subject of several pictures.

Augusta Savage showed her own work in the exhibition, lending an air of seriousness to the enterprise and establishing the high standard by which the student work was to be judged. Savage's piece, a head study of her young student and friend Gwendolyn Knight (plate 173 and fig. 3) had been first modeled in clay, then cast in plaster, and painted dark brown to emulate bronze. Although her training had been solidly in the classical tradition, Savage invested her work with a particular feeling for individualization. Thus the portrait head of Knight is clearly individualized, even with the classical elegance of its frontality, its simulation of bronze, its nonspecific gaze, and its gravitas; Knight's upswept hair itself recalls a classical Greek chignon. Knight was a stunning beauty, tall and graceful, but it was her reserve, her thoughtfulness and introspection, that truly impressed her friends. She was muse to more than one artist: Henry Bannarn made a pencil portrait of Knight at this same time, when both were at the Harlem Art Workshop; and Jacob Lawrence, whom she married in 1941, considered Knight his most trusted critic.[26]

In promoting African-American cultural identity, Savage pointed to the infinite diversity of that culture. Her interest was in individuals, not types. Gwendolyn Knight embodied that diversity

(opposite)
173 **Augusta Savage**
American, 1892–1962
Gwendolyn Knight, 1934–35
painted plaster, 18½ × 8½ × 9 in.
Gift of Gwendolyn Knight Lawrence, 2006.86

Figure 3. Augusta Savage with her portrait head of
Gwendolyn Knight, from the *New York Herald Tribune*,
February 15, 1935

especially well: born in Barbados of a white father and a black mother, she was the rare child of an interracial marriage to live comfortably in both worlds, black and white. Savage knew that the example of Knight's life challenged racial structures.

Only four weeks after the closing of Savage's expansive exhibition, Harlem erupted into massive, deadly violence. On March 19, 1935, rioting broke out when a young shoplifter was murdered by white police, unleashing a torrent of rage against all the inequities suffered by blacks in Harlem and in a city gripped by severe economic depression. The so-called Harlem Race Riot was a defining moment for the country, the city of New York, the community of Harlem, and Harlem's cultural leaders. Racism inherent in New Deal initiatives was suddenly exposed, for while other regions of the country, and other parts of New York City, were being lifted up by government support, Harlem was essentially shut out of economic recovery programs. For her part, with the riot Augusta Savage became increasingly politically active. She cofounded with artist Charles Alston and historian Arthur Schomburg the Harlem Artists Guild, a union of black artists dedicated to the economic and social needs of African Americans. In 1936 Savage was appointed to

a supervisory position within the Fine Arts Program of the New Deal's Works Progress Administration (WPA) and became a new, strong voice for African Americans, who were now entering the program in large numbers. The guild's work led that same year to the creation of the Harlem Community Art Center, an outgrowth of the Harlem Art Workshop, now under the auspices of the WPA. Savage was made its first director. It was there, under Savage's progressive leadership, that such artists as Jacob Lawrence, Norman Lewis, and Robert Blackburn—some of the most renowned African Americans in American art between the world wars—received their training and set a course for their respective careers.

New York has long stood as the art capital of the United States, the place that tests the mettle of this country's artists. The stories behind the early twentieth-century American works that have recently come to the Seattle Art Museum are as individual as the artists themselves. These particular New York episodes, as we have seen, in almost every instance coincided with a defining moment in an artist's career. Each in its way reflects the power of New York as a place for artists to live, learn, and work.

NOTES
1. "Around the Bulletin Boards," *New York Times*, November 4, 1903.
2. "Some Pastels by Shinn," *New York Times*, March 12, 1904.
3. Patrick Devlin, *Too Proud to Fight: Woodrow Wilson's Neutrality* (New York: Oxford University Press, 1975), 284.
4. "New York Ready for Big Parade," *New York Times*, May 13, 1916.
5. Hartley to Stieglitz, undated [week of May 18, 1913], in James Timothy Voorhies, ed., *My Dear Stieglitz: Letters of Marsden Hartley and Alfred Stieglitz, 1912–1915* (Columbia: University of South Carolina Press, 2002), 76.
6. Hartley to Stieglitz, October 23, 1914; ibid., 164.
7. Hartley to Stieglitz, undated [March 15, 1915]; ibid., 183.
8. Hartley to Stieglitz, October 29, 1914; ibid., 166.
9. Hartley's introduction survives in Stieglitz's *Camera Work*, no. 48 (October 1916): 12.
10. O'Keeffe to Kennerley, undated [fall 1922], reproduced in Jack Cowart, Juan Hamilton, and Sarah Greenough, *Georgia O'Keeffe: Art and Letters* (New York: New York Graphic Society Books, 1987), 172.
11. Henry McBride, "O'Keeffe at the Museum," *New York Sun*, May 18, 1946; quoted in Sarah Greenough, "Georgia O'Keeffe: A Flight to the Spirit," in Sarah Greenough et al., *Modern Art and America: Alfred Stieglitz and His New York Galleries* (Boston: Bulfinch Press for the National Gallery of Art, 2000), 450.

12. Marsden Hartley, *Adventures in the Arts: Informal Chapters on Painters, Vaudeville, and Poets* (New York: Boni and Liveright, 1921), 116.
13. Paul Rosenfeld, "American Painting," *The Dial* 71 (December 1921), 666–70, reprinted in Barbara Buhler Lynes, *O'Keeffe, Stieglitz, and the Critics, 1916–1929* (Chicago: University of Chicago Press, 1989), 171 (hereafter cited as Lynes).
14. O'Keeffe, in an interview with critic Grace Glueck, in the *New York Times*, October 18, 1970; quoted in Lynes, 68.
15. Georgia O'Keeffe, *Georgia O'Keeffe* (New York: Viking Press, 1976), opposite plate 14.
16. Helen Appleton Read, "Georgia O'Keeffe's Show an Emotional Escape," *Brooklyn Daily Eagle*, February 11, 1923; reprinted in Lynes, 191.
17. William Murrell Fisher, "The Georgia O'Keeffe Drawings and Paintings at 291," *Camera Work*, nos. 49–50 (June 1917): 5; reprinted in Lynes, 169.
18. See Barbara Buhler Lynes with Russell Bowman, *O'Keeffe's O'Keeffes: The Artist's Collection* (New York: Thames and Hudson, 2001), 58.
19. See J. A. G. Roberts, *China to Chinatown: Chinese Food in the West* (London: Reaktion Books, 2002), 138–39.

20. Betram Reinitz, "Chop Suey's New Role," *New York Times*, December 27, 1925.
21. "Chop Suey Resorts: Chinese Dish Now Served in Many Parts of the City," *New York Times*, November 15, 1903.
22. Reinitz, "Chop Suey's New Role."
23. Gail Levin, *Edward Hopper: An Intimate Biography* (New York: Alfred A. Knopf, 1995), 221.
24. Augusta Savage, as represented in a lengthy press piece, "Exhibition of Negro Art at Adult Education Project in Harlem YWCA," *New York Herald Tribune*, February 15, 1935. I am grateful to Daniel Schulman for sharing this newspaper article with me.
25. Gwendolyn Knight Lawrence, quoted in Sheryl Conkelton, "Gwendolyn Knight: A Life in Art," in *Never Late for Heaven: The Art of Gwen Knight* (Seattle: University of Washington Press for the Tacoma Art Museum, 2003), 23.
26. The Bannarn drawing is in the collection of the Seattle Art Museum.

Patricia Junker

The Seattle Art Museum and the Northwest School

174 Imogen Cunningham
American, 1883–1976
Morris Graves and Imogen in His Garden, 1973
gelatin silver print (estate print by Rondel Partridge, 1983),
8⅜ × 7⅜ in.
Gift of the Marshall and Helen Hatch Collection, in honor of
the 75th Anniversary of the Seattle Art Museum, 2005.142

In his annual report for the year 1935, Seattle Art Museum director Richard E. Fuller articulated for the first time his highest ambitions for the city's new museum: "One of the major functions of an art museum is the encouragement of creative talent in the field of art. Our desire to stimulate local talent has caused us to favor the purchase of their work." He went on, "I hope that this encouragement may assist in the eventual achievement of the national prominence to which some of them give promise."[1] Fuller's support of local artists proved to be well placed and prescient. The artists he enthusiastically nurtured did indeed achieve national prominence, and by their fame they in turn established Seattle as a place to serve the artistic imagination.

From the very beginning Fuller made the Seattle Art Museum a gathering place for the region's artistic vanguard. He warmly embraced those artists who shared his own uncommon vision, finding inspiration in the Asian art collection that Fuller was passionately building. His closest friends became Mark Tobey, Morris Graves, Kenneth Callahan, and Guy Anderson, artists who would most famously come to represent in the national art press the distinctly mystic painters of the Pacific Northwest.

Fuller, through the Seattle Art Museum, played a significant part, particularly in the late 1930s and early 1940s, in nurturing the extraordinary synergistic relationships among these four artists. He regularly offered exhibitions to showcase their latest work. He made purchases from these shows and encouraged others in Seattle to do the same, thereby helping to sustain them, he believed, in what was at the time an artistic outpost. Mark Tobey was hired by Fuller to teach art classes in the galleries. Kenneth Callahan became Fuller's assistant director. Morris Graves and Guy Anderson were both given museum jobs as acts of kindness on Fuller's part. One imagines that the museum brought these artists together in ways that would not have been possible without it. Surely the museum was a catalyst for what Callahan would later describe as the group's all-inspiring "prolonged discussions of the position of man and the artist in today's world." Callahan, perhaps thinking specifically of the new, central place of the museum in the region's art life at the time, claimed that the 1930s and early 1940s were for Seattle's artists a time of unprecedented aesthetic awakening and sustained creative exchange, and that this more than anything was the basis for commonly held aesthetic ideals among so many of them. "Over a period of some fourteen years," Callahan wrote in 1946, Seattle's artists "have mulled over such questions as the interrelation of man

212

and nature, the infinite, Picasso and cubism, Chinese painting, and Oriental and Christian philosophies. These irregular but consistent talks are one of the bases for a present major trend in the art of the Pacific Northwest region."[2]

The expanding world view of Pacific Northwest artists coincided with tragic political upheavals in Europe, against which the Seattle Art Museum, with its collections of Asian antiquities, must have seemed to stand as a kind of monument to enduring civilizations and alternative ideals. "The rise of fascism in Europe and Asia directed the artists' thoughts to problems of humanity and its fate under political direction," Callahan explained. "As world conditions became increasingly complicated and war spread over the world, the Northwest artists began to question the old ironclad conceptions. Why, one wondered, should America persist in looking to Europe for cultural guidance, turning its back on the Pacific and the Orient?"

175 **Morris Graves**
American, 1910–2001
Millennium Light, 1933–34
oil on canvas, 39 × 40 in.
Promised gift of the Marshall and Helen Hatch Collection,
in honor of the 75th Anniversary of the Seattle Art Museum,
T2001.144.1

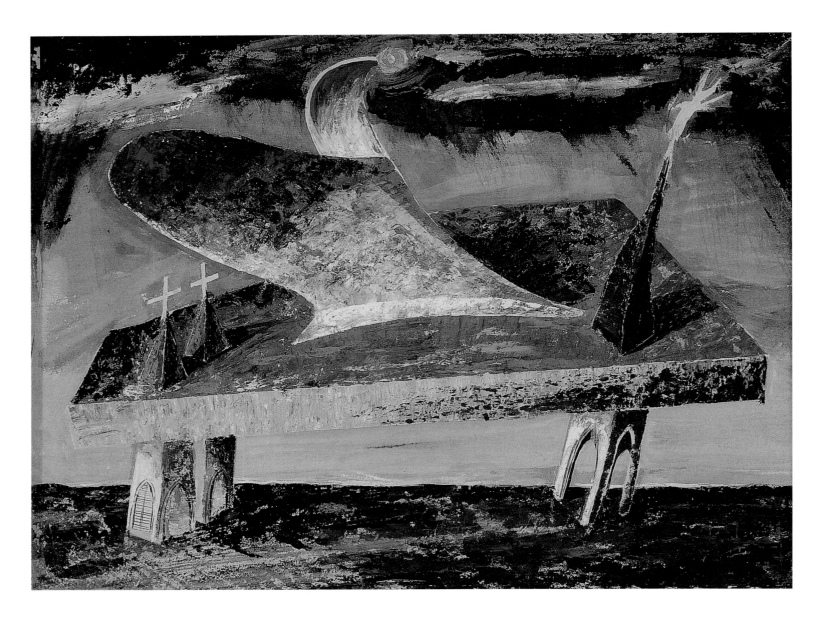

176 **Morris Graves**
American, 1910–2001
Altar, 1937
gouache on paper, 12 × 16 in.
Promised gift of the Marshall and Helen Hatch Collection,
in honor of the 75th Anniversary of the Seattle Art Museum,
T2005.108.23

Callahan made the claim that Pacific Northwest artists "had long concerned themselves instead with the ancient culture of the East, which had produced magnificent sculpture, beautiful Sung paintings, and great philosophies. Thus they decided that while the artist on the West Coast must look across America to New York and farther still to Europe, he must also direct his gaze across the Pacific to find and understand Asia directly from its source."[3] For those Seattle artists who did not have contact directly with Asian cultures, the collections at the Seattle Art Museum helped to make assimilation of Asian ideas possible.

After Fuller's tenure, key Seattle Art Museum benefactors made sure that the intertwined histories of the museum and the city's artists would be preserved in the institution's collections. The efforts of trustee John Hauberg and his wife Anne Gould Hauberg were honored when Mark Tobey, to whom they were especially close, bequeathed his estate to the museum in 1976.

But it was museum trustee Marshall Hatch and his wife, Helen, who, in their quiet way, built a collection that perhaps best defined the long period of artistic activity in Seattle that gave rise to the celebrated Northwest School. The Hatches built an extensive collection that truly reflects all the key figures who made Seattle an especially

vital art environment in these years, and not just the four artists—
Tobey, Graves, Callahan, and Anderson—made famous by *Life* magazine in 1953 through its feature, "Mystic Painters of the Northwest."[4]
The Hatches were close to many of the artists—especially to Morris
Graves, but also to Leo Kenney, George Tsutakawa, and others. They
collected from a deep understanding of each artist's own particular affinities, ambitions, temperament, and abilities. They also collected in depth, charting the high points of each individual artist's
career. Finally, they collected with the intention of creating what
would one day be a public collection, a defining historical collection
of Northwest art—a collection for the Seattle Art Museum.

177 **Mark Tobey**
American, 1890–1976
The Retreat of the Friend, 1947
tempera on board, 10 × 14½ in.
Promised gift of the Marshall and Helen Hatch Collection,
in honor of the 75th Anniversary of the Seattle Art Museum,
T2002.7.2

NOTES
1. Richard E. Fuller, "Report of the President and Director for the
Year 1935," in *Seattle Art Museum Annual Report for 1935* (1935), 506.
2. Kenneth Callahan, "Pacific Northwest," *Art News* 45, no. 5 (July
1946): 24.
3. Ibid.
4. [Dorothy Seiberling], "Mystic Painters of the Northwest," *Life*
(September 28, 1953): 84–89.

Chronology of the Seattle Art Museum

The museum opened up worlds beyond Seattle to the visiting public. A 1933 cartoon, published in the *Seattle Times*, captures the reaction of Seattleites to this new institution.

"The purpose . . . is to raise the artistic taste, to broaden the knowledge and appreciation of the products of both the past and the present, and to stimulate the creative genius of the artist. If in so doing the museum renders some of the ideals of other nations more intelligible to the general public, it, in a small measure, combats the present spirit of national intolerance that now besets the world, and brings recognition to our common heritage of creative achievements in the field of art, unprejudiced by the race or creed of their creators."

—Dr. Richard E. Fuller, 1939 annual report
of the Seattle Art Museum

1906 The Seattle Fine Arts Society is founded, only two years after the first exhibition of the Society of Seattle Artists is held. The annual exhibition continues for more than seven decades, until 1976.

1928 The Seattle Fine Arts Society is renamed the Art Institute of Seattle and continues its long search for permanent space while staging exhibitions in various locations.

1931 Dr. Richard E. Fuller, president of the Art Institute of Seattle, and his mother, Mrs. Eugene (Margaret MacTavish) Fuller, donate $250,000 to build a public museum. In the midst of the Depression, this building project brings jobs to the city. (The museum opens its doors the year President Franklin D. Roosevelt initiates his New Deal.) In return, the city of Seattle allows the museum to stand in Volunteer Park and assumes ownership of the building, in a plan similar to the precedent of the Metropolitan Museum of Art in New York City. The Fullers also announce plans to donate their collection to the new museum.

1933 The Seattle Art Museum—an art deco building, designed by architects Carl F. Gould and Charles Bebb—opens to the public. Richard Fuller never receives a salary in his forty years as director of the museum ("Please do not infer from the fact that I am acting in that capacity that I consider myself to be ideal for the job," he wrote in the museum's 1933 annual report). He envisions the museum

Without original European paintings in the collection, in the 1930s the museum acquires and displays a collection of five hundred color reproductions. Not until the 1950s is the museum able to mount exhibitions in this area without relying on facsimiles.

providing three things to the Seattle community: recreation, inspiration, and education.

1933 The museum's opening exhibitions include American paintings; oil paintings by Seattle artists; the greatest European paintings from the thirteenth to twentieth century, in facsimile; fifteenth- to twentieth-century European and American prints; contemporary American sculpture; the paintings of Seattle artist Kenjiro Nomura; and works by Seattle public school students.

1933 The museum's permanent collection consists of 1,926 works of art, including Chinese, Japanese, Korean, and Southeast Asian art from the Fuller collection, Classical glass, American prints, Northwest modern art, and reproductions of European old and modern master paintings.

1933 Three hundred thousand people visit the Seattle Art Museum in its first six months

1937 Kenneth Callahan, who had been assistant director since the museum's opening in 1933, is appointed the museum's first curator. His duties include registration, tracking objects, and installing art. A "struggling writer," he contributes a regular arts column to the *Seattle Times* starting in 1933. Callahan retires from the museum in 1953 to focus on painting.

1941 SAM has the first of four female directors (or acting directors). Mrs. Thomas D. (Emma Baillargeon) Stimson, vice-president of the board, takes on the role of acting director as Dr. Fuller serves in the Army Specialist Corps for the second half of the year.

1941–42 War brings the threat of danger to Seattle. 650 important works from the collection are removed from Seattle and stored in Denver for safe-keeping.

1944 For more than ten years, exhibitions had focused on Asian and European masterpieces (the European mainly in reproduction). In 1944 the museum presents a traveling exhibition of original works of abstract and surrealist art. Dr. Fuller explained this as a "controversial field . . . presented to permit our public and artists to become acquainted with some of the leading exponents of this rather esoteric form of art." (1944 annual report)

1944 *India, Its Achievements of the Past and Present:* This traveling exhibition—organized by the British Information Services and SAM—is the largest and by far the most comprehensive exhibition yet held at SAM. This look at the history of South Asian art is augmented by a photography exhibition and images illustrating British home rule in India.

India, Its Achievements of the Past and Present (1944) is so well received that more than thirty of the works loaned to the show are purchased by the museum and today remain on view in the Fuller Garden Court of the Seattle Asian Art Museum.

The successful partnership of the *Official Japanese Exhibition of Painting and Sculpture* (1953) comes fewer than ten years after the end of World War II, when Seattle so feared Japanese attack that artworks were evacuated from the city.

Tawaraya Sōtatsu (Japanese, 1576–1643) and Hon'ami Kōetsu (Japanese, 1558–1637), detail from *Poem Scroll with Deer*, 1610s, handscroll, ink, gold, and silver on paper, 13½ × 410¼ in. (overall). Gift of Mrs. Donald E. Frederick, 51.127.

1948 Sherman Lee joins the museum as assistant director. This "outstanding scholar of art history both in the Oriental and Occidental fields," according to Dr. Fuller, remains in this post until 1952. During his time at SAM, he initiates the gift of the Samuel H. Kress Collection (see 1952 and 1954), oversees publication of the first museum handbook and various catalogues, and himself publishes articles on numerous objects in the collection. Perhaps the most notable of the acquisitions spearheaded by Lee is the Japanese *Poem Scroll with Deer* (the Deer Scroll).

1952 The Samuel H. Kress Foundation loans twenty-three European paintings and sculptures to SAM, all of which are installed in a single gallery. Rush Kress of the foundation complains to a Seattle friend, "The hanging arrangement looks like an accumulation of three of four months' work on top of your desk." The foundation threatens to cancel the loan unless the museum creates more space for the collection.

1953 *Official Japanese Exhibition of Painting and Sculpture:* For the first time, Seattle is invited to participate in a prestigious international exhibition, and as a result the museum receives more publicity than ever before.

1953 Museum cofounder Margaret E. Fuller dies. She leaves the museum the largest bequest of art and funds in its twenty-year history. The first purchase—a rare, black Delft plate—using the

Though mainly interested in Asian art, Dr. Fuller oversaw the installation of the museum's Kress Collection when the paintings first arrived in 1954.

Margaret E. Fuller Purchase Fund is made in 1954. More than fifty years later, this endowment continues to fund museum acquisitions such as *Bird in Space*, by British artist Simon Starling, added to the collection in 2007.

1954 A newly constructed gallery dedicated to the Kress Collection opens. The Kress Foundation is so pleased with this installation that it lends ten additional works of art. One painting had been donated by the foundation in 1937; in 1961 the collection of thirty-five works is officially given to the museum.

1954 *Caravaggio and the Tenebrosi:* The museum's first major old master show, organized by Sherman Lee while at SAM, opens. The lenders to this ambitious exhibition include seven museums and three private art dealers from New York.

1958 Silver-anniversary exhibitions "emphasize the wealth of our collection after 25 years . . . successive exhibitions featuring our historical coverage of the creative art of successive regions and periods, as well as our indebtedness to our major donors" (Director Richard E. Fuller, 1958 annual report).

1958 One hundred forty-four objects from thirty-eight sources (including Peggy Guggenheim) are acquired in the museum's twenty-fifth year; the Silver Anniversary Fund and specific anniversary gifts bring more than a dozen new acquisitions in the areas of modern, Asian, European, and ancient Mediterranean art.

1959 *Paintings and Drawings by Vincent van Gogh:* Drawn from the private collection of Van Gogh's nephew, this spring show sets attendance records with 126,110 visitors.

1959 *Mark Tobey Retrospective:* In celebration of the Northwest master, the exhibition of 224 objects, organized by SAM, tours museums along the West Coast (Portland, Colorado Springs, Pasadena, and San Francisco).

1961 *18th-century porcelain:* The museum's first porcelain installation of scale is organized by honorary curator Mrs. William L. Harnan. SAM's small collection of porcelain is augmented by the private collections of members of the Seattle Ceramic Society.

1962 In conjunction with the Seattle World's Fair (the Century 21 Exposition), highlights of the museum's ancient Asian collections and Mark Tobey works are installed in the fair's Fine Arts Pavilion. Concurrently, the finest items in SAM's collection are placed on view at the museum in Volunteer Park.

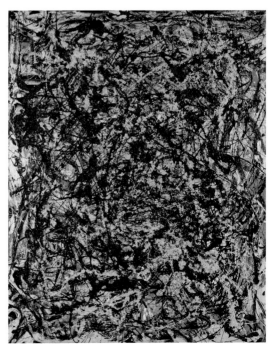

Jackson Pollock (American, 1912–1956), *Sea Change,* 1947, oil and pebbles on canvas, 57⅞ × 44⅛ in. Gift of Signora Peggy Guggenheim, 58.55.

The Art of the Ancient East was one of SAM's contributions to the World's Fair of 1962.

1963 After the World's Fair ends, the UK Pavilion is converted into a center for "all-year art activity" for the museum. The space is used, mainly for modern art exhibitions and projects, until 1987.

1964 The Contemporary Art Council (CAC) is founded, giving those in the community committed to emerging art and artists a voice in museum programming and acquisitions.

1968 The museum's curatorial division is officially founded with the hiring of Henry Trubner, curator of Asiatic art.

1969 The National Council on the Arts (later the National Endowment for the Arts, NEA), the Seattle Foundation (which Dr. Fuller helped to found), the city of Seattle, and Richard Fuller finance the acquisition and installation of Isamu Noguchi's *Black Sun* in front of the Seattle Art Museum in Volunteer Park. Part of the city's collection of public art, it is the NEA's first commission in Seattle.

1973 Upon the fortieth anniversary of the Seattle Art Museum, the permanent collection numbers more than ten thousand objects spanning five thousand years and six continents.

1973 Founding director Dr. Fuller retires. The Eugene Fuller Memorial Collection—given over the course of forty years by Fuller and his mother—now numbers more than 6,600 objects. The Fuller collection remains the core of SAM's holdings.

1973 The City of Seattle institutes one of the country's first percent-for-art programs. By requiring city capital improvement projects to dedicate 1 percent of total funds toward commissioning, purchasing, or installing art, more than 3,200 works of public art have been sited in Seattle, including Jonathan Borofsky's *Hammering Man*, installed in front of the Seattle Art Museum Downtown in 1992.

1974 Willis Woods becomes director. He remains at the Seattle Art Museum until 1978, when illness forces his resignation. At that time, Bagley Wright, president of the board of trustees, becomes interim director.

1974 The museum hosts its first retrospective of the work of American master Jacob Lawrence. Lawrence and his wife, Gwendolyn Knight Lawrence, who had moved to Seattle in 1970, live and work here for the next thirty years.

1974 The Asian Art Council (AAC) is founded.

1974 The independent Pacific Northwest Arts Center merges with the museum to create the Pacific Northwest Arts Council

In honor of the museum's fortieth anniversary in 1973, the museum's exterior is decorated with forty red birthday candles, a feat duplicated on the museum's "birthday" cake.

Exhibition activity at the Pavilion ramps up after the founding of the Modern Art Department in 1975. In 1976 Museum Week celebrations include a visit from Andy Warhol, concurrent with an exhibition of Warhol portraits, including one of SAM trustee Jane Lang Davis.

(PNAC). The council's focus is on modern and contemporary art of this region.

1975 The modern art department is founded with Charles Cowles as curator and Sarah Clark as assistant curator. Initially the department is funded by the CAC and PNAC.

1975–76 The museum begins charging public admission, a change approved by a City Council vote in April 1975.

1976 The Ethnic Arts Council (EAC) is founded.

1976 Martha and Henry Isaacson, who began donating European porcelain to the museum in the mid-1950s, give the majority of their collection to SAM.

1976–78 SAM undertakes three years of planning as a venue for the ambitious *Treasures of Tutankhamun*. SAM is awarded support from the National Endowment for the Humanities to fund educational outreach, additional staff, a lecture series, and a six-state slide lecture program. "When the planning for this exhibition was in its initial stages, no one truly comprehended the enormity of the project. . . . The exhibition had become a phenomenon" (Director Willis F. Woods, July–August 1978 museum newsletter).

1977–78 A $21 million capital campaign is undertaken to build a new downtown museum at Westlake Mall.

1977–78 The curatorial division grows with the hiring of William Rathbun to oversee Japanese art.

1977–78 The museum employs seventy-one staff members, thirty-one solely dedicated to *Tut*; by comparison, a decade earlier the entire staff had numbered thirty. For the first time, a development officer is hired, a gift-processing program is created, and membership, grants, and publications departments are founded. By the opening of the Seattle Art Museum Downtown in the early 1990s, the staff will grow to nearly two hundred.

1977–78 Fifteen hundred volunteers are recruited for *Tut*; thirty outside organizations partner with SAM on programming; museum membership explodes to more than twenty thousand. Prior to opening the exhibition that will forever change the museum, Director Willis Woods wrote: "The museum is on the brink of presenting an exhibition which will draw unprecedented crowds, focusing public attention upon the museum in a way that it has never before experienced . . . the phenomenon we call 'Tut.'" (1977–78 annual report)

The Isaacson collection forms the core of the museum's European porcelain holdings, now celebrated in the Porcelain Room.

The inaugural publication of the Seattle Art Museum publications department is *Johsel Namkung: An Artist's View of Nature* (1978).

1978 *Treasures of Tutankhamun*: The first international blockbuster exhibition is held at Seattle Center in the Flag Pavilion.

1978—79 The ethnic art department is founded with the hiring of assistant curator Pamela McClusky. *Nubia: Africa in Antiquity* is the first exhibition of the new department.

1978—79 The Photography Council is founded.

1979 Arnold Jolles becomes director. He remains at SAM until 1986.

1980—81 The department of European and American decorative arts is founded with the hiring of assistant curator Julie Emerson.

1980—81 The Westlake Mall expansion is held up in court, and by 1982 the site is abandoned. Director Arnold Jolles remarks in the 1981 annual report: "Throughout the country, governmental agencies are shedding cultural responsibilities they can no longer pay for."

1980—81 The Decorative Arts Council (later the Decorative Arts and Paintings Council—DAPC) is founded.

1981 Part-bequest of the owner and part-gift of the Boeing Company, the Katherine White collection of 2,100 works comes to the museum. One of the most important private collections of African art in the world, the acquisition increases the permanent collection by 15 percent.

1.3 million visitors view the finest ancient Egyptian art during the four months *Treasures of Tutankhamun* is in Seattle in 1978. Exhibition preparator Chris Manojlovic encounters the exhibition's most famous work of art.

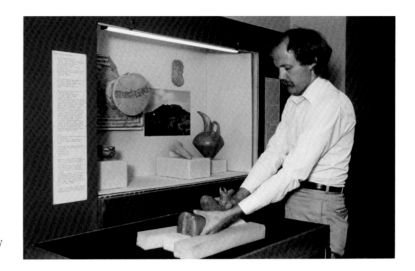

As part of the major curatorial initiatives that go into effect after *Tut*, exhibition space is returned to permanent collection installations in 1983. Exhibition designer Michael McCafferty installs works of ancient Near Eastern Art.

1982—84 The community marks the museum's fiftieth anniversary with 138 gifts of art from forty-three sources, plus numerous promised gifts. Several exhibitions are mounted to commemorate the occasion: *50 Years: A Legacy of Asian Art; Praise Poems: The Katherine White Collection; 200 Photographs from the Museum Collection;* and *The Anniversary Case* (a rotating installation highlighting small treasures from the collection).

1983—84 The museum acquires property downtown between First and Second Avenues, and University and Union Streets (the former JC Penney site), to bring to reality its long overdue expansion. The site is large enough to hold a new building and leave enough room for future expansion. Robert Venturi is appointed architect for the project.

1984 "The act of contributing to the richness of the collective human experience is at the very heart of what museums are all about. Museums are gathering places, places of discovery, places to find quiet, to contemplate, and to be inspired. They are our collective memory, our chronicle of human creativity, our window in the natural and physical world. This is what the new Seattle Art Museum is all about." (Langdon Simons, chairman of the board of trustees, 1984 annual report)

B View

TV-Radio
General News
Comics

Wednesday, January 8, 1975 The Seattle Times B 1

A preview of
primitive art

Guests came from as far away as New York and Los Angeles to attend a preview of primitive art objects from New York's Museum of Primitive Art yesterday evening at the Seattle Art Museum.

Tribal work from Africa, Oceania and the Pre-columbian Americas is included in the exhibit. It was organized by the Museum of Primitive Art, which was founded in 1957 by Nelson Rockefeller, and the American Federation of Arts.

The Seattle Art Museum is the first museum to host the traveling exhibition.

The exhibition features nearly 150 masks, vessels, blankets, ancestral figures and ceremonial objects. It opened to the public today and will remain on view through February 16.

Mrs. Katherine C. White of Los Angeles, trustee of the American Federation of Arts, studied a wood slit-drum head from Melanesia. She was accompanied on her visit here by 22 members of the Ethnic Arts Council of Los Angeles.

Katherine White had lived in Seattle only a short while before her untimely death in 1980. The acquisition of her collection immediately transforms SAM into an international destination for African art.

Robert Venturi unveils his model for the new downtown building to the press and public in 1987.

Jacob Lawrence and Gwendolyn Knight Lawrence, shown here in the galleries of the 1986 retrospective, maintained close ties to the museum throughout their thirty years in Seattle.

1986 *Jacob Lawrence: American Painter*: SAM organizes a major retrospective of Jacob Lawrence and publishes a catalogue to accompany the show, which travels to other major museums around the country.

1987 Jay Gates is named museum director (the head of the education division, Bonnie Pitman-Gelles, has been acting as interim director since 1986). He leads the institution through the expansion downtown, staying at SAM until 1993. This same year, he brings Patterson Sims to the museum, who oversees the curatorial division for more than eight years.

1989 Virginia and Bagley Wright donate their collection of nearly one hundred Japanese textiles. The Wrights first donated art to the collection in 1959 and have continued to do so through the seventy-fifth anniversary.

1990 The curatorial division expands as Steve Brown is hired as the new curator of Native American art and Chiyo Ishikawa founds the department of European painting. In 2007 Ishikawa leads the artistic program of the museum's expansion as deputy director of art.

1991 The original Seattle Art Museum in Volunteer Park closes to the public in the fall in preparation for the opening of the new downtown building. When the downtown museum opens in December, more than ten thousand visitors come through the building on the first day alone.

1991 The John H. Hauberg collection of Northwest Native art is given to SAM to celebrate the opening of the downtown museum. Collected over decades by the Pilchuck Glass School cofounder and former SAM board president and Ethnic Art Council president, the Hauberg collection is the basis of the museum's holdings in Native American art.

1992 *Dale Chihuly: Installations 1964–1992*: One of the most popular exhibitions ever presented in Seattle, the show draws huge crowds. Chihuly, a Pilchuck Glass School cofounder, first exhibited at SAM in 1977. For the 1992 show, he creates the first installation of his Chandelier series.

The Chinese Ming-dynasty tomb guardians that for decades sat outside the Volunteer Park museum are moved to a new home inside the downtown museum in 1990.

Works of Northwest Coast Native American art from the Hauberg collection have been on view since the Seattle Art Museum's downtown building first opened in 1991.

1994 Mimi Gardner Neill (Gates) is named director of SAM. (Gail Joice, head of the museum services division, had taken on the role of interim director in 1993.) Mimi Gates remains director through the museum's seventy-fifth anniversary, leading the institution through its downtown expansion, Sculpture Park construction, Asian Art Museum renovations, dozens of special exhibitions, and thousands of new acquisitions.

1994 The Seattle Art Museum's original art deco building in Volunteer Park reopens to the public as the Seattle Asian Art Museum. This transformation realizes one of the primary visions for the museum by founder Richard E. Fuller as a public institution that showcases superb Asian art.

1997 *A Passion for Possession: Visitors Buy African Art*: Thousands of visitors participate in an innovative acquisition partnership. By popular vote, one of eight potential African art acquisitions is chosen for purchase. African-American artist Marita Dingus's *400 Men of African Descent* wins by a huge margin and enters the collection.

President Bill Clinton (here with SAM board president Faye Sarkowsky) convenes the Asia-Pacific Economic Cooperation summit in a longhouse on Blake Island in 1993. Leaders of thirteen countries bordering the Pacific attend the summit and an event held in the Seattle Asian Art Museum in Volunteer Park.

Mimi Gardner Gates (right) has continued her curatorial work since assuming the directorship of SAM, contributing to special exhibitions, delivering public lectures, and leading tours of the SAM collections. After Dr. Fuller, she is the longest-serving director in museum history.

Bill Gates and curator Chiyo Ishikawa discuss Leonardo da Vinci and his legacy in art and science with a group of students during the 1997 *Leonardo Lives* exhibition.

1997 *Leonardo Lives: The Codex Leicester and Leonardo da Vinci's Legacy of Art and Science:* This exhibition spotlights a codex in the collection of Bill and Melinda Gates—the only Leonardo manuscript in the United States and the last such manuscript in private hands in the world. 236,000 visitors, more than half of whom had never been to SAM, come to see the codex as well as Renaissance and contemporary works influenced by Leonardo.

1999 *Impressionism: Paintings Collected by European Museums:* The most extensive exhibition of Impressionist art to ever be shown in the Northwest draws even more visitors than *Leonardo Lives*, setting an attendance record for the downtown museum at more than 315,000.

1999 SAM and the Trust for Public Land raise $17 million for the purchase of the 6-acre Olympic Sculpture Park site. The former Union Oil of California (Unocal) site had been a contaminated brownfield prior to its purchase.

2000–2001 Marion Weiss and Michael Manfredi are chosen as achitects for the Olympic Sculpture Park. Jon and Mary Shirley donate Alexander Calder's *Eagle*, the first acquisition for the future Olympic Sculpture Park. Until the Sculpture Park is finished, *Eagle* rests in front of the Seattle Asian Art Museum.

More than 6,000 visitors celebrate the opening of the Seattle Asian Art Museum on August 13, 1994.

2001 The museum invests in the future of its collections by hiring Nicholas Dorman, a paintings conservator, to found the conservation department.

2001 The Christensen collection of African and Japanese art is donated to the museum; the collection had been on long-term loan.

2001 *Treasures from a Lost Civilization: Ancient Chinese Art from Sichuan:* This major exhibition is organized by Asian art curator Jay Xu with cooperation from the Chinese government. The objects in the show are lent by the People's Republic of China. Five years of preparation culminate in a tour of American and Canadian museums.

2001 The events of September 11 do not leave Seattle, or SAM, untouched: "The events of the past two months have strengthened our belief that art affirms life—promoting understanding and healing. We are thankful that during times of uncertainty, the Seattle Art Museum can be a place of refuge and inspiration, bringing forth the best of the human spirit." (Director Mimi Gates and board president Susan Brotman, 2001 annual report)

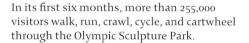

In its first six months, more than 255,000 visitors walk, run, crawl, cycle, and cartwheel through the Olympic Sculpture Park.

The largest work of art in the museum's collection, Cai Guo-Qiang's *Inopportune: Stage One* greets visitors to the "new" Seattle Art Museum.

2002 The innovative ContemporaryArtProject collective donates a collection of thirty-three works by twenty-eight international artists which had been formulated over three years with Seattle gallery owner Linda Farris.

2004 *Van Gogh to Mondrian: Modern Art from the Kröller-Müller Museum*: A testament to the enduring popularity of Vincent van Gogh and his art, a third major exhibition at SAM is dedicated to this artist.

2004 SAM's American art department, funded by a group of committed local collectors and enthusiasts, is founded with the hiring of curator Patricia Junker.

2007 The Olympic Sculpture Park opens in January as the third venue of the Seattle Art Museum.

2007 Closed for sixteen months, the Seattle Art Museum Downtown re-opens in May, with an expansion designed by Portland-based architect Brad Cloepfil and his firm, Allied Works Architects. Like the original museum opening in 1933, the inaugural installations are dedicated to the museum's collections.

2008 The Seattle Art Museum's seventy-fifth anniversary is celebrated with an ambitious art acquisition initiative, resulting in more than one thousand gifts (full, partial, pledged, intended) from more than seventy donors, bringing the permanent collection to nearly twenty-five thousand objects.

Photography Credits

Primary photography by Susan A. Cole
Additional photography by
Paul Macapia: pp. 16, 98, 132 (fig. 2), 219 (bottom), 221 (bottom); plates 22, 28, 30–32, 34, 42, 51, 54–55, 57–59, 69–70, 72, 74–76, 84, 86–88, 100, 110, 122, 130–131, 152, 153, 159
Eduardo Calderón: pp. 10, 174; plates 6–8, 10–11, 13, 15, 20–21, 23–26, 37, 41, 50, 53, 77, 79, 82, 149–150
Beth Mann: plates 106, 109

Photographs provided courtesy of the lenders: plates 1–2, 16–18, 75, 168, 171–172. Additional photographs provided courtesy of Adelson Galleries: plates 155–157; Timothy Aguero: p. 227 right; Carl Andre and the Paula Cooper Gallery, New York: plate 71; Photography © Art Institute of Chicago: p. 203 (fig. 1); BLUM and POE: plate 99; Edward Burtynsky and Charles Cowles Gallery, New York / Robert Koch Gallery, San Francisco / Nicholas Metivier Gallery, Toronto / Galerie Stefan Röpke, Köln / Flowers East, London / Galeria Toni Tapies, Barcelona: plate 93; Susan Dirk: p. 225 top; Gagosian Gallery, New York: plate 49; Gary Hill: plates 95–98, Candida Höfer: plate 94; Ryan Hyde: p. 227 left; Greg Kucera Gallery: plate 89; Spike Mafford: plate 184; Matthew Marks Gallery, New York: plate 85, 91; National Gallery of Art: p. 205 (fig. 2); General Research Division, The New York Public Library, Astor, Lenox and Tilden Foundations: p. 211 (fig. 3); The Power Plant Contemporary Art Gallery, Toronto, photo by Rafael Goldchain: plate 90; Stuart Pratt, for the Seattle Times: p. 216; James Prinze Photography: plate 56; Roger Schreiber: plate 3; Seattle Public Library: p. 191 (fig. 2); Cindy Sherman and Metro Picture Gallery: plate 4; Seiji Shirono, National Institute for Cultural Properties, Tokyo: p. 218; Teresa Tamura: p. 226 bottom; Tiffany and Company Archives: p. 185 (fig. 1); Mike Urban, for the Seattle Post-Intelligencer: p. 226 top; E. K. Waller Photography and Serindia Publications: plate 141; White Cube, London: plate 92; William Wicket Photo Services: plate 147.

Copyright Notices

Published by Seattle Art Museum
1300 First Avenue
Seattle, WA 98101-2003

Distributed by University of Washington Press
PO Box 50096
Seattle, WA 98145-5096
www.washington.edu/uwpress

Library of Congress Cataloging-in-Publication Data
Seattle Art Museum.
    A community of collectors: 75th anniversary gifts to the
Seattle Art Museum / edited by Chiyo Ishikawa; essays by
Barbara Brotherton . . . [et al.].
       p. cm.
    Includes bibliographical references.
    ISBN 978-0-932216-60-1 (hardcover: alk. paper)
    1. Seattle Art Museum. 2. Art—Washington (State)—Seattle.
3. Art—Collectors and collecting—Washington (State)—Seattle.
4. Art donors—Washington (State)—Seattle. I. Ishikawa, Chiyo.
II. Brotherton, Barbara. III. Title. IV. Title: 75th anniversary gifts
to the Seattle Art Museum.
N745.A83 2008
708.197'772—dc22   2008016781

page 1: Edward Hopper, *Chop Suey* (plate 142)
page 2: John Singleton Copley, *Dr. Silvester Gardiner* (plate 153)
page 4: Sonny Assu, *Breakfast Series* (plate 122)
page 6: Katsushika Hokusai, *Under the Wave, off Kanagawa*
(plate 147)
page 8: David Smith, *Cubi XXV* (plate 82)
endsheets: Gloria Petyarre, detail of *Leaves* (plate 59)

Edited by Suzanne Kotz
Designed by John Hubbard
Proofread by Sharon Rutberg
Typeset by Maggie Lee
Produced by Marquand Books, Inc., Seattle
    www.marquand.com
Color management by iocolor, Seattle
Printed and bound by CS Graphics Pte., Ltd., Singapore

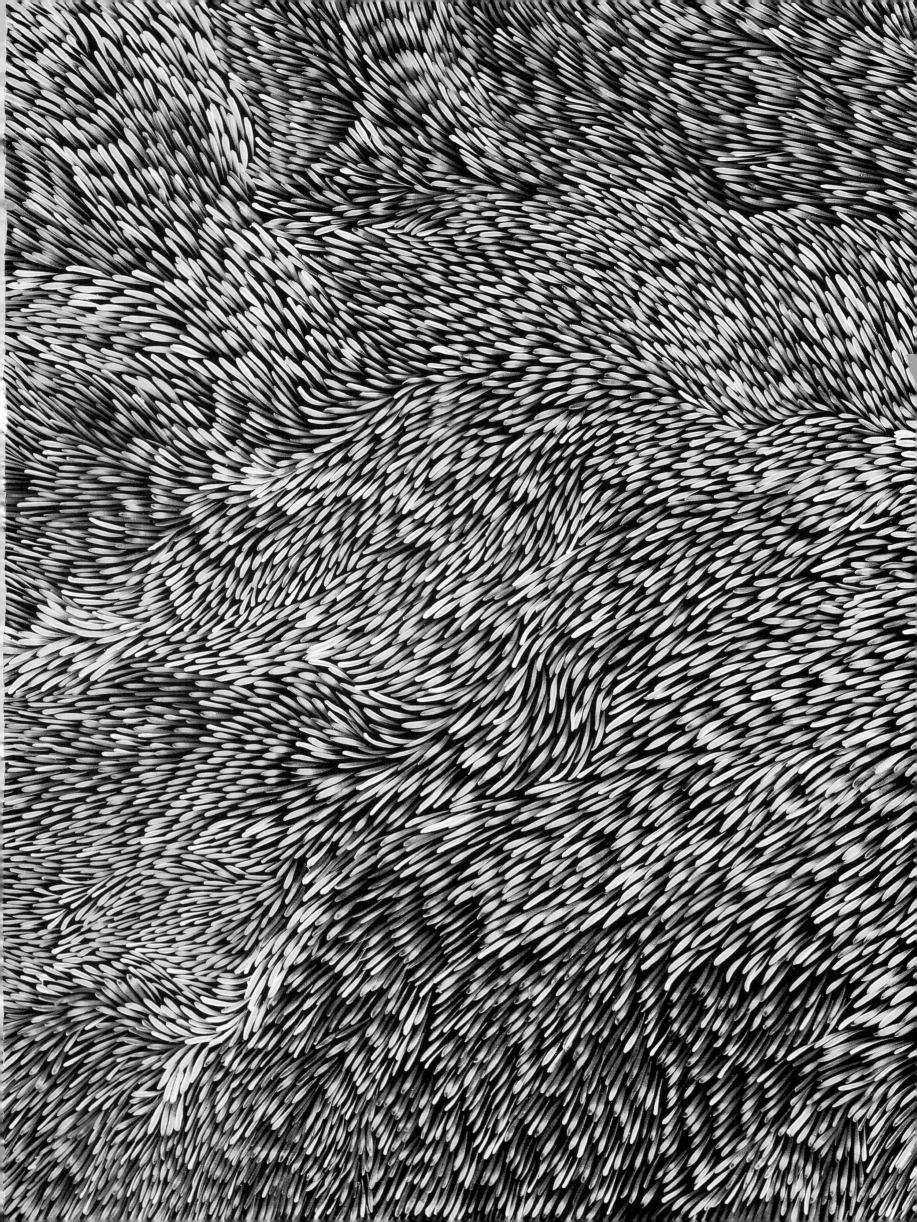